The
Human
Impact

DISCARD

W9-CCX-846

The Human Impact

Man's Role in Environmental Change

ANDREW GOUDIE

The MIT Press · Cambridge, Massachusetts

Second printing, September 1982
First MIT Press edition, 1982
© Andrew Goudie 1981

First published in 1981 by
Basil Blackwell Publisher Limited

All rights reserved. No part of this publication
may be reproduced, stored in a retrieval system,
or transmitted, in any form or by any means,
electronic, mechanical, photocopying, recording
or otherwise, without the prior permission of the
publisher.

Printed and bound in the United States of America

Library of Congress Cataloging in Publication Data

Goudie, Andrew.
  The human impact.

  Bibliography: p.
  Includes index.
  1. Man—Influence on nature. I. Title.
GF75.G68 1982   304.2   81-15643
ISBN 0-262-07086-3   AACR2
ISBN 0-262-57058-0 (pbk.)

Contents

Acknowledgements

In the Oxford School of Geography there is thankfully, though others might say unfashionably, a concern with the unity of Geography and an abomination of fissiparist tendencies. Such an atmosphere makes the writing of a book such as this a real possibility, for one receives many ideas and much information from colleagues which is germane to the theme of the volume. Some of the ideas come from the lecture courses of others, some ideas come from discourses in a house in Holywell, Oxford, and some ideas come from the overall atmosphere of the School. Mrs Pam Berry, Dr Alayne Street, Mr Bruce Atkinson (of Queen Mary College), Miss Ruth Goodwin, Mr Steve Lewitt, and Mr C. L. M. H. Gibbons have made comments on parts of an early draft, and the office, secretarial and technical staff of the School have assisted in many ways — especially Julie. Christine Zwart has assisted me greatly in obtaining illustrations for the book, and I am grateful to all those authors who have permitted me to use their figures and plates. I am also in the debt of the Faculty of Anthropology and Geography and of Hertford College for granting me a spell of sabbatical leave to facilitate the completion of this book. My main debt is to several generations of hapless undergraduates who, unknowingly, have provided a critical appraisal of some of this material in tutorials and lectures.

The publisher and author would like to thank the following for permission to redraw and reproduce figures: American Association for the Advancement of Science (3.5, 6.4, 7.13); American Scientist, journal of Sigma Xi, The Scientific Research Society (1.1, 6.19); D. W. Anderson (3.5); Edward Arnold (Publishers) Ltd (1.10); Association of American Geographers (7.6, 7.11); Ballinger Publishing Company (5.18); Bibliographisches Institut AG Mannheim (5.4); Blackwell Scientific Publications Ltd (5.20); Cambridge University Press (5.15); Chapman and Hall, Ltd (3.2, 3.11,

Acknowledgements

3.12); Colorado State University Patent Administration (5.23); Dowden Hutchinson and Ross Inc. (5.6, 5.7); Elsevier Scientific Publishing Co. (4.1, 4.2); Dr J. G. Evans (1.7); Fontana, London (2.11); Dr P. J. Fowler (1.7); Gower Publishing Co. Ltd (5.20); Dr M. J. Haigh (6.3); Hamilton, Inc. (6.13); Harper and Row, Publishers, Inc. (5.29); the Controller of Her Majesty's Stationery Office (6.11); J. J. Hickey (3.5); Institute of British Geographers (5.1, 7.8); Professor Mike Kirkby (4.7); Longman Group (5.5); Macmillan, London and Basingstoke (6.2); McGraw Hill, New York (2.2, 5.17); Manchester University Press (7.10); MIT Press (7.4, 7.5); Nature Conservancy Council (2.12, 2.13, 3.7, 3.8, 3.10); Newnes-Butterworth (5.24); *New Society*, London, the weekly review of the Social Sciences (3.6); Oxford University School of Geography (3.11); Pergamon Press (5.11, 7.8, 7.9, 7.12); Prentice-Hall, Inc. (6.17, 8.1); Professor Anders Rapp (2.6, 2.7); D. Reidel Publishing Co. (7.2); Royal Geographical Society (4.4, 4.5, 5.19, 5.21, 6.6); Scientific American Inc. (5.25, 5.26, 5.28); Soil Conservation Society of America (5.30, 6.14); Springer Verlag (6.15); Tajik Academy of Sciences (6.22); UNESCO (2.5); United States Geological Survey (5.8); University of Chicago Press (2.3); University Press of Virginia (5.27); *Water Resources Research* (5.9); A. Watson (6.5); Georg Westermann Verlag (3.1, 3.9); John Wiley and Sons Inc. (1.6, 1.8, 1.9, 5.16, 5.21, 6.12); John Wiley and Sons Ltd (5.10); V. H. Winston and Sons (5.14).

The publisher and author are grateful to the following for permission to use and for their help in supplying photographs: Michael Abrahams (4); Alexander Turnbull Library, Wellington (5); Argus Printing and Publishing Co. Ltd (33); Janet and Colin Bord (13, 31 top); Jean Bottin (9, 11); Cambridge University Collection, copyright reserved (16, 39); Camera Press, photo Colin Jones (8); J. Allan Cash Ltd (29); Louise Davies (37 bottom); Sonia Halliday (31 bottom); Grant Heilman, Lititz, PA (27, 28, 30); Hoa-qui, Paris (6); Eric Kay (36); Keystone Press Agency Ltd (35, 38); Jeremy Moeran (37 top and centre); Tony Morrison (7); Museum of Modern Art Collection, New York (23); Trustees of the National Portrait Gallery (1); National Resources Defence Council Inc., Washington (18); New Zealand High Commission (17); Novosti Press Agency (20, 26); Oxfam (10); G. R. Roberts, Nelson, New Zealand (14); John Topham Picture Library (15, 19); Transafrica Pix (12); Western Americana — Peter Newark (32); Xinhua News Agency (25). All other photographs are by the author.

The
Human
Impact

CHAPTER 1

Introduction

The development of ideas

In the history of Western thought three basic questions have been posed concerning the relationship of man to the habitable earth. The first of these is whether the earth, which is plainly a fit environment for man and other organic life, is a purposefully made creation, made perhaps by God for man. The second question is whether the climates, relief, and configuration of the continents have influenced both the moral and social nature of individuals and the character and nature of human cultures. The third question, the one with which this book is concerned, seeks to find out whether, and to what degree, man has during his long tenure of the earth changed it from its hypothetical pristine condition, for as Yi-fu Tuan (1971) has put it: 'The fact of diminishing nature and of human ubiquity is now obvious.'

The third of these questions received relatively little systematic attention until the eighteenth century, and overall it has been less central in the history of geographical thought than that second — the one which asks whether environment has an influence on man (Glacken, 1967). Indeed, in the late seventeenth century, when the Creation was deemed to have occurred in 4004 BC, a grand conception of nature as a divinely created order for the well-being of all life was formulated (Glacken, 1956). In other words it was the first question to which men addressed themselves. Man was seen to be a caretaker, a steward of God, and the task of man was thought to be to improve the primeval aspect of the earth through tillage and in other ways. These thinkers, such as John Ray, author of *The wisdom of God manifested in the works of the Creation* (1691), saw man living in a world — which he could change and improve — where the order and beauty of nature, manifestations of the Creator's skill and wisdom, could be seen everywhere. Indeed the Genesis

1

notion of man above and against nature, entitled to rule like an absolute despot (Passmore, 1974: 9), was formulated into a philosophy of science and progress by men like Francis Bacon, Galileo, and Descartes (Swift, 1974). Bacon foresaw the need to join knowledge with invention in order to give man control of nature. Also, for a time in the nineteenth century, biology was interpreted as fortifying man's belief in the right to deal with nature however he chose. Darwin's theory of natural selection was transformed by Spencer into the doctrine of 'the survival of the fittest'.

Count Buffon can be regarded as the first Western scientist to be concerned directly and intimately with the effects of man on the natural environment (Glacken, 1963). He contrasts the appearance of inhabited life with uninhabited lands: the anciently inhabited countries have few woods, lakes or marshes, but they have many heaths and scrub, their mountains are bare, and their soils are less fertile because they lack the organic matter which woods, felled in inhabited countries, supply, and the herbs are browsed. Buffon was also much involved with the domestication of plants and animals — one of the major transformations in nature brought about by human actions.

Studies of the torrents of the French and Austrian Alps, undertaken in the late eighteenth and early nineteenth centuries, deepened immeasurably the realization of man's power to change his environment. Fabre and Surrell studied the flooding, the siltation, the erosion, and the division of watercourses brought about by deforestation in the Alps. Similarly, de Saussure showed that Alpine lakes had suffered a lowering of their water levels in recent times because of deforestation. In Venezuela, at the valley of Aragua, von Humboldt concluded that the lake level of Lake Valencia in 1800 (the year of his visit) was lower than it had been in recent times, and that deforestation, clearing of plains, and the cultivation of indigo, were among the causes of the gradual drying up of the basin (see p. 159).

Comparable observations were made by the French rural economist, Boussingault (1845). He returned to the same lake basin some 25 years after Humboldt and noted that it was then actually rising. He ascribed this reversal in its regime to political and social upheavals following the granting of independence to the colonies of the erstwhile Spanish Empire. The freeing of slaves had led to a decline in agriculture, a reduction in the application of irrigation water, and a re-establishment of forest. Boussingault also reported some pertinent hydrological observations that had been made on Ascension Island (p. 685):

In the Island of Ascension there was an excellent spring situated at the foot of a mountain originally covered with wood; the spring became scanty and dried up after the trees which covered the mountain had been felled. The loss of the spring was rightly ascribed to the cutting down of the timber. The mountain was therefore planted anew. A few years afterwards the spring reappeared by degrees, and by and by flowed with its former abundance.

Charles Lyell, in his *Principles of Geology*, one of the most influential of all scientific works, referred to the role of man and recognized that tree-felling and drainage of lakes and marshes tended 'greatly to vary the state of the habitable surface'. Overall, however, he believed that the forces exerted by man were insignificant in comparison with those exerted by nature:

If all the nations of the earth should attempt to quarry away the lava which flowed from one eruption of the Icelandic volcanos in 1783, and the two following years, and should attempt to consign it to the deepest abysses of the ocean they might toil for thousands of years before their task was accomplished. Yet the matter borne down by the Ganges and Burrampooter, in a single year, probably very much exceeds, in weight and volume, the mass of Icelandic lava produced by that great eruption. (Lyell, 1835: 197)

One of the most important physical geographers to show concern with our theme was Mary Somerville (1858), who clearly appreciated the unexpected results that occurred as man 'dexterously avails himself of the powers of nature to subdue nature':

Man's necessities and enjoyments have been the cause of great changes in the animal creation, and his destructive propensity of still greater. Animals are intended for our use, and field-sports are advantageous by encouraging a daring and active spirit in young men; but the utter destruction of some races in order to protect those destined for his pleasure, is too selfish, and cruelty is unpardonable: but the ignorant are often cruel. A farmer sees the rook pecking a little of his grain, or digging at the roots of the springing corn, and poisons all his neighbourhood. A few years after he is surprised to find his crop destroyed by grubs. The works of the Creator are nicely balanced, and man cannot infringe His laws with impunity.

1
*Mary Somerville
(1780–1872)*

This is in effect a statement of one of the basic laws of ecology; namely that everything is connected to everything else and that one cannot change just one thing in nature.

The question of the influence of man on his environment was not, however, explored in detail, and on the basis of sound data, until George Perkins Marsh published *Man and*

3

The Human Impact

Nature (1864), in which he dealt with man's influence on the woods, the waters, and the sands. The following extract illustrates the width of his interests and the ramifying connections which he could identify between human actions and environmental changes:

Vast forests have disappeared from mountain spurs and ridges; the vegetable earth accumulated beneath the trees by the decay of leaves and fallen trunks, the soil of the alpine pastures which skirted and indented the woods, and the mould of the upland fields, are washed away; meadows, once fertilized by irrigation, are waste and unproductive, because the cisterns and reservoirs that supplied the ancient canals are broken, or the springs that fed them dried up; rivers famous in history and song have shrunk to humble brooklets; the willows that ornamented and protected the banks of lesser watercourses are gone, and the rivulets have ceased to exist as perennial currents, because the little water that finds its way into their old channels is evaporated by the droughts of summer, or absorbed by the parched earth, before it reaches the lowlands; the beds of the brooks have widened into broad expanses of pebbles and gravel, over which, though in the hot season passed dryshod, in winter sealike torrents thunder; the entrances of navigable streams are obstructed by sandbars, and harbors, once marts of an extensive commerce, are shoaled by the deposits of the rivers at whose mouths they lie; the elevation of the beds of estuaries, and the consequently diminished velocity of the streams which flow into them, have converted thousands of leagues of shallow sea and fertile lowland into unproductive and miasmatic morasses. (Marsh, 1965: 9)

More than a third of the book was concerned with 'the woods'; Marsh did not touch upon important themes like the modification of mid-latitude grasslands, and he was much concerned with Western civilization, but employing an eloquent style and copious footnotes, Marsh, the versatile Vermonter, stands as a landmark in the study of environment (Thomas, 1956).

Marsh, however, was not totally pessimistic about the future role of man or entirely unimpressed by his positive achievements (1965: 43—4):

...new forests have been planted; inundations of flowing streams restrained by heavy walls of masonry and other constructions; torrents compelled to aid, by depositing the slime with which they are charged, in filling up lowlands, and raising the level of morasses which their own overflows had created; ground submerged by the encroachment of the ocean, or exposed to be covered by its tides, have been rescued from its dominion by diking; swamps and even lakes have been drained, and their beds brought within the domain of agricultural industry; drifting coast dunes have been checked and made productive by plantation;

2

George Perkins Marsh in 1861. Marsh was the author of Man and Nature — *probably the most important landmark in the history of the study of man's role in changing the face of the earth*

4

seas and inland waters have been repeopled with fish, and even the sands of the Sahara have been fertilised by artesian fountains. These achivements are far more glorious than the proudest triumphs of war....

Reclus (1871), one of the most prominent French geographers of his generation, also displayed concern with the relationship between forests, torrents (p. 335) and sedimentation (p. 338):

It is, however, the improvidence of the inhabitants, and not so much the geological constitution of the soil, which is the principal cause of the devastating action of the streams. In the mountains of Dauphimy and Provence...during the course of centuries, the trees have been cut down by greedy speculators, and by senseless farmers who wished to add some little strips of land to the fields in the valleys and to the pastures on the summits; but when they destroyed the forest they also destroyed the very land it stood on.

Although the torrents lower the mounts, on the other hand they elevate the plains; but their deposits not being pulverised into clays and sands, are often the means of bringing another disaster on the inhabitants, who find their fertile land covered beneath enormous masses of rocks and pebbles.

Reclus obtained many of his ideas from Marsh and another important contributor, Woeikof (1842–1914) of St Petersburg, obtained some of his ideas from Reclus. He believed that the earth's surface was composed of mobile bodies (*corps meubles*), such as soil, subsoil, and gravels, and that man influenced them through an intermediary, vegetation. He refers to the effects of fire, the climatic effects of forest removal, the destruction of chernozems by ploughing, gullying, the siltation of streams, and the barrenness of karst.

In 1904 Friedrich coined the term 'Raubwirtschaft' which can be translated as economic plunder, robber economy, or, more simply, devastation. This concept has had a great influence but is open to criticism. He believed that destructive exploitation of resources leads of necessity to foresight and to improvements, and that after an initial phase of ruthless exploitation and resulting deprivation measures would, as in the old countries of Europe, lead to conservation and improvement measures:

I can conceive the Raubwirtschaft of our time as a depletion of land, wild plants, and animals, which will disappear quickly as the culture of northwest Europe is substituted for that of colonial and primitive peoples. Such a substitution will bring an intensive use of earth resources which aims at a firmer and firmer establishment of man on the earth. (Friedrich, cited in Whitaker, 1940: 157)

5

The Human Impact

This idea was opposed by Sauer (1938) and Whitaker (1940), the latter pointing out that some soil erosion could well be irreversible and irretrievable (p. 157):

It is surely impossible for anyone who is familiar with the eroded loessial lands of northwestern Mississippi, or the burned and scarred rock hills of north central Ontario, to accept so complacently the damage to resources involved in the process of colonization, or to be so certain that resource depletion is but the forerunner of conservation.

Nonetheless Friedrich's concept of robber economy was adopted and modified by the great French geographer, Jean Brunhes (1920) in his *Human geography*. He recognized the interrelationships involved in anthropogenic environmental change (p. 332): '...Devastation always brings about, not a catastrophe, but a series of catastrophes, for in nature things are dependent one upon the other.' Moreover, Brunhes recognized that the 'essential facts' of human geography included 'Facts of Plant and Animal Conquest' and 'Facts of Destructive Exploitation'. At much the same time other significant studies were made of the same theme. Shaler of Harvard (*Man and the Earth*, 1912) was very much concerned with the destruction of mineral resources (a topic largely neglected by Marsh).

In spite of this work, however, the theme of man's role in changing the face of the earth received relatively little attention from geographers in the nineteenth century and early decades of the twentieth century. One of the main features of the 'classical' view of geography as put forward by men like Ratzel (Wrigley, 1965: 5) was the investigation of the ways in which the physical environment affects the functioning and development of societies and environmentalism persisted as a potent force, notably in American geography, through the works of Davis, Brigham, Semple, and Huntington.

Very definite shifts of emphasis appeared, however, in the 1920s and 1930s when, under the influence of Harlan Barrows and Carl Sauer, there was an eager search for an alternative to so-called 'naive environmental determinism'. Sauer led an effective campaign against destructive exploitation (Speth, 1977), re-introduced Marsh to a wide public, recognized the ecological virtues of some primitive peoples, concerned himself with the great theme of domestication, concentrated on the landscape changes wrought by man, and gave clear and far-sighted warnings about the need for conservation (Sauer, 1938: 494):

We have accustomed ourselves to think of ever expanding productive capacity, of ever fresh spaces of the world to be filled with people,

3
Carl Ortwin Sauer (1889–1975), a cultural and historical geographer, whose studies included such central themes as domestication, the effects of resource exploitation, conservation, and the evolution of cultural landscapes

6

of ever new discoveries of kinds and sources of raw materials, of continuous technical progress operating indefinitely to solve problems of supply. We have lived so long in what we have regarded as an expanding world, that we reject in our contemporary theories of economics and of population the realities which contradict such views. Yet our modern expansion has been effected in large measure at the cost of an actual and permanent impoverishment of the world.

Likewise, in the USSR, in spite of the fact that in *Das Capital* Marx took an environmental line (Matley, 1966), the era of Stalin produced a strong attack on environmentalist views. Grandiose 'practical' schemes were developed for the alteration of the natural environment, such as the 1948 'Stalin Plan for the Transformation of Nature'. These views in turn, however, were recognized by some geographers as being excessive. Indeed, much recent Soviet geography has been concerned with the sometimes undesirable transformation of the natural environment by man (see Komarov, 1978).

Gerasimov and others (1971) point to some of the effects produced by the exploitation of natural resources in the USSR, including erosion and pollution and Gerasimov (1976: 77) has placed the effects of man in transforming nature in their historical context:

By taking energy and matter from the environment and returning them in converted — industrial, domestic and other — forms society interferes with the dynamically balanced cycles of natural processes. However, as a result of its long evolution, nature has acquired an ability to restore disrupted natural processes....Thus the natural environment taken as a whole was able, up to a point, to withstand anthropogenic disturbances, although there were also local irreversible changes. Since the industrial revolution, the general intensity of human impact on the environment has exceeded its potential for restoration in many large areas of the earth's surface, leading to irreversible changes not only on a local but also on a regional scale.

He also indicated that some systems had been more disrupted than others (p. 79):

Almost all European capitalist countries find themselves 'pressed' between the two jaws of a vice — the complex historical inheritance of a considerably disrupted natural environment and the increasing negative effects on the environment of industrialization and urbanization.

Gerasimov has written in the same work (p. 78) of a sub-discipline of *'constructive geography'* ('a science of the planned transformation and management of the natural environment for the sake of the future of mankind'). This

7

concept has been criticized as neither sufficiently distinctively geographical nor as having a distinctive object of study by Mil'kov and his co-workers (Nesterov, 1974), who propose an alternative subdiscipline, *'anthropogenic landscape science'* concerned with the human construction of entire landscapes. Isachenko (1974 and 1975) in turn attacks the Mil'kov school with vigour and urges the need to see natural and human influences working together in the landscape:

An oasis created in desert remains part of the desert just as a clearing and plot of cropped land in the tayga belongs to the tayga and will continue to belong to it as long as zonal and azonal external conditions will be preserved or until man acquires the ability to control incoming solar radiation, the circulation of air masses and tectonic processes. (Isachenko, 1974: 473)

To the non-Russian geographer the wonder is not so much that their Russian colleagues seem to hold such firmly divergent viewpoints, but that Gerasimov, Mil'kov and Isachenko are all so greatly concerned with the human impact.

The theme of the human impact on the environment has, however, been central to some Western historical geographers concerned with the evolution of the cultural landscape. The clearing of the woodland (Darby, 1956), the domestication process (Sauer, 1952), the draining of marshlands (Williams, 1970), the introduction of alien plants and animals (McKnight, 1959) and the reclamation of heathland are among some of the recurrent themes of a fine tradition of historical geography.

In the last 20 years too many Anglo-Saxon geographers have largely retreated from a concern with relationships between man and the physical environment. Much geography has been concerned with spatial and distributional analysis and has found little space for consideration of the natural environment (see, for example, Abler *et al.*, 1971). Nonetheless, this retreat has not been total, though it is salutory to reflect that at a time of increasing concern with environmental issues at the public and political levels, one of the main traditional concerns of geography — man—land relationships — has been effectively carried out by other disciplines under the guise of ecology, environmental studies, and the like.

There have, however, been notable exceptions to this tendency, and many geographers have contributed to, and been affected by, the phenomenon which is often called the environmental revolution or the ecological movement. The subject of the impact of man on his environment, dealing as it does with such matters as environmental degradation, pollution, and desertification, has close links with these developments, and is once again a theme in many textbooks and research monographs in geography (see, for example, Detwyler, 1971; Berry 1974; Manners and Mikesell, 1974; Wagner, 1974; Cooke and Reeves, 1976; Gregory and Walling, 1979 and Simmons, 1979).

The development of human population and stages of cultural development

At the start of the Ice Age, some three or so million years ago, human beings probably first appeared on earth. Their remains have been found in sediments from the Rift Valleys of East Africa, notably in Tanzania, Kenya, and Ethiopia. Since that time the human population has diffused over virtually the entire land surface of the planet (figure 1.1).

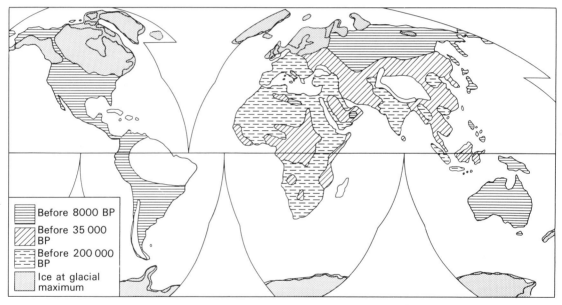

FIG. 1.1
The spread of Pleistocene man
(after Butzer, 1977)

Estimates of population levels in the early stages of man's development (figure 1.2) are not easy to manufacture with any degree of certainty. Before the agricultural 'revolution' some 10 000 years ago, human groups lived through hunting and gathering over parts of the world where this was possible. At that time the world population *may* have been of the order of 5 million people (Ehrlich *et al.*, 1977: 182) and large areas would only recently have witnessed human migration. The Americas and Australia, for example, were

9

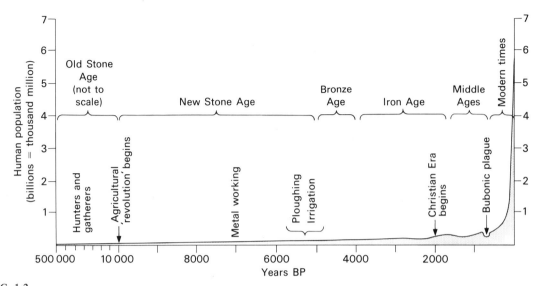

FIG. 1.2
*The growth of human numbers
for the past half-million years
(after Ehrlich et al., 1977,
figure 5.2)*

not inhabited by man to any significant degree until after about 30 000 years ago (or possibly even later).

The agricultural revolution (figure 1.3) probably enabled an expansion of the total human population to about 200 million by the time of Christ, and to 500 million by AD 1650. It is since that time, in association with the medical and industrial revolutions and developments in agriculture and colonization of new lands, that human population has exploded, reaching about 1 000 million by AD 1850, 2 000 million by AD 1930 and 4 000 million by AD 1975. The fifth billion should be attained by 1987. Victory over malaria, smallpox, cholera, and other diseases has been responsible for abrupt drops in death rates throughout the non-industrial world, but death rate control has not in general been matched by birth control. Thus the annual population growth rate at the present time in South Asia is 2.64%, Africa 2.66% and Latin America (where population increased sixfold between 1850 and 1950), 2.73%.

FIG. 1.3
*Human population growth
plotted on a log–log scale.
Plotted in this way, population
growth is seen as occurring in
three surges associated with
the so-called cultural,
agricultural, and industrial–
medical revolutions (after
Deevey in Ehrlich et al.,
1977, figure 5.1)*

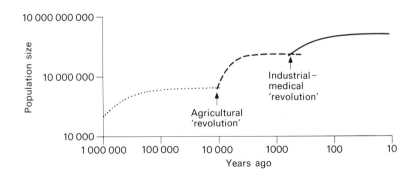

Clearly this growth of the human population of the earth is in itself a highly important cause of the transformation of nature. Of no lesser importance, however, has been the growth and development of culture and technology. Sears (1957: 51) has put the power of man into the context of other species:

Man's unique power to manipulate things and accumulate experience presently enabled him to break through the barriers of temperature, aridity, space, seas and mountains that have always restricted other species to specific habitats within a limited range. With the cultural devices of fire, clothing, shelter, and tools he was able to do what no other organism could do without changing its original character. Cultural change was, for the first time, substituted for biological evolution as a means of adapting an organism to new habitats in a widening range that eventually came to include the whole earth.

We now turn to a consideration of the major cultural and technical developments that have taken place during the past 2–3 million years. Three main phases will form the basis of this analysis: the phase of hunting and gathering; the phase of plant cultivation, animal keeping, and metal working; and the phase of modern urban and industrial man.

Man the hunter and gatherer

The definition of 'man' is something of a problem, not least because as is the case with all existing organisms new forms tend to emerge by imperceptible degrees from antecedent ones. Moreover, the fossil evidence is scarce, fragmentary, and rarely datable with any degree of precision. Although it is probably justifiable to separate the hominids from the great apes on the basis of their assumption of an upright posture, it is much less justifiable or possible to distinguish on purely zoological grounds between those hominids that remained prehuman and those that attained the status of man. To qualify as human, a hominid has to show evidence of cultural development: the systematic manufacture of implements as an aid to manipulating the environment.

The oldest records of human activity and technology, pebble tools, crude stone tools which consist of a pebble with one end chipped into a rough cutting edge, have been found in conjunction with human bone remains from various parts of Africa. For example, at Lake Rudolf (Turkana) in northern Kenya, and the Omo Valley in southern Ethiopia, a tool-bearing bed of volcanic material called tuff has been dated by isotopic means at about 2.6 million years old, while another bed at the Olduvai Gorge in Tanzania, made famous by the researches of the Leakey family, has been dated by similar means to 1.75 million years.

As the Stone Age progressed the tools became more sophisticated, more varied, and more effective. Greater exploitation of plant and animal resources became possible. It is possible to observe a clear progression during the Palaeolithic Age in the technology of working stone (figure 1.4), though it needs to be stressed that in reality the stages were not synchronous in different areas nor among different human groups in the same area. In addition particular industries are often seen to combine techniques from more than one stage of development.

The lithic technology in the Old Stone Age in Europe has been divided into five main modes: mode 1 (figure 1.4a) consists of chopper tools of Lower Palaeolithic type; mode 2 (figure 1.4b and c) consists of bifacially flaked hand-axes of the Lower Palaeolithic; mode 3 (figure 1.4d) consists of Middle Palaeolithic flake tools from prepared cores; mode 4 (figure 1.4e) consists of Upper Palaeolithic punch-struck blades with steep retouch; and mode 5 (figure 1.4f), of Mesolithic Age, consists of microlithic components of composite artefacts.

Stone may not, however, have been the only material used by early man. Sticks and animal bones, the preservation of which is less likely than stone, are among the first objects that may have been used as implements, though the sophisticated utilization of antler and bone as materials for weapons and implements appears to have developed surprisingly late in prehistory.

Another feature of early man which seems to have set him apart from the surviving non-human primates was his seemingly omnivorous diet. Biological materials recovered from his settlements in many different parts of the world indicate that Palaeolithic man secured a wide range of animal meat, whereas the great apes, though not averse to an occasional taste of animal food, are predominantly vegetarian. One consequence of enlarging the range of his diet was that in the long run man was able to explore a much wider range of environment (G. Clark, 1977b: 19).

Moreover, at an early stage man discovered the use of fire, and as Sparks and West (1972) have indicated, 'the regularity with which hearths are found associated with the Middle and Upper Palaeolithic sites leaves little doubt that Neanderthal Man and his successors were capable of fire production'. Fire, as we shall see (chapter 2), is a major agent by which man has had an impact on his environment. It has been found in association with Peking Man in deposits at Choukoutien

FIG. 1.4 (opposite)
Developments in stone tool technology:
(a) a primitive pebble tool from early Pleistocene strata – Mode 1
(b) a hand axe of Abbeville type from a younger level – Mode 2
(c) another Lower Palaeolithic hand axe, from Rajasthan, India – Mode 2
(d) a Middle Palaeolithic keeled scraper and core from Rajasthan – Mode 3
(e) Upper Palaeolithic burin and blade from Rajasthan – Mode 4
(f) Mesolithic artefacts from Rajasthan – Mode 5

12

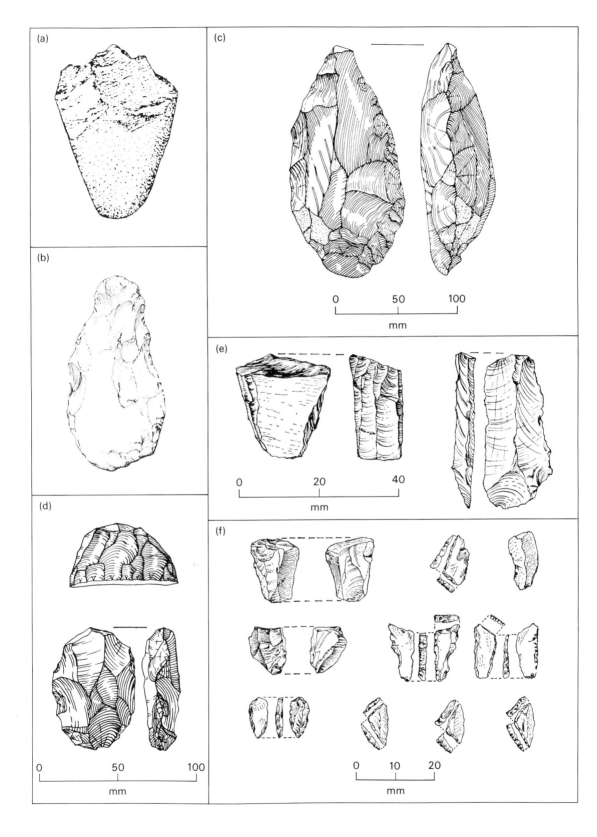

(a)

(b)

(c)

0   50   100
mm

(e)

0   20   40
mm

(d)

0   50   100
mm

(f)

0 10 20
mm

dating back to the early part of the Middle Pleistocene, and may have been employed even earlier in East Africa.

Another major development that set man above the beasts was the development of speech. Until hominids had developed words as symbols, the possibility of transmitting, and so accumulating, culture hardly existed. Animals can express and communicate emotions, never designate or describe objects.

Overall, at this stage of his cultural development, man had neither the numbers nor the technological skills to have a very substantial effect on his environment. Besides the effects of fire, which have already been mentioned, he may have caused some diffusion of seeds and nuts, and through his hunting activities (see chapter 3) may have had some effects on animal extinctions (the so-called 'Pleistocene overkill').

Locally some eutrophication may have occurred and around some archaeological sites phosphate and nitrate levels may be sufficiently raised to make them an indicator of habitation to archaeologists today (Holdgate, 1979).

Man the cultivator, keeper and metal worker

Some time around the beginning of the Holocene, about 10 000 years ago, man started in various parts of the world to domesticate rather than to gather food plants and to keep, rather than just hunt, animals. By domesticating food plants, man reduced enormously the space required for sustaining each individual by a factor of the order of 500 at least (Sears, 1957: 54). As a consequence we see shortly thereafter, notably in the Middle East, the establishment of the first major settlements — towns. So long as man had

to subsist on the game animals, birds and fish he could catch and trap, the insects and eggs he could collect and the foliage, roots, fruits and seeds he could gather, he was limited in the kind of social life he could develop; as a rule he could only live in small groups, which gave small scope for specialisation and the subdivision of labour, and in the course of a year he would have to move over extensive tracts of country, shifting his habitation so that he could tap the natural resources of successive areas. It is hardly to be wondered at that among communities whose energies were almost entirely absorbed by the mere business of keeping alive, technology, remained at a low ebb. (Clark, 1962: 76)

Although it is now recognized that some subsistence hunters and gatherers had considerable leisure, there is no doubt that through the control of breeding of animals and plants man was able, by hard work, to ensure himself a more reliable and readily expandable source of food and thereby create a solid and secure basis for cultural advance, an advance which included civilization, and the 'urban revolution' of Childe (1936) and others. Indeed, Isaac (1970) has termed domestication 'the single most important intervention man had made in his environment', while G. Clark (1977) has remarked that 'the milk-stool and the mattock were forerunners of the conveyor-belt and the punch-card'.

The whole question of the origin of agriculture remains a controversial one (Bender, 1975). Some early workers saw agriculture as a Divine Gift for man, while others thought that animals were domesticated for religious reasons. They argued that it would have been improbable that man could have predicted the usefulness of domestic cattle before they were actually domesticated. Wild cattle are large and fierce beasts and no one could have foreseen their utility for labour or milk until they were tamed — tamed for ritual sacrifice in connection with lunar goddess cults (the great curved horns being the reason for the association). Another major theory was that domestication was produced by crowding, possibly brought on by a combination of climatic deterioration (post-Glacial progressive desiccation) and population growth. Such pressure, according to Childe, gave the necessary stimulus to man to intensify his way of food production. Current palaeo-climatological research tends not to support this interpretation. Sauer (1952), a geographer, believed that domestication of plants was initiated in south-east Asia by fishing folk, who found that lacustrine and riverine resources would underwrite a stable economy and a sedentary or semi-sedentary life-style. He surmises, in an almost totally theoretical model, that the initial domesticates would be multi-purpose plants set out around small fishing villages to provide such items as starch foods, substances for toughening nets and lines and making them water-resistant, and drugs and poisons. He suggested that 'food production was one and perhaps not the most important reason for bringing plants under cultivation'. Yet another model was advanced by Jacobs (1969) which stood certain more traditional models on their heads. Instead of following the classic model whereby farming leads to village which leads to town which leads to civilization, she proposed that one could be a hunter—gatherer and live in a city and that agriculture originated in and around such cities rather than in the countryside. The argument is that even in primitive hunter—gatherer societies particularly valuable commodities such as fine stones, pigments, shells, and the like can create and sustain a trading centre which would possibly become large and stable. Food would be

15

exchanged for goods, but natural produce brought any distance would have to be durable, so meat would be brought in on the hoof, for example, but not all the animals would be consumed immediately; some would be herded together and might breed. This might be the start of domestication.

The process of domestication and cultivation also used to be thought of as a revolutionary system of land procurement that had evolved in one or two hearths and diffused over the face of the earth, replacing the older hunting–gathering system by stimulus diffusion. It was felt that the deliberate rearing of plants and animals for food was a discovery or invention so radical and so complex that it could have developed only once (or possibly twice) – the so-called 'Eureka model'.

The current evidence (Harlan, 1976) indicates otherwise; agriculture evolved through an extension and intensification of what people had already been doing for a long time, it evolved over wide areas and in different areas, and the innovative pattern was complex and diffuse. Harlan (1975b: 57) has gone so far as to write:

I am inclined to develop a no-model model which leaves room for whole arrays of motives, actions, practices and evolutionary processes. What applies in Southeast Asia may not apply in Southwest Asia.... A search for a single overriding cause for human behaviour is likely to be frustrating and fruitless.

A recent interpretation of this spatial and temporal complexity is shown in figure 1.5. Certainly the pre-eminence once accorded the Near East is now lessened (Simoons, 1974); while Jarman (1977) has stressed the continuity of man–animal relationships and cast doubt on any clear-cut wild–domestic dichotomy. Indeed, Jarman proposes six stages in the process of Human exploitation of animals:

1   *Random predation*, during which the human group makes no effort to control or benefit from the regularity of the animal behaviour pattern, simply exploiting the animal when it happens to be available.
2   *Controlled predation*, which would not necessarily amount to a year-round association between man and prey. The control of animal movement in game drives and corralling are examples.
3   *Herd following*, in which the human group, or part of it, echoes the animal movements, maintaining a degree of contact with it, such that a given human population tends to become associated with a given animal population.

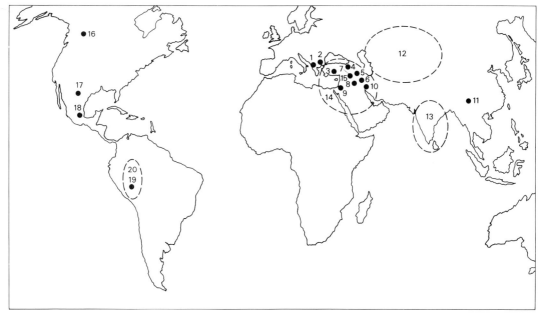

KEY

1 Franchthi (5000 BC): sheep, goats, pig, cattle
2 Argissa (6500 BC): cattle
3 Çatal Hüyük (6500 BC): cattle
4 Çayönü (7000 BC): einkorm, emmer, pea, lentil, sheep, pig, goat (?)
5 Shandidar (9000 BC): sheep?
6 Palegawra Cave (12 000 BC): dog
7 Jarmo (6700 BC): einkorm, emmer, barley, lentil, pea
8 Tell 'Awrab (3000 BC): zebu
9 Jericho (7000 BC): einkorn, emmer, barley, pea, lentil
10 Ali Kosh (7500 BC): sheep, goat (?)
    (7000 BC): einkorn, emmer (?)
11 Pan P'o (3750 BC): foxtail millet, cabbage
12 Central Asia (3000 BC): horse
    (1500 BC): Bactrian camel
13 India (2500 BC): buffalo
14 Egypt (3000 BC): donkey
15 Near East (2000 BC): dromedary
16 Jaguar Cave (11 000 BC): dog
17 Ocampo Cave (7000 BC): squash? gourd? scarlet runner bean
    (4000 BC): common bean
18 Tehuacan (6000 BC): maize? squash, gourds
    (5000 BC): maize
19 Ayacucho (6000 BC): lima bean, common bean
20 Highland South America (2000 BC): guinea pig
    (1500 BC): llama, alpaca

FIG. 1.5
Dates for the domestication of crops and animals (modified after Harlan, 1976)

4 *Loose herding*, in which some seasonal control is exerted.
5 *Close herding*, in which a high degree of control of herds is maintained throughout the year.
6 *Factory farming*, whereby animals are kept immobile throughout their lives, and maintained in a wholly artificial environment.

Recent studies in Egypt by Wendorf *et al.* (1979) have indicated the possibility that there was a broadly comparable continuity of man—plant relationships in that archaeological and stratigraphic evidence suggests that man was intensively exploiting barley (albeit possibly wild), living in settlements and grinding the grain as early as about 18 000 years ago. These investigations may place the origins of food production nearly 10 000 years earlier than previously believed, and might seriously question previous assumptions concerning the role of food production in stimulating the social changes which characterize the Neolithic.

One highly important development in agriculture, because of its rapid and early effects on environment, was irrigation. This came rather later than domestication. The earliest evidence for artificial irrigation is the mace-head of the Egyptian Scorpion King which shows one of the last Pre-dynastic kings ceremonially cutting an irrigation ditch around 5050 years ago (Butzer, 1976). The plough, so efficient at disturbing the soil, was also invented some 5000 years ago (Spencer and Thomas, 1978) and diffused rapidly (figure

FIG. 1.6
The spread of plough agriculture in the Old World (after Spencer and Thomas, 1978, figure 4.2)

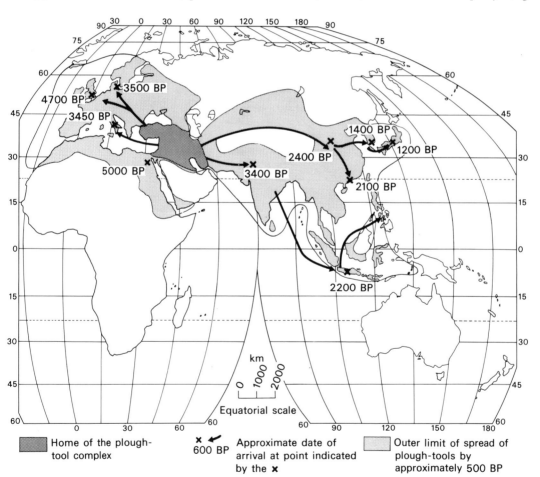

18

1.6). The remains of plough marks have been found beneath a burial mound at South Street, Avebury, in England, which has been dated at around 3000 BC (see figure 1.7) and ever since that time fields have been a dominant feature of the English landscape (Taylor, 1975). A little earlier came the wheel. This too diffused quickly from a similar part of western Asia and greatly enhanced the power of man to move materials (figure 1.8).

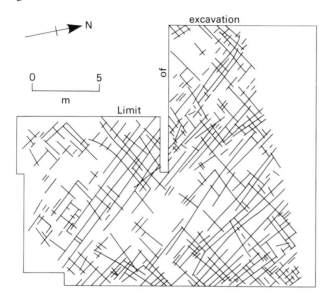

FIG. 1.7
Plan of Neolithic plough marks: some of the first tangible evidence of the first agricultural revolution in the British Isles (after Taylor, 1975, figure 1a)

The development of other means of transport preceded the wheel. Sledge-runners found in Scandinavian bogs have been dated to the Mesolithic (Cole, 1970: 42), while by the Neolithic era man had developed boats, floats, and rafts that were able to cross to Mediterranean islands and across the Irish Sea. Dugout canoes could hardly have been common before polished stone axes and adzes came into general use during Neolithic times, though some paddle and canoe remains are recorded from Mesolithic sites in northern Europe. The middens of the hunter—fishers of the Danish Neolithic contain bones of deep-sea fish such as cod, which shows that these people certainly had sea-worthy craft with which to exploit ocean resources.

Both domestication of animals and the cultivation of plants have been among the most significant causes of the human impact. Pastoralists have had many major effects — for example, on soil erosion — though Passmore (1974: 12) believes that the nomadic pastoralist is probably more conscious than the agriculturalist that he shares the Earth with other living things, which go their own way largely indifferent

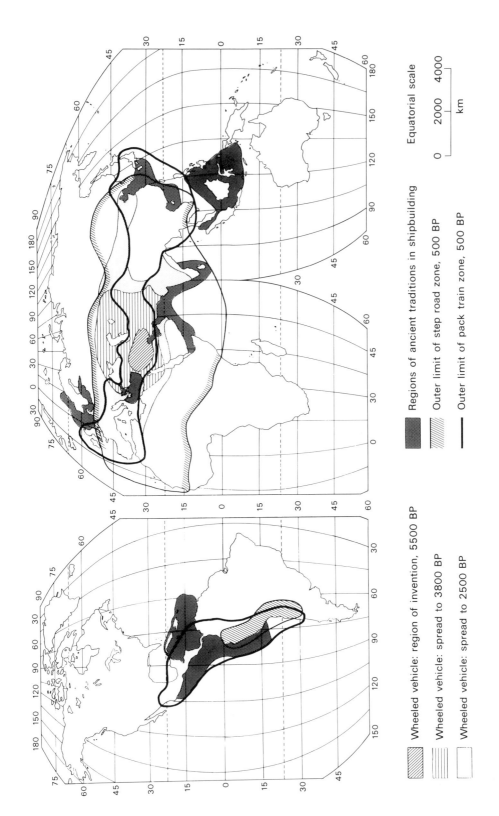

Regions of ancient traditions in shipbuilding

Outer limit of step road zone, 500 BP

Outer limit of pack train zone, 500 BP

Wheeled vehicle: region of invention, 5500 BP

Wheeled vehicle: spread to 3800 BP

Wheeled vehicle: spread to 2500 BP

Equatorial scale

0   2000   4000
        km

FIG. 1.8   *The early development of transport (after Spencer and Thomas, 1978, figure 4.5)*

to his presence. The agriculturalist, on the other hand, deliberately transforms nature in a sense which the nomadic pastoralist does not. His main role has been to simplify the world's ecosystems. Thus in the prairies of North America by ploughing and seeding the grasslands the farmer has eliminated a hundred species of native prairie herbs and grasses, which he replaces with pure stands of wheat, corn, or alfalfa. This simplification may reduce stability in the ecosystem. Indeed, on a world basis (see Harlan, 1976) such simplification is evident. Whereas man once enjoyed a highly varied diet, and has used for food several thousand species of plants and several hundreds of species of animals, with domestication the sources he employs are greatly reduced. For example, four crops (wheat, rice, maize, and potatoes) at the head of the list of food supplies contribute more tonnage to the world total than the next twenty-six crops combined. Simmonds (1976) provides an excellent account of the history of most of the major crops produced by man.

It is becoming increasingly clear that Neolithic and Bronze Age peoples were able to achieve very notable changes in the soils, plants, and animals of large areas of Europe and the Near East (see, for example, Dimbleby, 1974).

One further development in man's cultural and technological life which was to increase his power was the mining of ores and the smelting of metals. This may have started around 5700 years ago, possibly in what is today north-west Iran, with the smelting of copper-oxide ores into metallic copper. Recent finds of copper and bronze implements in north-east Thailand, however, raise questions about the dating and the place of origin, since tentative dates of between 7000 and 6000 years ago have been given to the Thailand finds. The spread of metal working into other areas was rapid (figure 1.9) and by 2500 BC bronze products were in use from Britain in the west to northern China in the east. The smelting of iron ores may date back to as late as 1500 BC (Spencer and Thomas, 1978).

Modern industrial and urban man

The Modern era, especially since the late seventeenth century, has witnessed another major transformation of, or revolution in, culture and technology — the development of major industries (Pawson, 1978). This, like the adoption of domestication, has reduced the space required for sustaining each individual and has increased the utilization of resources. Modern science and modern medicine have compounded

21

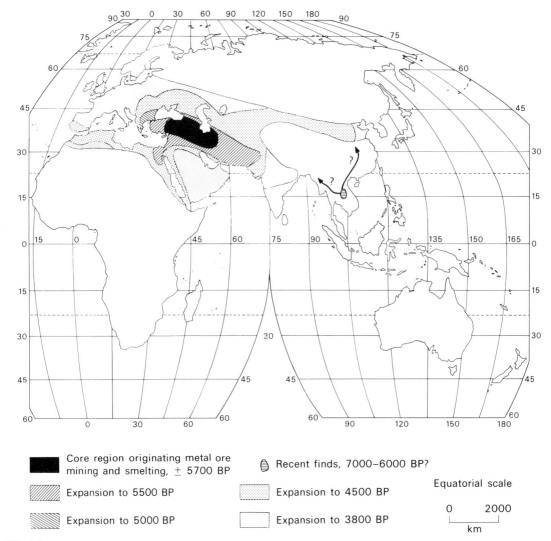

FIG. 1.9
*The diffusion of mining and
smelting in the Old World
(after Spencer and Thomas,
1978, figure 4.4)*

Core region originating metal ore mining and smelting, ± 5700 BP

Expansion to 5500 BP

Expansion to 5000 BP

Recent finds, 7000–6000 BP?

Expansion to 4500 BP

Expansion to 3800 BP

Equatorial scale

0   2000
          km

these effects, leading to accelerating population increase even in non-industrial societies.

Figure 1.10 illustrates the way in which, during the present century, not only has population increased but also the consumption of resources (e.g. coal, fish, oil) and the production of goods (e.g. cars).

The perfecting of sea-going ships in the sixteenth and seventeenth centuries was part of the transformation, and this was the time when mainly self-contained but developing regions of the world coalesced so that the ecumene became to all intents and purposes continuous. The development of the steam engine in the late eighteenth century and the internal combustion engine in the late nineteenth century

22

gave man a massively increased access to energy, and lessened his dependence on animals, wind, and water.

Modern science, technology, and industry have also been applied to agriculture and in recent decades some spectacular progress has been attained through such developments as the use of fertilizers and the selective breeding of plants and animals.

To conclude we can recognize certain trends in man's manipulation of his environment which have taken place in the Modern era. The first of these is that the number of ways in which man is affecting his environment is proliferating. For example, nearly all the powerful pesticides post-date the Second World War, and the same applies to the increasing construction of nuclear reactors (see figure 1.11). Secondly, environmental problems that were once locally confined have become regional problems or even global problems. An instance of this is the way in which substances such as DDT, lead, and sulphates are found at the poles, far removed from the industrial societies that produced them. Thirdly, the complexity, magnitude and frequency of impacts is probably increasing; for instance a massive modern dam like that at Aswan has a very different level of impact to a small Roman dam. Finally, compounding the effects of greatly expanding populations is a general increase in *per capita* consumption and environmental impact.

FIG. 1.10
The development of human population and some indices of technological development and production over the last hundred years

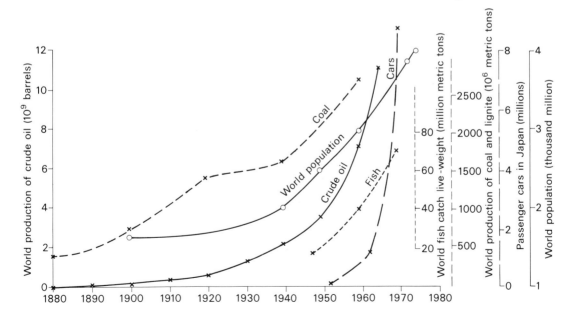

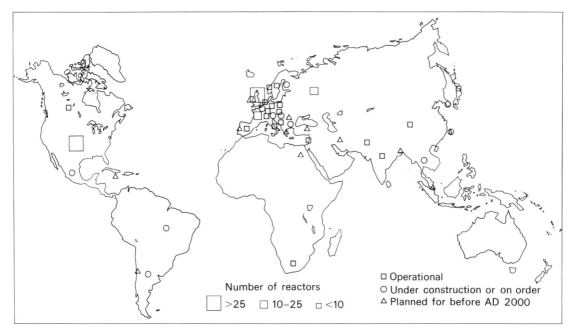

FIG. 1.11
The world distribution of nuclear reactors in 1975 (by countries) (after Eyre, 1978, figure 1)

Number of reactors

☐ >25   ☐ 10–25   ☐ <10

☐ Operational
○ Under construction or on order
△ Planned for before AD 2000

4
The nuclear installation at Windscale in northern England, an example of one of the new technological innovations spreading throughout the world and causing fear over possible environmental consequences

24

CHAPTER 2

Man's Impact on Vegetation

Introduction

In starting any consideration of the impact of man on his environment it is probably appropriate to start with vegetation, for man has possibly had a greater influence on plant life than on any of the other components of his environment. Through the changes he has brought about in plant cover he has modified soils (see chapter 4), influenced climates (see chapter 7), affected geomorphic processes (see chapter 6), and changed the quality (see chapter 5) and quantity of some natural waters. Indeed the nature of whole landscapes has been transformed by man-induced vegetation change (figure 2.1). Following Hamel and Dansereau (1949, cited by Frenkel, 1970) we can recognize five principal degrees of

FIG. 2.1
Some ramifications of man-induced vegetation change

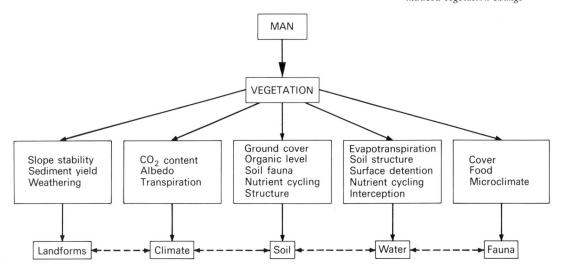

interference with increasing remoteness from pristine conditions. These are:

1 *Natural habitats*: those that develop in the absence of human activities.
2 *Degraded habitats*: those produced by sporadic, yet incomplete, disturbances; for example the cutting of a forest (see p. 36), burning (see p. 28) and the non-intensive grazing of natural grassland (see p. 33).
3 *Ruderal habitats*: where disturbance is sustained but where there is no intentional substitution of vegetation. Roadsides are an example of a ruderal habitat (see p. 57).
4 *Cultivated habitats*: when complete disturbance is accompanied by the intentional introduction of plants.
5 *Artificial habitats*: which are developed when man modifies the ambient climate and soil as in greenhouse cultivation.

In this chapter we shall mainly be concerned with degraded and ruderal habitats, and first we need to consider some of the processes that man employs; notably fire, grazing, and physical removal of forest.

The use of fire

Man is known to have used fire since Palaeolithic times (see p. 12), and so, for example, at the famous Kalambo Falls archaeological site on the Tanzania–Zambia border there is evidence of its use as long as 60 000 years ago. As Sauer (1969), one of the great proponents of the role of fire in environmental change, has put it (pp. 10–11):

Through all ages the use of fire has perhaps been the most important skill to which man has applied his mind. Fire gave to man, a diurnal creature, security by night from other predators.... The fireside was the beginning of social living, the place of communication and reflection.

Man has utilized fire for a great variety of reasons (Bartlett, 1956; Stewart, 1956; Wertine, 1973) including: to clear forest for agriculture; to improve grazing land for domestic animals or to attract game; to deprive game of cover; to drive game from cover in hunting; to kill or drive away predatory animals, ticks, mosquitoes, and other pests; to repel the attacks of enemies, or to burn them out of their refuges; for cooking; to expedite travel; to break up stone for tool-

5
Large areas of the world's forests are being destroyed by fires started by man, such as this one in eastern New Zealand. On steep slopes serious erosion may follow such fires

making; to protect settlements or encampments from great fires by controlled burning; to satisfy the sheer love of fires as spectacles; to make pottery; to smelt ores; to harden spears; to provide warmth; to make charcoal; and to assist in the collection of insects like crickets for eating. Given this remarkable utility it would be surprising if it had not been much used. Indeed it is still much used, especially by pastoralists such as the cattle-keepers of Africa (Lemon, 1968), and by the practitioners of shifting agriculture. For example, the Malaysian and Indonesian *ladang* and the *milpa* system

6
One of the prime reasons for burning woodland is to clear a small plot for shifting cultivation

of the Maya in Latin America involved the preparation of land for planting by felling or deadening forest, letting the debris dry in the hot season, and burning it before the commencement of the rainy season. With the first rains holes are dibbled in the soft ash-covered earth with a planting stick. This system was adapted to areas of low population density with sufficiently extensive forest that there could be long intervals of 'forest fallow' between burnings. Land which was burned over too frequently became overgrown with perennial grasses, which tended to make it useless for agricultural exploitation with primitive tools. Land which was cultivated for too long rapidly suffered a deterioration in fertility, while land recently burned was temporarily rich in nutrients (see figure 8.1).

The use of fire, however, has not been restricted to primitive peoples in the tropics. Remains of charcoal are found in Neolithic soil profiles in highland Britain, large parts of North America appear to have suffered fires at regular intervals prior to European settlement, and in the case of South America the 'great number of fires' observed by Magellan during the historical passage of the Strait that bears his name resulted in the toponym, 'Tierra del Fuego'. Indeed, says Sternberg (1968: 718): 'for thousands of years, man has been putting the New World to the torch, and making it a "land of fire" '.

Fires: natural and man-made

Although man has used fire for all the reasons that have been mentioned, before one can assess the role of this facet of man's impact, one must ascertain how important man-made fires are in comparison with those caused naturally, especially by lightning activity, which on average strikes the land surface of the globe 100 000 times each day (Yi-fu Tuan, 1971). Some of the available data on the causes of fires are summarized in table 2.1. In the forest lands of the western United States about half the fires are caused by lightning; in the pine savanna of Belize, Central America, over half the fires are caused by lightning; in the bush of Australia only about 8% are caused by lightning; while in the south of France nearly all the fires are caused by man.

Some natural fires may result from spontaneous combustion (Vogl, 1974) for in certain ecosystems heavy vegetal accumulations may become compacted, rotted, and fermented, thus generating heat.

One method of gauging the long-term frequency of fires is to look at tree rings, for these are affected when fires take

28

place. Such studies in the USA indicate that over wide areas fires have occurred with sufficient frequency to have effects on annual tree rings and lake cores every 7–80 years (table 2.2) in pre-European times.

Fires can sometimes extend over very great areas. In 1963 in Paraná, Brazil, no less than 2 million hectares of forest were consumed in 3 weeks.

TABLE 2.1

Fire frequencies and their causes for selected areas

1 WESTERN UNITED STATES

State	Total average yearly number of fires	Percentage caused by lightning
Arizona	1 486	84
California	3 608	26
Colorado	413	36
Idaho	1 458	69
Montana	852	71
Nevada	86	34
New Mexico	614	79
Oregon	1 860	52
South Dakota	173	62
Utah	236	35
Washington	1 807	28
Wyoming	157	62
TOTAL	12 750	49

Source: Brown and Davis (1973)

2 MONTANE SAVANNA, BELIZE

Year	Total number of fires	Percentage caused by by lightning
1963	7	43
1964	11	55
1965	7	43
1966	2	100
1967	5	80
1968	8	100
1969	3	67
1970	7	71
1971	4	25
1972	12	42
TOTAL	66	59

Source: Kellman (1975)

29

TABLE 2.1 (continued)　　　　3　BUSH FIRES IN AUSTRALIA

Cause	Percentage of total
Deliberate burning off	35
Cigarettes and matches	7
Camp fires	6
Lightning	8
Trains	6
Tractors	5
Motor vehicles	6
Domestic	9
Miscellaneous	18

Source: Luke (1961)

4　MEDITERRANEAN FRANCE (BOUCHES DU RHONE), 1962

Cause	Percentage of total
Children playing with fire	39
Cigarettes	17
Agricultural accidents	12.5
French railways	11.8
Rubbish tips	6.8
Spontaneous fires	6.4
Others	6.0

Source: Nicod, cited by Wright and Wanstall (1977)

Tree or forest type	Location	Interval	Source
Ponderosa pine	Eastern Oregon	18	H. Weaver (1974)
	Southern Nevada	8—10	H. Weaver (1974)
	Eastern Washington	8	H. Weaver (1974)
Sequoias	South-west USA	7—9	H. Weaver (1974)
Coniferous forest	Minnesota	80	Wright (1974)
Coniferous forest	Ontario	80	Cwynar (1978)
Sequoia—mixed conifer forest	California	9—16	Kilgore and Taylor (1979)

TABLE 2.2
Long-term forest burning frequencies in North America determined from tree-ring analyses and lake-core studies

The temperatures attained in fires

The effects which fires have on the environment depend very much on their size, duration, and intensity. Some fires are relatively quick and cool, and only affect ground vegetation. Other fires, crown fires, affect whole forests up to crown level and generate very high temperatures (table 2.3). In general forest fires are hotter than grassland fires. Perhaps

30

TABLE 2.3
Temperatures attained in fires (maxima)

Vegetation	Source	Temperature (°C)
Minnesota Jack pine	Ahlgren (1974)	800
Chaparral scrub	Ahlgren (1974)	538
British heath	Whittaker (1961)	840
Senegal savanna	Daubenmire (1968)	715
Japanese grassland	Daubenmire (1968)	887
Chaparral scrub	Mooney and Parsons (1973)	1 100
Nigerian savanna	Hopkins (1965)	> 538; 640
Sudanese savanna	Hopkins (1965)	850

more significantly in terms of forest management, fires which occur with great frequency do not attain too great a temperature level because there is inadequate inflammable material available to fire them. However, when man deliberately suppresses fire, as has frequently been normal policy in forest areas (see figure 2.2), large quantities of such inflammable materials build up; this means that when there is a fire it is of the hot, crown type. Such fires can be ecologically disastrous and there is now much debate about the wisdom of fire-suppression policies given, that in many forests, fires under so-called 'natural' conditions appear, as we have seen, to have been a relatively frequent and regular phenomenon.

Some consequences of fire-suppression

Given that fire has long been a feature of many ecosystems, and irrespective of whether the fires were or were not caused by man, it is clear that any deliberate policy of fire-

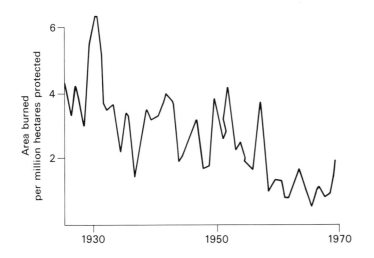

FIG. 2.2
Graph showing the reduction in the number of hectares burned per million hectares protected for the USA between 1926 and 1969 as a result of fire-suppression policies (after Brown and Davis, 1973, figure 2.1)

31

suppression will have important consequences for vegetation.

Fire-suppression, as has already been suggested, can magnify the adverse effects of fire. The position has been well stated by Sauer (1969: 14):

The great fires we have come to fear are effects of our civilisation. These are the crown fires of great depths and heat, notorious after-maths of the pyres of slash left by lumbering. We also increase fire hazard by the very giving of fire protection which permits the indefinite accumulation of inflammable litter. Under the natural and primitive order, such holocausts, that leave a barren waste, even to the destruction of the organic soil, were not common.

Recent studies have indicated that rigid fire-protection policies have often had undesirable results and as a consequence many foresters stress the need for 'environmental restoration burning' (Vankat, 1977). So, for example, in the coniferous forests of the middle and upper elevations in the Sierra Nevada mountains of California fire-protection since 1890 means that the stands have become denser, shadier, and less park-like and sequoia seedlings have decreased in number. Likewise, at lower elevations the Mediterranean semi-arid shrubland, called chaparral, has had its character changed. The vegetation has increased in density, the amount of combustible fuel has risen, fire-intolerant species have encroached, and vegetation diversity has decreased, resulting in a monotony of old-age stands instead of a mosaic of different successional stages. Mosquito invasion may also be related to fire-suppression (Harris, 1966). Unfavourable consequences of fire-suppression have also been noted in Alaska (Oberle, 1969). It has been found that when fire is excluded from many lowland sites an insulating carpet of moss tends to accumulate and raise the permafrost level. Permafrost close to the surface encourages the growth of black spruce, a low-growing species with little timber or food value. In the Kruger National Park, in South Africa, fires have occurred less frequently after the establishment of the game reserve, when it became uninhabited by natives and hunters. As a result of this, bush encroachment has taken place in areas that were formerly grassland, and the carrying capacity for grazing animals had declined. Controlled burning has been reinstituted as a necessary game-management operation.

Some effects of fire on vegetation

There are various major types of vegetation where there is evidence that fire has played a great role in their formation. This applies, for instance, to some savannas, mid-latitude grasslands, and shrublands (like the garrigue and maquis of the Mediterranean lands and the chaparral of the south-west United States). Before examining these, however, it is worth looking at some of the general consequences of burning.

Fire may assist in seed germination. For example, the abundant germination of dormant seeds on recently burned chaparral sites has been reported by many investigators and it seems that some seeds of chaparral species require scarification by fire. The better germination of those not requiring scarification may be related to removal by fire of competition, litter, and some substances in the soils which are toxic to plants (Hanes, 1971). Fire alters seedbeds. If litter and humus removal are substantial, large areas of this ash, bare soil, or thin humus may be created. Some trees, such as Douglas fir and the giant sequoia benefit from such seed beds (Heinselman and Wright, 1973). Fire sometimes triggers the release of seeds (as with the Jack pine), and seems to stimulate the vegetative reproduction of many woody and herbaceous species. Fire can control forest insects, parasites and fungi – a process termed 'sanitization'. It also seems to stimulate the flowering and fruiting of many shrubs and herbs, and to modify the physicochemical environment of the plants. Mineral elements are released both as ash and through increased decomposition rates of organic layers. Above all, areas subject to fire often show greater species diversity, which is a factor that tends to favour stability.

The role of grazing

Many of the world's grasslands have long been grazed by wild animals like the bison of North America or the large game of East Africa, but the introduction of pastoral economies also affects their nature and productivity (Coupland, 1979).

Light grazing may increase the productivity of wild pastures (Warren and Maizels, 1976). Nibbling, for example, may increase the vigour and growth of plants, and in some species such as the valuable African grass, *Themeda triandra*, the removal of coarse, dead stems permits succulent sprouts to shoot. Likewise the seeds of some plant species are spread efficiently by being carried in cattle guts, and are then placed in favourable seedbeds of dung or are trampled into the soil surface. Moreover, the passage of herbage through the gut and out as faeces modifies the nitrogen cycle, so that grazed pastures tend to be richer in nitrogen than ungrazed ones. Also, like fire, grazing can increase species diversity by opening out the community and creating more niches.

7
Grazing of domestic animals has many environmental consequences and assists in the maintenance of grassland such as the Pampas at Entre Rios in Argentina. Excessive grazing can compact the soil and contribute to both wind and water erosion

On the other hand, heavy grazing may be detrimental. Excessive trampling when conditions are dry will reduce the size of soil aggregates and plant litter to a point where they are subject to aeolian deflational processes. Trampling, by puddling the soil surface, can accelerate this soil deterioration and erosion as infiltration capacity is reduced. Heavy grazing can kill plants or lead to a great reduction in their level of photosynthesis. In addition, when relieved of competition from palatable plants or plants liable to trampling damage, resistant and usually unpalatable species expand their cover. Thus in the western USA poisonous burroweed has become dangerously common, and many woody species have invaded. These include the Mesquite (*Prosopis juliflora*), the big sagebrush (*Artemisia tridentata*) (Vale, 1974), the one-seed juniper (*Juniperus monosperma*) (Harris, 1966), and the Pinyon Pine (Blackburn and Tueller, 1970). Some of the plants that have invaded grasslands in California are aliens, and these have been studied in detail by Burcham (1970). It is clear from his long-term analysis of their spread (see table 2.4) that the aliens have spread in four distinct stages. These are stages of progressively less desirable species and indicate increasing intensities of grazing use. In general he demonstrates that perennials have tended to be replaced through time by greater numbers of annuals, which have the ability to germinate quickly, grow rapidly, and produce great quantities of viable seed.

In Australia (R. M. Moore, 1959) the widespread adoption of sheep grazing led to great changes in the nature of grasslands over extensive areas. In particular, the introduction of sheep led to the removal of kangaroo grass (*Themeda australis*) — a predominantly summer-growing species — and its replacement by essentially winter-growing species such as *Danthonia* and *Stipa*.

TABLE 2.4
*Stages in the invasion of
Californian grasslands by aliens*

Stage 1 (1845 →)
  Wild oats (*Avena fatua* + *A. barbata*) + black mustard (*Brassica nigra*)

Stage 2 (1855 →)
  Filarees (*Erodium* spp.), wild barleys (*Hordeum* spp.), nitgrass (*Gastridium ventricosum*) and native annuals.

Stage 3 (1870 →)
  Mouse barley (*Hordeum leporinum*), red brome (*Bromus rubens*), silver hairgrass (*Aira caryophyllea*), Chile tarweed (*Madia sativa*) + star thistles (*Centaurea*).

Stage 4 (1900 →)
  Medusa-head (*Taeniatherum asperum*), barb goatgrass (*Aegilops triuncialis*), dogtail grass (*Cynosaurus echinatus*) and annual false-brome (*Brachypodium distachyon*).

Source: data in Burcham (1970)

Similarly in Britain many plants are avoided by grazing animals because they are distasteful, hairy, prickly or even poisonous (Tivy, 1971). The persistence and continued spread of bracken (*Pteridium aquilinium*) on heavily grazed rough pasture in Scotland is aided by the fact that it is slightly poisonous, especially to young stock. The success of bracken is furthered by its reaction to burning, for with its extensive system of underground stems (rhizomes) it tends to be little damaged by most fires.

The survival and prevalence of shrubs such as elder (*Sarnbucus nigra*), gorse (*Ulex* spp.), broom (*Sarothamus scoparius*) and the common weeds rag-wort (*Senecio jacobaea*) and creeping thistle (*Cirsium arvense*), in face of grazing, can be attributed to their lack of palatability.

The role of grazing in causing marked deterioration of habitat has been the subject of further discussion in the context of upland Britain. Darling (1956: 780–1) has written:

It may be said in general that man's ecological dominance by pastoralism of domesticated animals over wild lands has resulted in marked deterioration of habitat. Vegetational climaxes have been broken insidiously rather than by some grand traumatic act, and, just as cultivation of food plants involves setting back ecological succession to a primary stage, pastoralism deflects succession to the xeric, a profound and dangerous change.

In particular, Darling stresses that while trees bring up nutrients from rocks and keep the mineral matter in circulation, pastoralism means the export of calcium phosphate and nitrogenous organic matter. The vegetation gradually deteriorates, the calcicoles go and the herbage becomes deficient in both minerals and protein. Progressively more xerophytic plants come in: *Nardus stricta, Molinia caeruleea, Erica tetralix*, and then *Scirpus caespitosa*.

In general terms it is clear that in many parts of the world the grass family is well equipped to withstand grazing. Many plants have their growing points located on the apex of leaves and shoots, but grasses have the bulk of the reproduction of fresh tissue taking place at the base of the grass leaves. This part is least likely to be damaged by grazing and allows regrowth to continue at the same time as material is being removed.

Communities severely affected by the treading activities of animals (and, indeed man) tend to have certain distinctive characteristics. These include diminutiveness (since the smaller the plant is the more protection it will get from soil surface irregularities), strong ramification (the plant stems and leaves spread close to the ground), small leaves (which are less easily damaged by treading), tissue firmness (so that by cell wall strength and thickness plants will resist mechanical damage), a bending ability, strong vegetative increase and dispersal (e.g. by stolons), small hard seeds which can be easily dispersed, and the production of a large number of seeds per plant (which is particularly important because the mortality of seedlings is high under treading and trampling conditions).

Deforestation

The deliberate removal of forest is one of the most long-continued and most significant of the ways in which man has modified his environment, whether achieved by fire or by cutting. Pollen analysis shows that temperate forests were removed in Mesolithic and Neolithic times and at an accelerating rate thereafter. Sometimes the removal has been to allow agriculture, at others to provide fuel for domestic purposes, at others to provide charcoal, at others to provide wood for construction, at others to fuel locomotives, at others to smoke fish, and at others to smelt metals. The Phoenicians were exporting cedars as early as 4600 years ago (Mikesell, 1969) both to the Pharaohs and to Mesopotamia. Attica in Greece was laid bare by the fifth century BC and classical writers alude to the effects of fire, cutting, and the destructive nibble of the goat. The great phase of deforestation in central and western Europe, described by Darby

(1956: 194) as 'the great heroic period of reclamation' occurred from AD 1050 onwards for about 200 years (figure 2.3). In particular the Germans moved eastward: 'What the new west meant to young America in the nineteenth century, the new east meant to Germany in the Middle Ages' (Darby, 1956: 196).

The landscape of Europe was transformed, just as that of North America, Australia, New Zealand, and South Africa was to be as a result of the European expansions, especially in the nineteenth century.

With regard to the equatorial rain forests, the researches of Flenley and others (Flenley, 1979) have indicated that

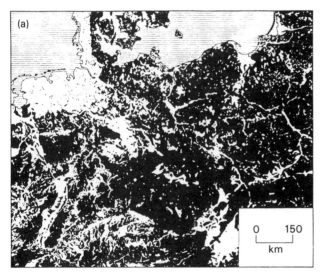

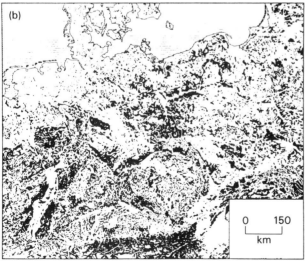

FIG. 2.3
The changing distribution of forest in Central Europe between (a) AD 900 and (b) AD 1900 (reprinted from Darby, 1956: 202, 203, in Man's role in changing the face of the Earth, *ed.* W. L. Thomas, *by permission of The University of Chicago Press © The University of Chicago 1956)*

37

forest clearance for agriculture has been going on since at least 3000 BP in Africa, 7000 BP in South and Central America and possibly since 9000 BP or earlier in India and New Guinea.

8

One of the most serious environmental problems in tropical areas is the removal of the rain forest. Removal of trees in Amazonia on slopes as steep as these will cause accelerated erosion, loss of soil nutrients and may promote lateritization

One of the great phases of forest clearance occurring at the present time is that in the humid tropics. The results of detailed investigations of the reported regression rates for tropical moist forests in thirteen selected countries representing about 18% of the world total area for these forests (table 2.5) indicate that the annual regression rate for these countries is greater than 2 million hectares (or 1.2% of their tropical moist forest area). If these figures are extrapolated (Scott, 1978) the yearly regression rate for the world's tropical moist forests is about 11 million hectares per year (10.9 ha/min). Already West Africa has lost 72% of its moist forests and southern Asia 63.5%. This is potentially extremely serious because as Poore (1976: 138) has stated these forests are 'a source-book of potential foods, drinks, medicines, contraceptives, abortifacients, gums, resins, scents, colourants, specific pesticides, and so on, of which we have

TABLE 2.5
*Reported regression rates for
tropical moist forests in thirteen
selected countries*

Country	Area of forest reported to be lost per year (million ha)
Bangladesh	0.01
Colombia	0.25
Costa Rica	0.06
Ghana	0.05
Ivory Coast	0.40
Laos	0.30
Madagascar	0.30
Malaysia	0.15
North Vietnam	0.01
Papua—New Guinea	0.02
Philippines	0.26
Thailand	0.30
Venezuela	0.05 (?)

Source: after Sommer, in Scott, 1978, table 1

scarcely turned the pages'. Their removal may also create lateritization (see p. 116), climatic change (see p. 241) and increased rates of erosion (see p. 127).

Some traditional societies have developed means of exploiting the rain forest environment which tend to minimize the problems posed by soil fertility deterioration, soil erosion, and vegetation degradation. Such a system is shifting agriculture (*swidden*). As Geertz (1963: 16) has remarked:

In ecological terms, the most distinctive positive characteristic of swidden agriculture...is that it is integrated into and, when genuinely adoptive, maintains the general structure of the pre-existing natural ecosystem into which it is projected, rather than creating and sustaining one organised along novel lines and displaying novel dynamics.

The tropical rain forest and the swidden plots have certain common characteristics. Both are closed cover systems, in part because in swidden some trees are left standing, in part because some tree crops (such as banana, papaya, areca, etc.) are planted, but also because food plants are not planted in an open field, crop-row manner, but helter-skelter in a tightly woven, dense botanical fabric. It is in Geertz's words (1963: 25) 'a miniaturized tropical forest'. Secondly, swidden agriculture normally involves a wide range of cultigens, thereby having a high diversity index like the rain forest itself. Thirdly, both swidden plots and the rain forest have high quantities of nutrients locked up in the biotic community (Douglas, 1969) compared to that in the soil. The primary concern of 'slash-and-burn' activities is not mere clearing of the land but rather the transfer of the rich store of nutrients locked up in the prolific vegetation of the rain forest to a botanical complex whose yield to man is a great deal larger. If the period of cultivation is not too long and the period of fallow is long enough, an equilibrated, non-deteriorating and reasonably productive farming regime can be sustained in spite of the rather impoverished soil base upon which it rests.

Unfortunately this system is susceptible to breakdown, especially when population increase precludes the maintenance of an adequately long fallow period. When this happens, the rain forest cannot recuperate and is replaced by a more open vegetation assemblage which is often dominated by the notorious *Imperata* savanna grass which has turned so much of south-east Asia into a green desert. *Imperata cylindrica* is a tall grass which springs up from rhizomes. Because of its rhizomes it is fire-resistant, but because it is a tall grass it helps to spread fire (Gourou, 1961).

Having considered the importance of the three basic processes of fire, grazing, and deforestation, we can now turn to a consideration of some of the major changes in vegetation types that have taken place over extensive areas as a result of such activities.

Secondary rain forest

When an area of rain forest that has been cleared for cultivation or timber exploitation is abandoned by man, the forest begins to regenerate, but for an extended period of years the type of forest that occurs — secondary forest — is very different in character from the virgin forest that it replaces. The features of such secondary forest, which is widespread in many tropical regions, have been summarized by Richards (1952) and Ellenberg (1979).

First, secondary forest is lower and consists of trees of smaller average dimensions than those of primary forest, but since it is comparatively rare that an area of primary forest is clear-felled or completely destroyed by fire, occasional trees much larger than the average are usually found scattered through secondary forest. Secondly, very young secondary forest is often remarkably regular and uniform in structure, though the abundance of small climbers and young saplings gives it a dense and tangled appearance which is unlike that of primary forest and makes it laborious to penetrate. Thirdly, secondary forest tends to be much poorer in species than primary, and is sometimes, though by no means always, dominated by a single species, or a small number of species.

Fourthly, the dominant trees of secondary forest are light-demanding and intolerant of shade, most of the trees possess efficient dispersal mechanisms (having seeds or fruits well adapted for transport by wind or animals), and most of them can grow very quickly. Some species are known to grow at rates of up to 12 m in 3 years, but they tend to be short-lived and to mature and reproduce early. One consequence of their rapid growth is that their wood often has a soft texture and low density.

The role of man in the creation and maintenance of savanna

The savannas can be defined, following Hills (1965: 2181−9), as:

a plant formation of tropical regions, comprising a virtually continuous ecologically dominant stratum of more or less xeromorphic plants, of which herbaceous plants, especially grasses and sedges, are frequently the principal, and occasionally the only, components, although woody plants often of the dimension of trees or palms generally occur and are present in varying densities.

They are extremely widespread in low latitudes, covering about 18 million square km(an area about 2.6 million square km greater than that of the tropical rain forest). Their origin has been the subject of great contention in the literature of biogeography, though common ground which is conceded by most savanna research workers is that no matter what savanna origins may be, the agent which seems to maintain them is intentional or inadvertent burning (Scott, 1977). As with most major vegetation types there are a great number of interrelated factors involved in causing savanna and too many arguments about origins have neglected this fact (figure 2.4). Confusion has also arisen because of the failure to distinguish clearly between predisposing, causal, resulting, and maintaining factors (Hills, 1965). It appears, for instance, that in the savanna regions around the periphery of the Amazon basin, the climate *predisposes* the vegetation towards the development of savanna rather than forest. The geomorphic evolution of the landscape may be a *causal* factor; increased laterite development a *resulting* factor; and fire, a *maintaining* factor.

Originally, however, savanna was envisaged as being a predominantly natural vegetation type of climatic origin (see, for example, Schimper, 1903) and the climatologist Köppen used the term 'savanna climate' implying that a specific type

9

The Serengeti area of Tanzania provides a fine example of savanna vegetation

of climate is associated with all areas of savanna origin. According to supporters of this theory savanna is better adapted than other plant formations to withstand the annual cycle of alternating soil moisture: rain forests could not resist the extended period of extreme drought, while dry forests could not compete successfully with perennial grasses during the equally lengthy period with a large water surplus (Sarmiento and Monasterio, 1975).

Other workers have championed the importance of edaphic (soil) conditions, including poor drainage, soils which have a low water-retention capacity in the dry season, soils with a shallow profile due to the development of a lateritic crust, and soils with a low nutrient supply (either because they are developed on a poor parent rock such as quartzite or because

42

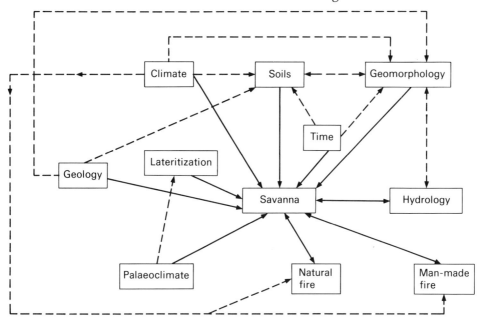

FIG. 2.4
*The interrelated factors
involved in the formation of
savanna vegetation*

the soil has undergone an extended period of leaching on an old land surface). Associated with soil characteristics, ages of land surfaces and degree of drainage is the geomorphology of an area (as stressed, for example, by Cole, 1963). This may also be an important factor in savanna development. Some other workers — for example, Eden (1974) — find that savannas are the product of former drier conditions (such as late Pleistocene aridity) but that in spite of a moistening climate they have been maintained by fire. He points to the fact that the patches of savanna in southern Venezuela occur in forest areas of similar humidity and soil infertility, suggesting that neither soil nor drainage nor climate was the cause. Moreover, the present 'islands' of savanna are characterized by species which are also present elsewhere in tropical American savannas and whose disjunct distribution conforms to the hypothesis of a previous widespread continuity of that formation.

The importance of fire in maintaining and originating some savannas is suggested by the fact that many of the savanna trees are fire-resistant. Controlled experiments in Africa (Hopkins, 1965) demonstrate that some tree species, such as *Burkea africana* and *Lophira lanceolata* withstand repeated burning better than others. There are also many observations of the frequency with which, for example, African herdsmen and agriculturalists burn over much of tropical Africa and thereby maintain grassland. On the other hand Morgan and

The Human Impact

Moss (1965) express some doubts about the role of fire in western Nigeria, and point out that fire is not itself necessarily an independent variable:

The evidence suggests that some notions of the extent and destructiveness of savanna fires are rather exaggerated. In particular the idea of an annual burn which affects a large proportion of the area in each year would seem to be false. It is more likely that some patches, peculiarly susceptible to fire, as a result of edaphic or biotic influences upon the character of the community itself, are repeatedly burned, whereas others are hardly, if ever, affected....It is also important to note that there is no evidence anywhere along the forest fringe...to suggest that fire sweeps into the forest, effecting notable destruction of forest trees.

Some savannas are undoubtedly natural, for pollen analysis in South America shows that savanna vegetation was present before the arrival of man. Nonetheless even natural savannas, when subjected to human pressures, change their characteristics. For example, the inability of grass cover to maintain itself over long periods in the presence of heavy stock grazing may be documented from many of the warm lands of the world (Johannessen, 1963). Heavy grazing tends to remove the fuel (grass) over much of the surface. The frequency of fires is therefore much reduced and tree and bush invasion takes place. As Johannessen (p. 111) wrote:

Without intense, almost annual fires, seedlings of trees and shrubs are able to invade the savannas where the grass sod has been opened by heavy grazing...the age and size of the trees on the savannas usually confirm the relative recency of the invasion.

In the case of the savannas of interior Honduras he reports that they only had a scattering of trees when the Spaniards first encountered them, whereas now they have been invaded by an assortment of trees and tall shrubs (table 2.6).

TABLE 2.6
Invasive trees and shrubs involved in bush encroachment in Honduras

Mimosa tenuiflora	*Acacia riparoides*
Acacia farnesiana	*Prosopis juliflora*
Acacia costaricensis	*Xylosma flexuosum*
Acacia pennatula	*Zanthoxylum culantillo*

Source: Johannessen (1963)

Elsewhere in Latin America changes in the nature and density of population have also led to a change in the nature and distribution of savanna grassland. C. F. Bennett (1968: 101) noted that in Panama the decimation of the Indian population saw the re-establishment of trees:

44

Large areas which today are covered by dense forest were in farms, grassland or low second growth in the early sixteenth century when the Spaniards arrived. At that time horses were ridden with ease through areas which today are most easily penetrated by river, so dense has the tree growth become since the Indians died away.

The spread of desert vegetation on desert margins

One of the most contentious and important environmental issues of recent years has been the debate surrounding the question of the alleged expansion of deserts.

This has variously been termed 'desertization' and 'desertification'. Rapp (1974: 3) defines desertization as 'the spread of desert-like conditions in arid or semi-arid areas, due to man's influence or to climatic change'. In this definition lies one of the problems of desertization — its cause. The question has been asked whether this process is caused by temporary drought periods of high magnitude, whether it is due to long-term climatic change towards aridity (either as alleged post-Glacial progressive desiccation or as part of a 200-year cycle), whether it is caused by man-induced climatic change (see p. 250), or whether it is the result of human action through man's degradation of the biological environments in arid zones. There is little doubt that severe droughts do take place, and have taken place (Nicholson, 1978), and that their

10
In the Sahel zone of West Africa and on other desert margins human activities such as wood collection, overgrazing and cultivation in drought prone areas has led to the process of desertization

effects become worse as human and domestic animal populations increase. The devastating drought in the African Sahel from 1968 to 1973 caused ecological stress of a higher order than the broadly comparable droughts of 1910–15 and 1944–8, largely because of the increasing anthropogenic pressures.

The venerable idea that climate is deteriorating through the mechanism of post-Glacial progressive desiccation is now descredited (see Goudie, 1972, for a critical analysis), though the idea that the Sahel zone is currently going through a 200-year cycle of drought has been proposed (Winstanley, 1973). However, numerous studies of available meteorological data (which in some cases date back as far as 130–135 years) do not allow any conclusion as to systematic long-term changes in rainfall, and the case for climatic deterioration — whether natural or aggravated by man — is not proven. Indeed, in a judicious review, Rapp (1974: 29) wrote that after consideration of the evidence for the role of climatic change in desertization his conclusion was 'that the reported desertization northwards and southwards from the Sahara could not be explained by a general trend towards drier climate during this century'.

It is, therefore, evident that it is largely a combination of man's activities (figure 2.5) with occasional runs of dry years that leads to presently observed desertization. The process also seems to be fiercest not in desert interiors but on the less arid marginal areas around them. It is in the semi-arid areas, where biological productivity is much greater than in the extremely arid zones, where precipitation is frequent enough and intense enough to cause rapid erosion of unprotected soils, and where man is prone to mistake short-term economic gains under temporary favourable climatic conditions for long-term stability, that there is to be found the combination of circumstances particularly favourable to desert expansion. It is in these marginal areas that dry farming and cattle rearing can be a success in good years so that susceptible areas are ploughed and cattle numbers become greater than the vegetation can support in dry years.

Therefore depletion of vegetation has occurred which has set in train such insidious processes as water erosion (see p. 126) and deflation. The vegetation has been removed by clearance for cultivation, by the cutting and uprooting of woody species for fuel, by overgrazing, and by burning of vegetation for pasture and charcoal.

An attempt to illustrate the shift in the boundary of desert vegetation at the expense of sub-desert scrub and

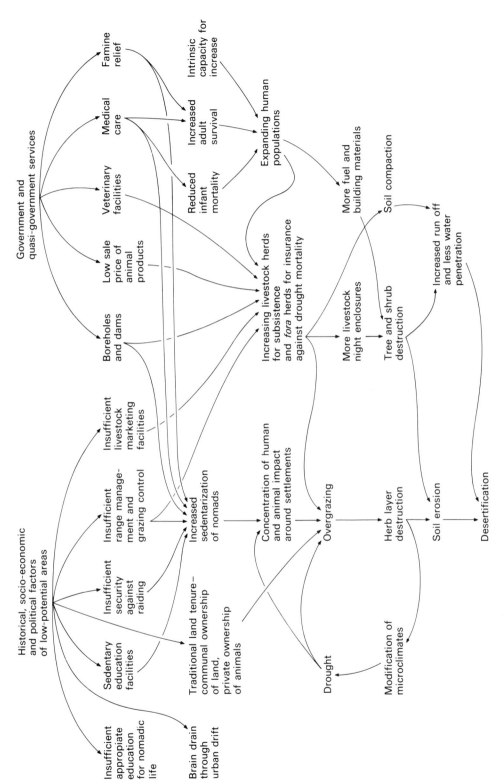

FIG. 2.5   *Some causal factors in desert encroachment in northern Kenya (after Lamprey, 1978, figure 2)*

47

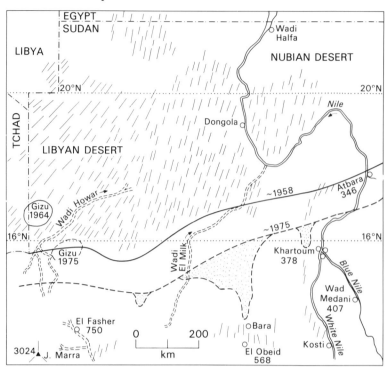

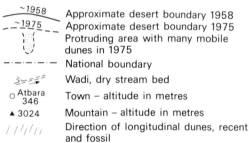

~1958	Approximate desert boundary 1958
~1975	Approximate desert boundary 1975
	Protruding area with many mobile dunes in 1975
	National boundary
	Wadi, dry stream bed
o Atbara 346	Town – altitude in metres
▲ 3024	Mountain – altitude in metres
/ / / / /	Direction of longitudinal dunes, recent and fossil

FIG. 2.6
Map showing desert encroachment in the northern Sudan, 1958–75, as represented by the position of the boundary between sub-desert scrub and grassland and the desert (after Rapp et al., *1976, figure 8.5.3)*

grassland in the Sudan between 1958 and 1975 is shown in figure 2.6. In a sense, however, such diagrams are misleading for very often the vegetation degradation occurs as a 'rash' around settlements rather than as an advance over a broad front. Woodcutting is a very serious cause of vegetation decline around almost all towns and cities of the Sahelian and Sudanian zones of Africa. Likewise, the installation of modern boreholes has allowed extreme multiplication of livestock numbers and large-scale destruction of the vegetation in a radius of 15–30 km around boreholes (figure 2.7). Given this localization of degradation, amelioration schemes such as local tree planting may be of some effectiveness, but ideas of planting green belts as a 'cordon sanitaire' along the desert edge (whatever that is)

48

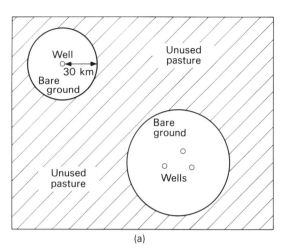
(a)

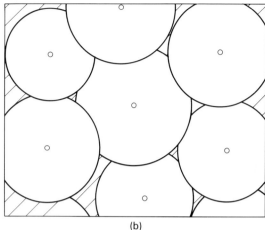
(b)

FIG. 2.7
Relation between spacing of wells and over-grazing:
(a) Original situation. End of dry season 1. Herd size limited by dry season pasture. Small population can live on pastoral economy
(b) After well-digging project, but no change in traditional herding. End of dry season 2. Large-scale erosion. Larger total subsistence herd, and more people can live there until a situation when grazing is finished in a drought year. Then the system collapses (after Rapp, 1974)

would not halt deterioration of the situation beyond this Maginot line (Warren and Maizels, 1977: 222). The deserts are not invading from without: the land is deteriorating from within.

There has been considerable debate as to whether the vegetation change and environmental degradation associated with desertization is irreversible.

In many cases where ecological conditions are favourable because of the existence of such factors as deep sandy soils, or favourable hydrologic characteristics, vegetation is able to recover once the excess pressures on it are eliminated. There is evidence of this in arid zones from all over the world where temporary or permanent enclosures have been set up (Le Houérou, 1977). The speed of recovery will depend on the stage of deterioration reached, the size of the area which is degraded, the nature of the soils and moisture resources, and the character of the local vegetation. It needs to be remembered in this connection that much desert vegetation is adapted to drought and to harsh conditions and that it often has built-in adaptations which enable a rapid response to improved circumstances.

Nonetheless, elsewhere experiments as well as observations in natural conditions tend to show that in certain specific circumstances recovery is so slow and so limited that it may be appropriate to talk of 'irreversible desertization'. Le Houérou (1977: 419), for example, has pointed to such a case in North Africa:

…in southern Tunisia, tracks made by the tanks and wheeled vehicles of Allied and Axis armies are still apparent on the ground and in the devastated and unregenerated vegetation 35 years after the conclusion

49

of the fighting. The perennial species have not re-established themselves in spite of several series of years with long-term, above-average rainfall in the 1950's, the late 1960's, and the early 1970's, although in this area grazing pressure is very low due to the absence of permanent water.

The suggestion has sometimes been made that not only are deserts expanding because of the activities of man but that the deserts themselves are man-made. There are authors who have suggested, for example, that the Thar Desert of India is a post-Glacial and possibly post-Medieval creation (see Allchin *et al.*, 1977, for a critique of such views), while Ehrlich and Ehrlich (1970) have written: 'The vast Sahara desert itself is largely manmade, the result of overgrazing, faulty irrigation, deforestation, perhaps combined with a shift in the course of a jet stream.' Nothing could be further from the truth. The Sahara is many millions of years old, predates man, and is the product of the nature of the general atmospheric circulation, occupying an area of dry descending air.

The maquis of the Mediterranean lands

Around much of the Mediterranean basin there is a plant formation called *maquis*. This consists of a stand of xerophilous non-deciduous bushes and shrubs which are evergreen and thick and whose trunks are normally obscured by low-level branches. It includes such plants as holly oak (*Quercus ilex*), kermes oak (*Quercus coccifera*), tree heath (*Erica arborea*), broom heath (*Erica scoparia*) and strawberry trees (*Arbutus unedo*).

Some of the maquis may represent a stage in the evolution towards true forest in places where the climax has not yet been reached, but in large areas it represents the degeneration of the forest. Considerable concern has been expressed about the speed with which degeneration to and degeneration beyond maquis is taking place as a result of human influences (Tomaselli, 1977), of which cutting, grazing, and fire are probably the most important and long-continued. Charcoal burners, goats and frequent fires of the resinous plants in the dry Mediterranean summer have taken their toll.

There is considerable evidence that the maquis vegetation is in part adapted to, and in part a response to, fire. One effect of fire is to reduce the frequency of standard trees and to favour species which after burning send up a series of suckers from ground level. Both *Quercus ilex* and *Quercus coccifera* seem to respond in this way. Similarly, a number of

11
The maquis of the Mediterranean lands illustrated here in Corsica is a vegetation type in which man has played a major role. It represents the degeneration of the natural forest cover

species (e.g. *Cistus albidus*, *Erica arborea* and *Pinus halepensis*) seem to be positively favoured by fire, perhaps because it suppresses competition, or perhaps because (as with the comparable chaparral of the south-west USA) a short burst of heat encourages germination (Wright and Wanstall, 1977).

The prairie problem

The mid-latitude grasslands of North America — the prairies — are another major vegetation type that can be used to examine the role of man, though as in the case of savanna grasslands in the tropics, his role is the subject of controversy.

It used to be fairly generally believed that the prairies were essentially a climatically related phenomenon. Workers like J. E. Weaver (1954) believed that under the prevailing conditions of soil and climate the invasion and establishment of trees was greatly hindered by the presence of a dense sod. High evapotranspiration levels combined with low precipitation were thought to give a competitive advantage to herbaceous plants with shallow, densely ramifying root systems and capable of completing their life-cycles rapidly.

51

An alternative view was, however, put forward by Stewart (1956: 128):

The fact that throughout the tall-grass prairie planted groves of many species have flourished and have reproduced seedlings during moist years and, furthermore, have survived the most severe and prolonged period of drought in the 1930s suggests that there is no climatic barrier to forests in the area.

Other arguments along the same lines have been advanced. Wells (1965), for example, has noted that in the Great Plains a number of woodland species, notably the Junipers, are remarkably drought-resistant and that their present range extends into the Chihuahua Desert where they often grow in association with one of the most xerophytic shrubs of the American deserts, the creosote bush (*Larrea divaricata*). He remarks (p. 247): 'There is no range of climate in the vast grassland climate of the central plains of North America which can be described as too arid for all species of trees native to the region.' Moreover, confirming Stewart, he points out that numerous plantations and shelter-belts have indicated that trees can survive for at least 50 years in a 'grassland' climate. One of his most persuasive arguments is that when one looks at the distribution of vegetation types in the plains one of the most striking vegetational features is the widespread but local occurrence of woodlands along escarpments and other abrupt breaks in topography remote from fluvial irrigation. A probable explanation for this is that fire effects are greatest on flat level surfaces where there are higher wind-speeds and no breaks to the travel of fire. It has also been noted that where burning has been restricted there has been extension of woodland into grass-land. The reason why fire tends to promote the establishment of grassland has been summarized by Cooper (1961: 150–51).

In open country fire favours grass over shrubs. Grasses are better adapted to withstand fire than are woody plants. The growing point of dormant grasses from which issues the following year's growth, lies near or beneath the ground, protected from all but the severest heat. A grass fire removes only one year's growth, and usually much of this is dried and dead. The living tissue of shrubs, on the other hand, stands well above the ground, fully exposed to fire. When it is burned, the growth of several years is destroyed. Even though many shrubs sprout vigorously after burning, repeated loss of their top growth keeps them small. Perennial grasses, moreover, produce seeds in abundance one or two years after germination; most woody plants require several years to reach seed-bearing age. Fires that are frequent enough to inhibit seed production in woody plants usually restrict the shrubs to a rela-tively minor part of the grassland area.

Thus as with savanna (see p. 41), anthropogenic fires may be a factor which maintains, and possibly forms, grasslands in the Great Plains, though again following the analogy with savanna, it is possible that some of the American prairies may have developed in a post-Glacial dry phase and that with a later increase in rainfall re-establishment of a forest cover was impeded by man through his use of fire and by grazing animals. The grazing animals concerned were not necessarily domesticated, however, for Larson (1940) has suggested that some of the short-grass plains were maintained by wild bison. These, he believed, stocked the plains to carrying capacity so that the introduction of domestic livestock such as cattle after the destruction of the wild game was merely a substitution so far as the effect of grazing on plants is concerned. There is indeed pollen analytical evidence that shows the presence of prairie in the western mid-west over 11 000 years ago, prior to man's arrival (Bernabo and Webb, 1977). Some of it at least may therefore be natural.

Comparable arguments have attended the origin of the great Pampa grassland of Argentina. The first Europeans who penetrated into the landscape were much impressed by the treeless open country and it was always taken for granted, and indeed became a dogma, that the grassland was a primary climax unit. However, this interpretation was successfully challenged, notably by Schmieder (1927a, 1927b) who noted that planted trees did well, that precipitation levels were quite adequate to maintain tree growth, and that in topographically favourable locations such as the steep gullies (*barrancas*) near Buenos Aires there were numerous endemic representatives of the former forest cover (*monte*). Schmieder saw the Pampa grasslands as having been produced by a pre-Spanish aboriginal hunting and pastoral population, the density of which had been underestimated, but whose efficiency in the use of fire was proven.

Post-glacial vegetational change in Britain

The classic interpretation of the vegetational changes of post-Glacial (Holocene) times — that is, over the past 11 000 or so years — has been in terms of climate. That changes in the vegetation of Britain and elsewhere in western Europe took place was identified by pollen analysts and palaeobotanists, and these changes were used to construct a model of climatic change — the Blytt–Sernander model (table 2.7). There was thus something of a chicken-and-egg situation; vegetational evidence was used to reconstruct past climates, and past climates were used to explain vegetational change.

53

Blytt and Sernander period	Climate	Date of boundary
Sub-Atlantic	Cold and wet Oceanic	
		c. 2500 BP
Sub-Boreal	Warm and dry Continental	
	Elm decline	*c.* 5000 BP
Atlantic	Warm and wet Oceanic	
		c. 7500 BP
Boreal	Warmer than before and dry	
		c. 9600 BP
Pre-Boreal	Sub-Arctic	

One vegetational change which has occasioned particular interest is the fall in *Ulmus* pollen — the so-called elm decline — which appears in all pollen diagrams from north-west Europe. A very considerable number of radiocarbon dates have shown that this decline was approximately synchronous over wide areas and took place at about 5000 BP (Pennington, 1974). It is now recognized that various hypotheses can be advanced in an attempt to explain this major event in vegetation history: the original climatic interpretation; progressive soil deterioration; the spread of disease; or the role of man. Man may have contributed to soil deterioration (see p. 117) and affected elms thereby. Troels-Smith (1956), however, postulated that around 5000 years ago a new technique of keeping stalled domestic animals was introduced into Europe by Neolithic peoples, and that these animals were fed by repeated gathering of heavy branches of those trees known to be nutritious — the elms. This, it is held, would reduce very greatly the pollen production of the elms. In Denmark it was found that the first appearance of the pollen of a weed, Ribwort plantain (*Plantago lanceolata*), always coincided with the fall in the elm pollen levels, confirming the association with man.

Experiments have also shown that Neolithic man, equipped with polished stone axes, could cut down mature trees and clear by burning a fair-sized patch of established forests within about a week. Such clearings were used for cereal cultivation. In Denmark a genuine chert Neolithic axe was fitted into an ash-wood shaft (figure 2.8). Three men managed to clear about 600 m^2 of birch forest in 4 h. Remarkably, more than 100 trees were felled with one axe-head, which had not been sharpened for about 4000 years (Cole, 1970: 38).

Thus far we have essentially been considering man's general impact on general assemblages of vegetation over broad zones. However, when one turns to questions such as the

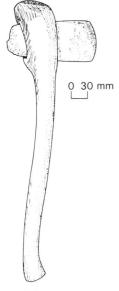

0 30 mm

FIG. 2.8
*A Neolithic chert axe-blade
from Denmark, of the type
which has been shown to be
effective at cutting forest in
experimental studies (after
S. Cole, 1970, figure 25)*

range of individual plant species the role of man is no less significant.

Introduction, invasion, and explosion

Man is an important agent in the spread of plants and other organisms (Bates, 1956). Some plants are introduced deliberately by man to new areas; these include crops, ornamentals and miscellaneous landscape modifiers (trees for reafforestation, cover plants for erosion control, etc.). Indeed, some plants such as bananas and breadfruit have become completely dependent on man for reproduction and dispersal, and in some cases they have lost the capacity for producing viable seeds and depend on man-controlled vegetation propagation. Most cultigens have not been able to survive without human attention, partly because of this low capacity for self-propagation, but also because they usually cannot compete with the better-adapted native vegetation.

However, some domesticated plants have, when left to their own devices, shown that they are capable of at least ephemeral colonization, and a small number of them have successfully naturalized themselves in areas other than their supposed region of origin (Gade, 1976). Examples of such plants include several umbelliferous annual garden crops (fennel, parsnip, and celery) which though native to Mediterranean Europe have colonized waste places in California. The Irish potato, which is native to South America, grows without human control in the mountains of Lesotho. The peach (in New Zealand), the guava (in the Philippines), coffee (in Haiti) and the coconut palm (on Indian Ocean island strands) are perennials that have established themselves as wild-growing populations, though the last-named is probably within the hearth region of its probable domestication. In Paraguay, orange trees (originating in south-east Asia and the East Indies) have demonstrated their ability to survive in direct competition with natural vegetation.

Plants that have been introduced deliberately because they have perceived virtue (Jarvis, 1979) can be usefully divided into an economic group (for example, crops, timber trees, etc.) and an ornamental or amenity one. In the case of the British Isles Jarvis believes that it can be argued that the great bulk of the deliberate introductions before the sixteenth century had some sort of economic merit, but that only a handful of the species introduced thereafter were brought in because of their utilitarian merit. Plants were introduced increasingly for their curiosity or decorative value.

Many plants, however, have been dispersed accidentally

as a result of man's activities: some by adhesion to moving objects such as man himself or his vehicles, some among crop seed, some among other plants (like fodder or packing materials), some among minerals (such as ballast or road metal), and some by the carriage of seed for purposes other than planting (such as drug plants). As illustrated in figure 2.9, based on California, the establishment of alien species proceeds rapidly. In the Pampa of Argentina, Schmieder (1927b) estimates that invasion of the country by European plants has taken place on such a large scale that at present only one-tenth of the plants growing wild in the Pampa are native.

The accidental dispersal of such plants and organisms can have serious ecological consequences. In Britain, for instance, many elm trees died in the 1970s because of the accidental introduction of the Dutch elm disease fungus which arrived on imported timber at certain ports, notably Avonmouth and the Thames Estuary ports (Sarre, 1978). Ocean islands have often been particularly vulnerable. The simplicity of their ecosystem inevitably leads to diminished stability, and

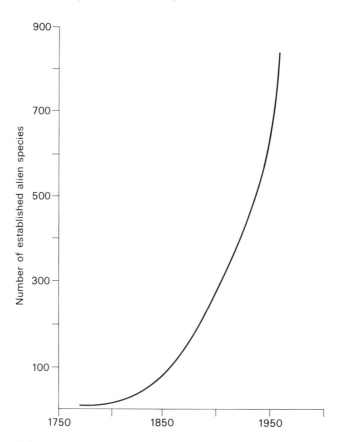

FIG. 2.9
Estimation of the establishment of alien plant species in California, USA, since 1750 (modified after Frenkel, 1970, figure 3)

introduced species often find that the relative lack of competition enables them to broaden their ecological range to one wider than on the continents. Moreover, because the natural species inhabiting remote islands have been selected primarily for their dispersal capacity, they have not necessarily been dominant or even highly successful in their original continental setting. Therefore, introduced species may prove more vigorous and effective (Holdgate and Wace, 1961). There may also be a lack of indigenous species to adapt to conditions such as bare ground caused by man. Thus introduced weeds may catch on.

There are many other examples of ecological explosions caused by man through his creation of new habitats. Some of the most striking are associated with the establishment of man-made lakes in place of rivers. Riverine species which cannot cope with the changed conditions tend to disappear, while others that can exploit the new sources of food, and reproduce themselves under the new conditions, multiply very fast in the absence of competition (Lowe-McConnell, 1975). Vegetation on land flooded as the lake waters rise decomposes to provide a rich supply of nutrients which allow explosive outgrowth of organisms as the new lake fills. In particular floating plants may form dense mats of vegetation, which in turn support large populations of invertebrate animals, may cause fish deaths by deoxygenating the water, and can create a serious nuisance to turbines, navigators, and fishermen. On Lake Kariba in Central Africa there were explosive growths of the South American water fern (*Salvinia*), bladderwort (*Utricularia*) and the African water lettuce (*Pistia stratiotes*); on the Nile behind the Jebel Aulia Dam there was a great development of the water hyacinth (*Eichhornia crassipes*); and in the Tennessee Valley lakes there was a massive spreading of the Eurasian water-millfoil (*Myriophyllum*).

The introduction of new animals can have an adverse effect on plant species. A clear demonstration of this comes from the atoll of Laysan. Rabbits and hares were introduced in 1903 in the hope of establishing a meat cannery. The number of native species of plants at this time was 25; by 1923 it had fallen to 4. In that year all the rabbits and hares were systematically exterminated to prevent the island turning into a desert, but recovery has been slower than the destruction. By 1930 there were nine species and by 1961, sixteen species on the island (Stoddart, 1968).

Roads have been of major importance in the spread of plants. As Frenkel (1970) has pointed out in a notable survey of this aspect of anthropogenic biogeography:

12
Water weed, Salvinia molesta, *which has developed since the construction of the Kariba Dam across the Zambezi river in Central Africa*

57

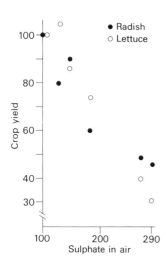

FIG. 2.10
The effect of air quality on plant growth in Leeds, England, in 1913. Values for yield and for air sulphate in a low pollution area taken as 100 and other values are scaled in proportion (data of Cohen and Rushton in Barrass, 1974: 187)

The Human Impact

By providing a route for the bearers of plant propagules — man, animal and vehicle — and by furnishing, along their margins, a highly specialised habitat for plant establishment, roads may facilitate the entry of plants into a new area. In this manner roads supply a cohesive directional component, cutting across physical barriers, linking suitable habitat to suitable habitat.

Roadsides tend to possess a distinctive flora in comparison with the natural vegetation of an area. As Frenkel has again written:

Roadsides are characterized by numerous ecologic modifications including: treading, soil compaction, confined drainage, increased runoff, removal of organic matter and sometimes additions of litter or waste material of frequently high nitrogen content (including urine and faeces), mowing or crushing of tall vegetation, herbicide application, removal of woody vegetation but occasionally the addition of wood chips or straw, substrate maintained in an ecologically open condition by blading, intensified frost action, rill and sheetwash erosion, snow deposition (together with accumulated dirt, gravel, salt and cinder associated with winter maintenance), soil and rock additions related to slumping and rock-falls, and altered microclimatic conditions associated with pavement and right-of-way structures. Furthermore, road rights-of-way may be used for driving stock in which case unselective, hurried but often close grazing may constitute an additional modification. Where highway landscaping or stability of cuts and fills is a concern, exotic or native plants may be planted and nurtured. (Frenkel, 1970: 1)

The speed with which plants may invade roadsides is impressive. A study by Helliwell (1974) demonstrated that the M1 motorway in England, less than 12 years after its construction, had on its cuttings and embankments not only the thirty species which had been deliberately sown or planted, but also over 350 species that had not been sown or planted.

Railways have also played their role in plant dispersal. The classic example of this is provided by the Oxford ragwort, *Senecio squalidus*, a species native to Sicily and southern Italy. It spread from the Oxford Botanical Garden (where it had been established since at least 1690) and colonized the walls of Oxford. Much of its dispersal to the rest of Britain (Usher, 1973) was achieved by the Great Western Railway, in the vortices of whose trains the plumed fruits were carried, and in its cargoes of ballast and iron ore. The distribution of the plant was very much associated with railway lines, railway towns and waste ground.

Indeed, by clearing forest, cultivating, depositing rubbish, and many other activities man has opened up a whole series of environments which are favourable to colonization by plants with the ability to make use of the opportunity provided to them. Such plants are generally thought of as weeds. Indeed it has often been said that the history of weeds is the history of man (though the converse might equally be true), and that such plants follow man like fruit flies follow a ripe banana or a gourd of unpasteurized beer (see Harlan, 1975b).

Air pollution and its effects on plants

Some of the air pollutants which man has put into the atmosphere (see p. 271) have had detrimental impacts on plants and, for example, sulphur dioxide is toxic to them. This was shown by Cohen and Rushton (in Barrass, 1974) who grew plants in containers of similar soil in different parts of Leeds, Yorkshire, in 1913. They found a close relationship between the amount of sulphate in the air and in the plants, and in the yield obtained (figure 2.10). In the more polluted areas of the city the leaves were blackened by soot and there was a smaller leaf area. The whole theme of urban vegetation has been studied in the North American context by Schmid (1975).

Lichens are also sensitive to air pollution effects and have been found to be rare in the central areas of cities like Bonn, Helsinki, Stockholm, Paris, and London. There appears to be a zonation of lichen types around big cities as shown for north-east England (figure 2.11a) and Belfast (figure 2.11b). Moreover, when a healthy lichen is transplanted from the county to a polluted atmosphere, the algal component gradually deteriorates and then the whole plant dies (see Gilbert, 1970). Overall it has been calculated (Rose, 1970) that over one-third of England and Wales, extending in a belt from the London area to Birmingham, broadening out

FIG. 2.11
(a) *Air pollution in north-east England and its impact upon growth areas for lichens (after Gilbert in Barrass, 1974, figure 73)*
(b) *The increase of lichen cover on trees outside the city of Belfast, Northern Ireland (after Fenton in Mellanby, 1967, figure 3)*

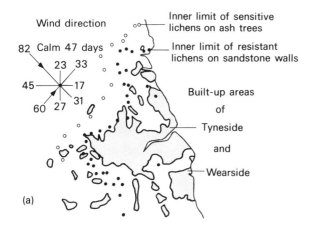

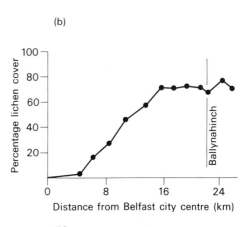

to include the industrial Midlands and most of Lancashire and West Yorkshire, and reaching up to Tyneside, has lost nearly all its epiphytic lichen flora, largely because of sulphur dioxide pollution.

Local concentrations of industrial fumes also kill vegetation. In the case of the smelters of the Sudbury mining district of Canada 2 million tonnes of noxious gases annually affect a 1900 square km area and White pine now only exists on about 7—8% of the productive area. Likewise in the lower Swansea valley, Wales, the fumes from a century of coal-burning resulted in almost complete destruction of the vegetation, with concomitant soil erosion. The area became a virtual desert. In Norway a number of the larger Norwegian aluminium smelters built immediately after the Second World War were sited in deep, narrow, steep-sided valleys at the heads of fjords. The relief has not proved conducive to the rapid dispersal of fumes, particularly of fluoride. In one valley a smelter with a production of 110 000 tonnes per year lead to the death of pines (*Pinus sylvestris*) for over 13 km in each direction up and down the valley. To about 6 km from the source all pines are dead. Birch, however, seems to be able to withstand the conditions, and to grow vigorously right up to the factory fence (Gilbert, 1975).

Photochemical smog is also known to have adverse effects on plants both within cities and on their margins. In California, Ponderosa pines in the San Bernadino mountains as much as 129 km to the east of Los Angeles have been extensively damaged by smog. In summer months in Britain ozone concentrations produced by photochemical reactions have reached around 17 pphm (parts per hundred million) compared with a maximum of 4 pphm associated with clean air, while in Los Angeles ozone concentrations may reach 70 pphm (Marx, 1975). Fumigation experiments in the USA show that plant injury can take place at levels only marginally above the natural maximum and well within the summertime levels now known to be present in Britain and the USA (table 2.8). Ozone appears to reduce photosynthesis and to cause reduced flowering and germination (W. H. Smith, 1974). It also seems to predispose conifers to bark-beetle infestation and to microbial pathogens.

The adverse effects of pollution on plants are not restricted to air pollution, for water and soil pollution can also be serious. Excessive amounts of heavy metals may prove to be toxic to them (Hughes *et al.*, 1980), high salt levels (see p. 114) in irrigated soils may kill all but the more resistant halophytes, and industrial effluents may smother and poison some species. At the Fawley Oil Refinery on Southampton

Ozone concentration (parts per hundred million)	Exposure time	Species	Type of injury
10	4 hours	*Solanum tuberosum* L.	Leaf damage
5	3 days	*Phaseolus vulgaris* L.	Reduction in leaf growth and early senescence
5	5 weeks (40 hours per week)	*Raphanus sativus* L.	Fresh weight reduction
5	18 weeks	*Pinus Elliottii*; *Pinus taeda* L.	Reduction in photosynthesis
5	10 days (12 hours per day)	*Pinus strobus*	Needle spotting
6.5	4 hours	*Pinus strobus*	Needle-tip burn

Source: data from various sources in Bell and Cox (1975)

TABLE 2.8
Examples of low levels of ozone producing plant injury in the course of fumigation experiments in the USA

Water, Dicks (1977) has shown how the salt marsh vegetation has been transformed by the pollution created by films of oil, and over extensive areas *Spartina anglica* has been killed off. Likewise heavy metals in soils may be toxic to microbes and especially to fungi which may in turn change the environment by reducing rates of leaf litter decomposition (W. H. Smith, 1974).

Miscellaneous causes of plant decline

Some of the main causes of plant decline have already been referred to: deforestation, grazing, fire, and pollution. However, there are many records of species being affected by other forms of human interference. For example, casual flower-picking has resulted in local elimination of previously common species, and has been held responsible for decreases in some species like the primrose (*Primula vulgaris*) on a national scale in England. However, the serious naturalist or plant collector, using his botanical knowledge to seek out rare, local, and unusual species can lead to eradication of rare species in an area. In Britain the progressive extermination of *Cypripedium calceolus* (Ladies' slipper orchid) is often cited as an example, though the species appears to be suffering the same fate in other parts of Europe and in the USA.

More significantly agricultural 'improvements' mean that many types of habitat are disappearing or that the range of such habitats is diminishing (see figure 3.7). Plants associated with distinctive habitats suffer a comparable reduction in their range. This is brought out for two British plants (figure 2.12a and b), the Corncockle (*Agrostemma githago*) and the Pasque flower (*Pulsatilla vulgaris*). The former was characteristic of unmodified cornfields while the latter was

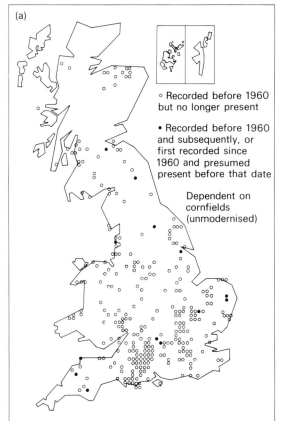

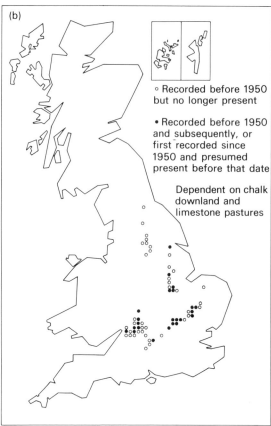

FIG. 2.12 (this page)
Reduction in the range of specie species related to habitat loss:
(a) corncockle (Agrostemma githago)
(b) pasque flower (Pulsatilla vulgaris) (after Nature Conservancy Council, 1977, figures 8 and 9)

FIG. 2.13 (opposite)
Reduction in the range of species related to habitat loss associated with drainage activities:
(a) pillwort (Pilularia globulifera)
(b) marsh clubmoss (Lycopodiella inundata)
(c) marsh gentian (Gentiana pneumonanthe)
(d) small fleabane (Pulicaria vulgaris) (after Nature Conservancy Council, 1977, figures 4–7)

characteristic of traditional chalk downland and limestone pastures. Both these types of habitat have contracted with recent agricultural change (Nature Conservancy Council, 1977). Other plants have suffered a reduction in range because of drainage activities (see figure 2.13).

The introduction of pests either deliberately or accidentally can lead to a reduction in the range and numbers of a particular species. Reference has already been made to the decline in the fortunes of the elm in Britain because of the unintentional establishment of Dutch elm disease. There are, however, many cases where 'pests' have been introduced deliberately to check the explosive invasion of a particular plant. One of the most spectacular examples of this involves the history of the Prickly pear (*Opuntia*) into Australia from the Americas. It was introduced at some time before 1839 (Dodd, 1959), and spread dramatically. By 1900, 4 million ha carried it, and by 1925, more than 24 million. Of this latter figure approximately one half was occupied by dense growth (1200–2000 tonnes/ha) and other more useful plants were excluded. To combat this menace one of *Opuntia*'s natural

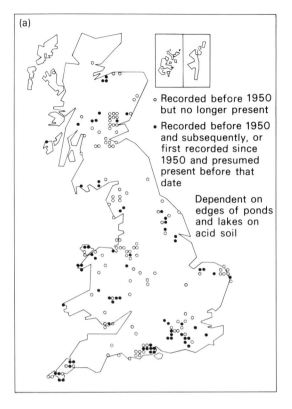

(a)

○ Recorded before 1950 but no longer present

● Recorded before 1950 and subsequently, or first recorded since 1950 and presumed present before that date

Dependent on edges of ponds and lakes on acid soil

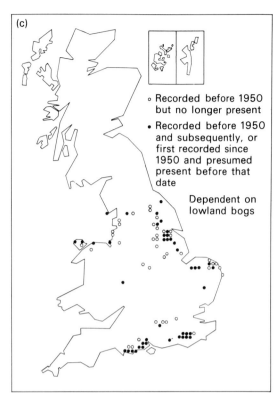

(c)

○ Recorded before 1950 but no longer present

● Recorded before 1950 and subsequently, or first recorded since 1950 and presumed present before that date

Dependent on lowland bogs

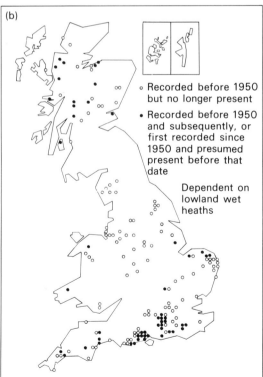

(b)

○ Recorded before 1950 but no longer present

● Recorded before 1950 and subsequently, or first recorded since 1950 and presumed present before that date

Dependent on lowland wet heaths

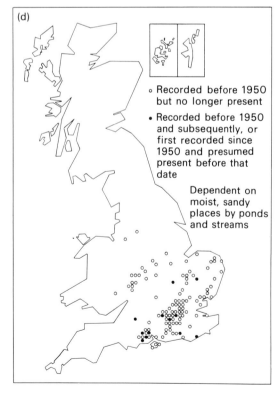

(d)

○ Recorded before 1950 but no longer present

● Recorded before 1950 and subsequently, or first recorded since 1950 and presumed present before that date

Dependent on moist, sandy places by ponds and streams

13
Dutch Elm disease has transformed the landscape of much of lowland England in the 1970s and 1980s. Accidentally introduced fungus caused the death of these elms in Leicestershire

14
The Prickly Pear (Opuntia) *in Queensland is a plant which was introduced by man and spread explosively. Recently this has been controlled by the introduction of moths and beetles*

enemies, a South American moth, *Cactoblastus*, was introduced to remarkable effect. 'By the year 1940 not less than 95% of the former 50,000,000 acres [20 million ha] of prickly pear in Queensland had been wiped out' (Dodd, 1959: 575).

Finally, the growth of leisure activities is placing greater pressure on more and more fragile plant communities, notably in tundra and high-altitude areas. These areas tend to recover but slowly from disturbance and both the trampling of human feet and the actions of vehicles can be severe (see, for example, Bayfield, 1979).

64

The change in genetic diversity

The application of modern science, technology, and industry to agriculture has led to some spectacular progress in recent decades through such developments as the use of fertilizers and the selective breeding of plants and animals. The latter has created some concern, for domesticated plants have in the process of evolution become strikingly different from their wild progenitors. Plant species that have been cultivated for a very long time and have wide distributions display this particularly clearly. Crop evolution through the millennia has been shaped by complex interactions involving both artificial and natural selection pressures. Alternate isolation of stocks followed by migration and seed exchanges brought distinctive stocks into new environments and permitted new hybridizations and recombination of characteristics. Great genetic diversity arose.

There are fears, however, that since the Second World War the situation has begun to change (Harlan, 1975a). Modern plant-breeding programmes have been established in many parts of the developing nations in the midst of genetically rich centres of diversity. Some of these programmes, associated with the so-called Green Revolution, have been successful and new, uniform high-yielding varieties have begun to replace the great range of old, local strains that have evolved over the millenia. This may lead to a serious decline in genetic resources which could potentially serve as reservoirs of variability. Ehrlich *et al.* (1977: 344) have warned:

Aside from nuclear war, there is probably no more serious environmental threat than the continued decay of the genetic variability of crops. Once the process has passed a certain point, humanity will have permanently lost the coevolutionary race with crop pests and diseases and will no longer be able to adapt crops to climatic change.

CHAPTER 3

Man's Impact on Animals

Introduction

The range of impacts that man has had on animals, though large, can be grouped conveniently into certain main categories: domestication, dispersal, extinction, expansion and contraction. As with plants man has helped to disperse animals deliberately, though many have also been dispersed accidentally (Yi-fu Tuan, 1971: 10)

The number of animals that accompany man without his leave are enormous, especially if we include the clouds of microorganisms that infest his land, his food, clothes, shelter, domestic animals and his own body.

Man has also domesticated many animals (see p. 16), an action that greatly intrigued Count Buffon, to the extent that, as with many plants, they depend on man for their survival and, in some cases, for their reproduction. The extinction of animals by the human predator has been extensive over the past 20 000 years, and in spite of recent interest in conservation policies continues at a high rate. In addition the presence of man has led to the contraction in the distribution and welfare of many animals (because of factors like pollution), though in other cases his alteration of the environment and modification of competition has favoured the expansion of some species, both numerically and spatially. Man now has the highest biomass of any animal species, some 100 million tonnes of dry weight (Jacobs, 1975).

Domestication of animals

We have already made some brief reference to one of the great themes in the study of man's influence on nature: domestication. This has been one of the most profound ways in which man has affected animals, for during the ten or eleven millennia that have passed since this process was initiated the animals that man has selected as useful to him have undergone major changes. The consequences are so substantial that the differences between breeds of animals of the same species often exceed those between different species under natural conditions. A cursory and superficial comparison of the tremendous range of shapes and sizes of modern dog breeds (as, for example, between a wolfhound and a chihuahua) is sufficient to establish the extent of alteration brought about by domestication and the speed at which domestication has accelerated the process of evolution. In particular man has changed the characters for which he originally chose to domesticate the animals. For example, the wild ancestors of cattle gave no more than a few hundred millilitres of milk; the best milk cow can today yield up to 15 000 litres of milk during its lactation period. Likewise, big changes have been created in sheep (Ryder, 1966). Wild sheep have a short tail whereas modern domestic sheep have long tails which may have arisen during man's selection of a fat tail. Wild sheep also have an overall brown colour whereas some domestic sheep have a tendency to be mainly white. Moreover, the woolly undercoat of the wild sheep has developed at the expense of the bristly outer coat. In the ancestors of domestic sheep wool (which served as a protection for the skin and as a means of insulation) consisted mainly of thick rough hairs and a small amount of down; the total weight of wool grown per year probably never reached 1 kg. The wool of present-day fine-fleeced sheep consists of uniform, thin down fibres and the total yearly weight may now reach 20 kg. Wild sheep also undergo a complete spring moult whereas domestic sheep have almost lost this tendency to shed wool.

Indeed, one of the most important consequences of, or manifestations of, domestication of animals consists of a sharp change in the seasonal biology. Whereas wild ancestors of domesticated beasts tend to be characterized by relatively strict seasonal reproduction and moulting rhythms, most domesticated species can reproduce themselves at almost any season of the year and moult little or not at all to a seasonal pattern.

67

Dispersal and invasions of animals

Most textbooks on zoogeography devote much time to dividing the world up into regions with distinctive animal life — the great "Faunal Realms" of Wallace and subsequent workers. This pattern of wildlife distribution evolved slowly over geological time. The most striking dividing line between such realms is probably that between Australasia and Asia — Wallace's Line. Australasia, with its relative absence of placental mammals, its well-developed marsupials, and the egg-laying monotremes (like the platypus), because of isolation from the Asian land mass developed this distinctive fauna.

Modern man, by moving wildlife from place to place, deliberately and non-deliberately, is breaking down this concept of distinct Faunal Realms. Highly adaptable and dispersive forms are spreading, perhaps at the expense of more specialized organisms. Worldwide, the diversity of species is thereby probably being reduced.

Deliberate introductions of new animals to new areas has been done for many reasons (Roots, 1976): for food, for sport, for revenue, for sentiment, for control of other pests, and for aesthetic reasons. Such deliberate actions probably account, for instance, for the widespread distribution of trout (see figure 3.1). Accidental introductions have been many, especially since the development of ocean-going

FIG. 3.1

The original area of distribution of the brown trout and areas where it has been artificially naturalized (after MacCrimmon in Illies, 1974, figure 3.2)

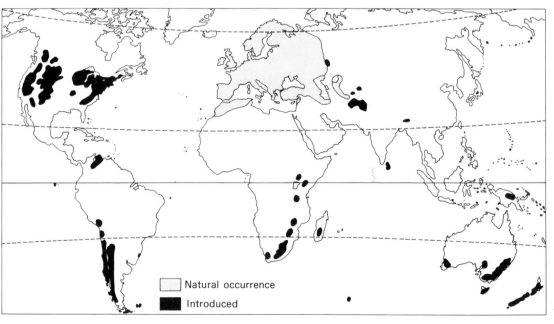

Natural occurrence

Introduced

vessels. The pace is increasing, for whereas in the eighteenth century there were few ocean-going vessels of more than 300 tonnes, today there are thousands. Because of this, in the words of Elton (1958, p. 31), 'we are seeing one of the great historical convulsions in the world's fauna and flora'. Many of the animals indeed are introduced with vegetable products for 'just as trade followed the flag, so animals have followed the plants'.

One of the most striking examples of the accidental introduction of animals given by Elton is the arrival of some chafer beetles, *Popillia japonica* (the Japanese beetle), in New Jersey in a consignment of plants from Japan. From an initial population of about one dozen beetles in 1916 the centre of population grew rapidly outwards to cover many thousands of square kilometres in only a few decades (figure 3.2).

Some animals arrive accidentally with other beasts that were introduced deliberately. In northern Australia, for instance, water buffalo were introduced (McKnight, 1971) and brought their own bloodsucking fly, a species which bred in cattle dung and transmitted an organism sometimes fatal to cattle. Australia's native dung beetles, accustomed only to the small sheep-like pellets of the grazing marsupials, could not tackle the large dung pats of the buffalo. Thus untouched pats abounded and the flies were able to breed undisturbed. Eventually African dung beetles were introduced to cope (Roote, 1976).

A study conducted in California (Moyle, 1976) gives an indication of the causes and significance of fish introductions in the state, for no less than 50 of the 133 fish species are introduced, and the rate of introduction appears to be increasing (figure 3.3). The prime reason for introductions, both authorized and unauthorized, has been sport fishing, but other reasons include the provision of forage for game fish, the escape of live bait, the release of pets, and the provision of fish for the biological control of insects.

While domesticated plants tend not to have been able to survive in most cases without human help (see p. 55), the same is not so true of domesticated animals. There are a great many examples of cattle, horses (see, for example, McKnight, 1959), donkeys, and goats which have effectively adapted to new environments and have virtually become wild. Frequently they have both ousted native animals and, particularly in the case of goats on ocean islands, have created desertization. Sometimes, however, introduced animals have spread so effectively and rapidly and have led to such a change in the environment to which they were

69

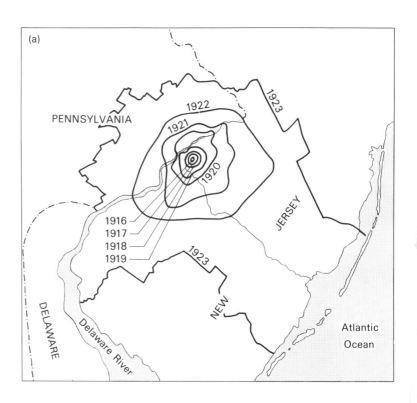

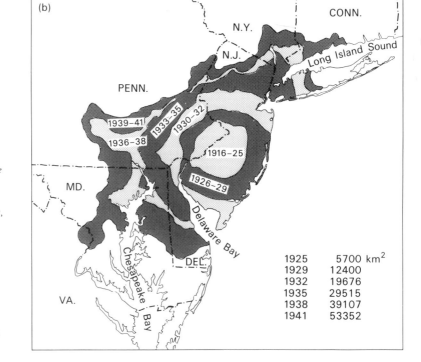

FIG. 3.2
The spread of the Japanese beetle, Popillia japonica, *in the eastern USA:*

(a) from its point of introduction in New Jersey, 1916–23 (after Elton, 1958, figure 14, and L. B. Smith and Hadley, 1926)

(b) from its point of introduction to elsewhere, 1916–41 (after Elton, 1958, figure 15, and US Bureau of Entomology, 1941)

1925	5700 km^2
1929	12400
1932	19676
1935	29515
1938	39107
1941	53352

70

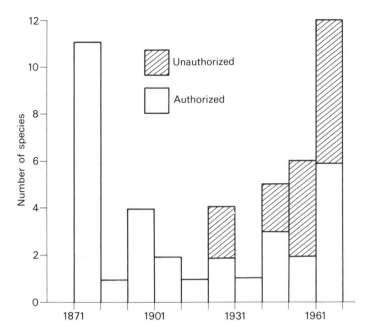

FIG. 3.3
The introduction of fish species into California (adapted from Moyle, 1976). 1871, when the graph begins, was the period of railroad arrival, the US Fish Commission and California Fish Commission

ntroduced that they have sown the seeds of their own demise. The reindeer, for example, was brought from Lapland to Alaska in 1891–1902 to make a new resource for the Eskimos, and the herds increased and spread to something over half a million animals. By the 1950s, however, there were not more than a twentieth of that number left, the reason being that they were allowed to eat off the lichen supplies that are essential to winter survival; as lichen grows very slowly their food supply was drastically reduced (Elton, 1958: 129).

The accidental dispersal of animals can be facilitated by means other than transport on ship or introduction with plants. This applies particularly to aquatic life which can be spread because of man's alteration of waterways by such means as canalization. Wooster (1969) gives the example of the way in which the construction of the Suez Canal has facilitated the exchange of animals between the Red Sea and the Eastern Mediterranean. In the early days of the canal the high salinity of the Great Bitter Lake acted to prevent movement, but the infusion of progressively fresher waters (figure 3.4) by way of the Suez Canal means that this barrier has gradually lost its effectiveness. This type of movement has recently been termed Lessepsian migration. The construction of the Welland Canal, linking the Atlantic with the Great Lakes, has permitted similar kinds of movement with more disastrous consequences. Much of the native fish fauna has been displaced by alewife (*Alosa pseudoharengus*) through competition for food, and sea-lamprey

71

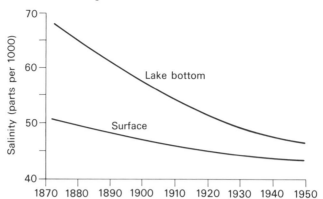

FIG. 3.4
*Decrease in the salinity of the
Great Bitter Lake, Egypt,
resulting from the infusion
of fresher water by way of the
Suez Canal (after Wooster,
1969)*

(*Petromyzon marinus*) as a predator, so that the once common Atlantic salmon (*Salmo salar*), lake trout (*Salvelinus namaycush*) and lake herring (*Leucihthys artedi*) have been nearly exterminated (Aron and Smith, 1971).

From time to time man has sought to rectify some earlier wrongs by reintroducing animals that were once native but which had been displaced by his actions in earlier times. There are three particularly good examples of such reintroductions in the British Isles: the reindeer (*Rangifer tarandus*), the capercaillie (*Tetrao urogallus*) and the great bustard (*Otis tarda*).

Miscellaneous causes of animal contractions and decline

The extreme point of man's interference with animals is extinction, but before that point is reached man may cause major contractions in both their numbers and their distribution. Some of the decline may be brought about by purposeful killing for subsistence and commercial purposes, but much wildlife decline results through indirect means (Doughty, 1974), such as pollution (Waldichuk, 1979; Holdgate, 1979).

Particular concern has been expressed about the role of certain pesticides in creating undesirable and unexpected changes. The classic case of this concerns DDT and related substances. These were introduced on a world-wide basis after the Second World War and proved highly effective in the control of insects like malarial mosquitoes. However, evidence accumulated that DDT was persistent, capable of wide dispersal, and reached high levels of concentration in certain animals at the top trophic levels (see figure 5.22). This tendency for DDT to become concentrated as one moves up the food chain is illustrated further by the data in

72

table 3.1c. DDT levels in river and estuary waters may be low, but the zooplankton and shrimps contain higher levels, the fish that feed on them higher levels still, while fish-eating birds have the highest levels of all.

One major effect of DDT is on sea-birds. Their egg shells become thinned to the extent that reproduction fails in fish-eating birds. Similar correlations between eggshell thinning and DDT residue concentrations have been demonstrated for various raptorial land-birds. The bald eagle (*Haliaeetus leucocephalus*), peregrine falcon (figure 3.5) (*Falco peregrinus*), and osprey (*Pandion haliaetus*) all showed decreases in eggshell thickness and population decline from 1947 to 1967, a decline which correlated with DDT usage and subsequent reproductive and metabolic effects upon the birds (Johnston, 1974).

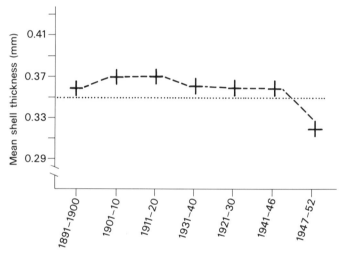

FIG. 3.5
Changing eggshell thickness versus time, associated with DDT use since the Second World War (modified after Hickey and Anderson, 1968)

Another example serves to make the same point about the 'magnification' effects associated with pesticides (Southwick, 1976: 45—46). At Clear Lake in California, periodic appearances of large numbers of gnats caused problems for tourists and residents. An insecticide, DDD, was applied at a low concentration (up to 0.05 ppm) and killed 99% of the larvae. Following the application of the DDD, western grebes were found dead, and tissue analysis showed concentrations of DDD in them of 1600 ppm, representing a concentration of 32 000 times the application rate. DDD had accumulated in the insect-eating fish at levels of 40 000—120 000 ppm and the grebes feeding on the fish received lethal doses of the pesticide. There are also records elsewhere of trout reproduction ceasing when DDT levels build up (Chesters and Konrad, 1971).

73

However, appreciation of the undesirable side-effects of DDD and DDT brought about by ecological concentration has led to severe controls on their utilization. For example, DDT reached a peak in terms of utilization in the USA in 1959 (35×10^6 kg) and by 1971 was down to 8.1×10^6 kg. Monitoring of birds in Florida over the same period indicated a parallel decline in the concentration of DDT and its metabolites (DDD and DDE) in their fat deposits (Johnston, 1974).

Other substances are also capable of concentration effects. For example, heavy metals and methyl mercury may build up in marine organisms, and filter feeders like shellfish have a strong tendency to concentrate the metals from very dilute solutions, as is shown very clearly in table 3.1a and b.

It is possible, however, that the importance of biological accumulation and magnification has been overplayed in some textbooks. G. W. Bryan (1979) reviews the situation and notes that although the absorption of pollutants from food is often the most important route for bioaccumulation, and that transfer along food chains certainly occurs, this does not automatically mean that predators at high trophic levels will always contain the highest levels. He writes (p. 497):

although, for a number of contaminants, concentrations in individual predators sometimes exceed those of their prey, when the situation overall is considered only the more persistent organochlorine pesticides, such as DDT and its metabolites and methyl mercury, show appreciable signs of being biologically magnified as a result of food-chain transfer.

TABLE 3.1

Examples of biological magnification

(a) ENRICHMENT FACTORS FOR THE TRACE ELEMENT COMPOSITIONS OF SHELLFISH COMPARED WITH THE MARINE ENVIRONMENT

Element	Enrichment factor		
	Scallops	*Oysters*	*Mussels*
Ag	2 300	18 700	330
Cd	2 260 000	318 000	100 000
Cr	200 000	60 000	320 000
Cu	3 000	13 700	3 000
Fe	291 500	68 200	196 000
Mn	55 000	4 000	13 500
Mo	90	30	60
Ni	12 000	4 000	14 000
Pb	5 300	3 300	4 000
V	4 500	1 500	2 500
Zn	28 000	110 300	9 100

Source: Merlini, 1971, in King, 1975, table 8.8, p. 303

TABLE 3.1 (continued)

(b) MEAN METHYL MERCURY CONCENTRATIONS IN ORGANISMS
FROM A CONTAMINATED SALT MARSH

Organism	Parts per million
Sediments	<0.001
Spartina	<0.001–0.002
Annelids	0.13
Bivalves	0.15–0.26
Gastropods	0.25
Crustaceans	0.28
Echinoderms	0.01
Fish muscle	1.04
Fish liver	1.57
Mammal muscle	2.2
Bird muscle	3.0
Mammal liver	4.3
Bird liver	8.2

Source: Gardner *et al.*, 1978, in Bryan, 1979

(c) THE CONCENTRATION OF DDT IN THE FOOD CHAIN

Source	Parts per million
River water	0.000003
Estuary water	0.00005
Zooplankton	0.04
Shrimps	0.16
Insects–*Diptera*	0.30
Minnows	0.50
Fundulus	1.24
Needlefish	2.00
Tern	2.80–5.17
Cormorant	26.40
Immature gull	75.50

Source: King, 1975, table 8.7, p. 301

Attempts at the chemical control of rodents and jackals in Israel to increase agricultural productivity had had certain unintended impacts on other beasts. Thallium-sulphate-coated wheat was used for rodent control but caused a heavy toll on birds of prey which lived on the rodents. It was found that all the birds of prey found dead contained large amounts of thallium. By 1955–6, breeding as well as wintering populations of those species of birds of prey which fed mainly on rodents had been almost entirely eliminated. The only bird of prey to succeed in keeping its numbers at about the same level was the short-toed eagle, *Circaetus gallicus*, which feeds exclusively on reptiles. Attempts were also made to exterminate jackals (*Canis aureus*) by means of poisoned baits, mainly strychnine. The undesirable results of this included the poisoning (and serious decline) of many Griffon vultures (*Gyps fulvus*), hooded crows (*Corvus corone*), crested cuckoos (*Clamator glandarius*) and the mongoose. This in turn meant that there was a great increase in the number of hares (*Lepus europaeus*) and in the Palestine viper (*Vipera xanthina palaestinae*) — the latter thriving because of the reduction in the mongoose population (Mendelssohn, 1973).

Oil pollution is an increasingly serious problem for marine and coastal fauna and flora, though some of it derives from natural seeps (Landes, 1973; Blumer, 1972). Sea-birds are especially vulnerable for oil clogs their feathers, while the ingestion of oil when birds attempt to preen themselves leads to enteritis and other complaints. Local bird populations may be seriously reduced though probably no extinction has resulted (Bourne, 1970). Fortunately, though oil is toxic it becomes less so with time and the oil spilt from the *Torrey Canyon* in March 1967 was almost biologically inert when it was stranded on the Cornish beaches (Cowell, 1976). There are natural oil-degrading organisms in nature. Much of the damage caused to marine life as a result of this particular disaster resulted not from the oil itself but from the use of 2.5 million gallons of detergents to disperse it (J. E. Smith, 1968).

Other industrial pollutants have a clear impact on aquatic systems but space requires that only a few examples can be given (from Southwick, 1976: 19–22). In Biscayne Bay, Florida, industrial and municipal wastes from Miami are thought to be responsible for a high prevalence of dermal tumours in several species of marine fish, while in Bellingham Bay, north of Seattle, sulphite wastes from pulp mills lead to abnormal growth of oyster larvae. The Lower Mississippi River, from which New Orleans obtains its drinking water, contains at least thirty-six chemical compounds of industrial origin, even after water treatment, which are known to be harmful to laboratory animals. Fish kills can sometimes involve massive populations. In San Diego Harbour in 1962 an estimated 37.8 million fish were killed by pollution. Such kills are often produced by industrial accidents.

The widespread phenomenon of 'acid rain' (see p. 271) brought about by sulphate emissions into the atmosphere has also been noted as a cause of decline in some species of lake fish. Studies by Beamish *et al.* (1975) demonstrated that between 1961 and 1975 pH had declined by 0.13 pH units per year in George Lake, Canada. Coincident with this, lake

15 (opposite)
The wreck of the great tanker, Amoco Cadiz, caused widespread pollution of beaches in Brittany, northern France

trout, wall-eye, burbot and small-mouth bass have disappeared, other species no longer reproduce successfully and deformities have become more frequent. A comparable picture emerges from Sweden where Almer *et al.* (1974) found that the pH in some lakes had decreased by as much as 1.8 pH units since the 1930s. When the pH falls below 5.8 most of the green algae and diatoms have been observed to disappear, while roach, arctic char, trout and perch have been wiped out from acidified lakes.

As yet the role of pollution from nuclear industries seems to be of limited importance to plants and animals (although its health effects on men are proven). Mellanby (1967: 63) has written:

I do not myself think that, except in the vicinity of nuclear test explosions, fall-out has caused measurable damage so far to animals and plants...up to the present man-made radiation can seldom have had important ecological effects.

Industrial air pollution has been known since the late nineteenth century to have an adverse effect on domestic animals, but there is less information about its effects on wildlife. Nonetheless, there is some evidence that it does affect wild animals (Newman, 1979). Arsenic emissions from silver foundries are known to have killed deer and wild rabbits in Germany, sulphur emissions from a pulp mill in Canada are known to have killed many songbirds, industrial fluorosis has been found in deer living in the USA and Canada, asbestosis has been found in free-living baboons and rodents in the vicinity of asbestos mines in South Africa, and oxidants from air pollution are recognized as having caused blindness in bighorn sheep in the San Bernardino Mountains near Los Angeles in California.

One could list many other indirect means of causing wildlife decline. Vehicle speed, noise, and mobility upset remote and sensitive wildlife populations, and this has become an increasing problem with the rapid development in the use of off-road recreation vehicles. In California there are an estimated 1.2 million motorcycles and 500 000 dune buggies which are regularly used in the fragile desert ecosystems (Busack and Bury, 1974). The effects of roads become greater with increasing traffic levels, vehicle speed, and road width. Many animals are now killed by vehicles, and roads also act as barriers to movement, particularly of small, cover-loving animals. As Orley *et al.* (1974) have put it, "a four-lane divided highway is as effective a barrier to the dispersal of small forest mammals as a body of fresh water twice as wide".

Leisure activities in general may create problems for some species (Speight, 1973). A survey of the breeding status of the little tern (*Sterna albifrons*) in Britain gave a number of instances of breeding failure by the species, apparently caused by the presence of fishermen and bathers on nesting beaches. The presence of even a few people inhibited the birds from returning to their nests. Likewise, species building floating nests on inland waters are very prone to disturbance by water-skiers and power-boating; for example great crested grebes (*Podiceps cristatus*). In the Murchison Falls National Park, Uganda, the Nile crocodile (*Crocodilus niloticus*) was a major tourist attraction and, when political conditions allowed, regular boat trips were organized to view the riverbank breeding areas. Female crocodiles actively protect their eggs and defend their young. The presence of tourist boats has the effect of driving females from the bank into the water and this allows predators, particularly monitor lizards and olive baboons, to move in and take buried eggs or young (see table 3.2) (Cott, 1969).

Breeding grounds	Number of nests	Nests destroyed by predators	
Tourist sites			
Sand-river 4	13	13	(100%)
Namsika	10	10	(100%)
Bee-eater slope	13	7	(54%)
Sites not visited by tourists			
Falls Bay	36	17	(47%)
Frog Bay	7	2	(29%)
Sand-river 2	22	4	(18%)
Paraa South	7	0	(0%)

TABLE 3.2
The effect of tourists on the loss of crocodile nests to predators

Source: table 2.6 in Edington and Edington, 1977; Cott, 1969

New types of construction can create problems. As Doughty (1974) has remarked '"wirescapes", tall buildings, and towers can become to birds what dams, locks, canals and irrigation ditches are to the passage of fish'. The construction of canals can cause changes in aquatic communities (see p. 71).

Likewise turbines associated with hydroelectric schemes can cause substantial fish deaths, either directly through ingesting them, or through gas-bubble disease. This resembles the 'bends' in divers and is produced if a fish takes in water supersaturated with gases. The excess gas may come out of solution as bubbles which can lodge in various parts of the fish's body and cause injury or death. Such supersaturation of water with gas can be produced in turbines or when a spillway plunges into a deep basin (Baxter, 1977).

Agricultural change can also have consequences in terms of animal decline. Forest clearance and the development of open farming landscapes benefits seed- and insect-eating birds, but is at the expense of arboreal animals. Likewise the adoption of increasing mechanization in crop production has increased the average size of fields and has led to a loss of the cover provided by hedgerows (figure 3.6). In 1962 there were almost one million km of hedge in Great Britain, probably covering the order of 181 000 ha, an area greater than that covered by National Nature Reserves, but the figure before Enclosure would not have been this high (see table 3.3) whereas in many areas sharp declines seem to be occurring at the present day. Bird numbers and diversity are likely to be greatly reduced if the removal of hedgerows continues, for most British birds are essentially of woodland type and because woods only cover about 5% of the land surface of Britain they very much depend on hedgerows (Moore *et al.*, 1967). Other types of habitat have also been disappearing at a quick rate with the agricultural changes of recent years (Nature Conservancy Council, 1977) (see figure 3.7). For example, the botanical diversity of grasslands is reduced by replacing them with grass leys or by treating them with selective herbicides and fertilizers, and this can mean that the habitat does not contain some of the basic requirements which are essential for many species. One can illustrate this by reference to the larva of the common blue butterfly (*Polyommatus icarus*) which feeds upon birds-foot trefoil (*Lotus corniculatus*). This plant disappears when pasture is ploughed and converted into a ley, or when it is treated with a selective herbicide. Once the plant has gone the butterfly goes too because it is not adapted to feeding on the plants that are grown in leys or improved pasture. Figure 3.8 illustrates the way in which the distribution of the silver-spotted skipper butterfly (*Hesperia comma*) has contracted with the reduction in the availability of chalk downland and

16

An air photograph of part of Suffolk in eastern England shows the traces of hedgerows that have been removed in the interests of modern farm technology. Hedgerows provide cover for many birds and animals

TABLE 3.3
Changes in the length of hedgerows in three parishes in Huntingdonshire, England over 600 years

	Date	Kilometres of hedge		Date	Kilometres of hedge
Prior to	1364	32		1780	93
	1364	40		1850	122
	1500	45		1946	114
	1550	52		1963	74
	1680	74		1965	32

Source: from Moore *et al.*, 1967

80

County (selected areas in each county only)

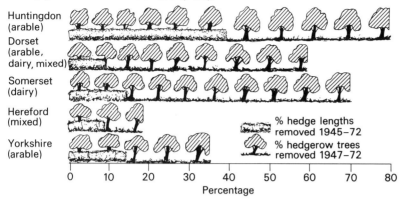

Huntingdon
(arable)

Dorset
(arable,
dairy, mixed)

Somerset
(dairy)

Hereford
(mixed)

Yorkshire
(arable)

% hedge lengths
removed 1945–72
% hedgerow trees
removed 1947–72

0   10   20   30   40   50   60   70   80
Percentage

FIG. 3.6
*Recent changes in hedgerows
in parts of England (from*
New Society, *June 1979,
p. 650)*

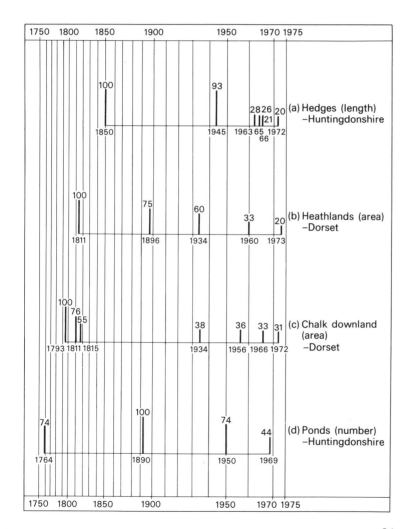

FIG. 3.7
*Examples of habitat loss in
England since the mid-
eighteenth century (after
Nature Conservancy Council,
1977, figure 3). All values
are expressed as percentages
of the largest value recorded
in each case*

81

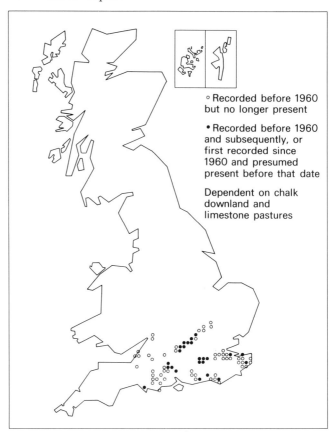

° Recorded before 1960 but no longer present

• Recorded before 1960 and subsequently, or first recorded since 1960 and presumed present before that date

Dependent on chalk downland and limestone pastures

FIG. 3.8

Reduction in the range of the silver-spotted skipper butterfly (Hesperia comma) *as a result of the reduction in the availability of the chalk downland and limestone pastures upon which it depends (after Nature Conservancy Council, 1977, figure 3.8)*

limestone pastures upon which it depends. Likewise, the large blue butterfly,*Maculinea arion*, has decreased in Britain. Its larvae live solely on the wild thyme, *Thymus drucei*, a plant which thrives on close-cropped grassland. Since the decimation of the rabbit by myxomatosis (see p. 94) conditions for the thyme have been less favourable and so both it and the large blue butterfly have declined. Another group of animals which has suffered from agriculture are the species implicated in disease cycles involving farm stock. Recently in Britain it has been thought necessary to eliminate some badgers (*Meles meles*) from a number of farms in the west of England in an attempt to reduce the threat of them transmitting tuberculosis to cattle. Likewise in parts of southern Africa wild ungulates are slaughtered to prevent them acting as a reservoir for the trypanosome parasite which causes the disease, *nagana*, in cattle. This measure is also said to check the vector of the disease, the tsetse fly, by reducing its opportunities to obtain blood meals.

Overall, as table 3.4 shows, the number of species occur-

Groups of animals	Unmodernized farms		Modern farms	
	Habitat	No. of species	Habitat	No. of species
	(a) Hedges* and semi-natural grass verges		(a) Wire fences with (i) sown grass (ii) semi-natural grass verges	
Mammals		20		(i) 5 (ii) 6
Birds		37		(i) 6 (ii) 9
Lepidoptera (butterflies only)		17		(i) 0 (ii) 8
	(b) Permanent pasture † (untreated)		(b) Grass leys	
Lepidoptera (butterflies only)		20		0
	(c) Permanent ponds and ditches		(c) Temporary ditches and piped water	
Mammals (aquatic)		2		0
Amphibia		5		2
Fish		9		0
Odonata (dragonflies)		11		0
Mollusca (gastropods only)		25		3

* Includes hedgerow trees
† Includes grasslands on chalk
Source: Nature Conservancy Council, 1977, table 2

TABLE 3.4
Approximate number of species occurring in equivalent habitats in unmodernized and modern farms

ring in England on unmodernized farms as compared to modernized farms is relatively great.

The replacement of natural oak-dominated woodlands in Britain by conifer plantations, another major land-use change of recent decades, also has its implications for wild life. It has been estimated that where this change has taken place the number of species of birds found has been approximately halved. This is illustrated by some data for Wales presented in table 3.5. Likewise the replacement of upland sheep walks with conifer plantations has led to a sharp reduction in raven numbers in southern Scotland and northern England. The raven (*Corvus corax*) obtains much of its carrion from open sheep country (Marquiss *et al.*, 1978).

In the USSR the ambitious ploughing-up of the so-called Virgin Lands of Central Kazakhstan in the late 1950s and early 1960s led to the replacement of herbaceous steppe and grass steppe by cultivated fields. As a result the animal inhabitants of the steppe became increasingly restricted to smaller areas of suitable habitat. The population of the fur-bearing marmot or bobac (*Marmot bobac*) steadily declined from about 3 million in the middle 1950s to 318 000 in 1969.

TABLE 3.5
Estimated numbers of breeding songbirds in two broad-leaved and two coniferous woods in Wales

	Broad-leaved woods		Coniferous woods	
	(1) (275 trees/ha, relict)	(2) (375 trees/ha, relict)	(3) (450 trees/ha, planted)	(4) (275 trees/ha, planted)
Chaffinch	7	4	4	7
Wren	13	15	34	9
Robin	7	4	3	3
Dunnock	—	—	2	—
Goldcrest	2	4	9	31
Coal Tit	6	3	7	4
Blue Tit	5	2	—	—
Great Tit	6	2	—	—
Marsh Tit	—	—	—	—
Nuthatch	3	—	—	—
Tree Creeper	1	1	—	—
Blackbird	3	—	—	—
Song Thrush	—	—	—	—
Mistle Thrush	—	—	—	3
Wood Warbler	3	3	—	—
Willow Warbler	4	10	—	—
Blackcap	—	—	—	—
Chiffchaff	—	—	—	—
Pied Flycatcher	6	7	—	—
Redstart	2	2	—	—
TOTAL	68	57	59	58
No. of species	14	12	6	6
Index of diversity	2.47	2.21	1.31	1.37

Source: Edington and Edington, 1977, table 2.1, p. 8

The animals are further threatened because the increase in human population following the extension of agriculture means that trapping activity to obtain pelts has expanded (Zimina *et al.*, 1972).

Soil erosion, by increasing stream turbidity, may adversely affect fish habitats (Ritchie, 1972). The reduction of light penetration inhibits photosynthesis, which in turn leads to a decline in food and a decline in carrying capacity. Decomposition of the organic matter, which is frequently deposited with sediment, uses dissolved oxygen, thereby reducing the oxygen supply around the fish; sediment restricts the emergence of fry from eggs; and turbidity reduces the ability of fish to find food (though conversely it may also allow young fish to escape predators).

Turbidity has also been increased by mining-waste, by construction (Barton, 1977), and by dredging. In the case of some of the Cornish rivers in china clay-mining areas river turbidities reach 5000 mg/l and trout are not present in streams so affected. Indeed, the non-toxic turbidity tolerances of river fish are much less than that figure. Alabaster (1972), after reviewing data from a wide range of sources, believes that in the absence of other pollution, fisheries are unlikely to be harmed at chemically inert suspended sediment concentrations of less than 25 mg/l, that there should be good or moderate fisheries at 25–80 mg/l, that good fisheries are unlikely at 80–400 mg/l, and that at best only poor fisheries would exist at more than 400 mg/l.

The role of mining in affecting animals is referred to in the world's first mining textbook, *De Re Metallica* by Georgius Agricola (1556), which contains an excellent description of the destruction caused by mining in Germany (Down and Stocks, 1977: 7).

the strongest argument of the detractors is that the fields are devastated by mining operations....The woods and groves are cut down, for there is need of an endless amount of wood for timbers, machines and the smelting of metals. And when the woods and groves are felled, then are exterminated the beasts and birds, very many of which furnish a pleasant and agreeable food for man. Further, when the areas are washed, the water which has been used poisons the brooks and streams and either destroys the fish or drives them away.

It needs to be stressed, however, that the changes of habitat brought about by urbanization, industry (B. N. K. Davis, 1976) and mining need not be detrimental. Indeed Ratcliffe (1974, p. 368) has described the present situation thus:

I think it is true to say that while mineral exploitation has caused some damage to nature conservation interest in Britain, this has been mostly on a local and minor scale, and on the whole the gains have outweighed the losses, especially in the creation of interesting new habitats.

He does, however, express some doubts about the future:

The anxiety about future mineral extraction stems from the scale and method of operation. Many mineral workings in the past were mainly subterranean, and surface disturbance was limited largely to waste tipping. Future workings are likely to use strip or opencast mining techniques increasingly, and the demand to rehabilitate new workings is often disadvantageous from the wildlife angle.

The Human Impact

It might also be thought that man's use of fire could be directly detrimental to animals, though the evidence is not conclusive. Many forest animals appear to be able to adapt to fire, and fire also tends to maintain habitat diversity. Thus, after a general review of the available ecological literature Bendell (1974) found that fires did not seem to produce so much change in birds or small mammals as one might have expected. Some of his data are presented in table 3.6. The amount of change is fairly small, though some increase in species diversities and animal densities is evident. Indeed Vogl (1977) has pointed to the diversity of fauna associated with fire-affected ecosystems (p. 281):

> Birds and mammals usually do not panic or show fear in the presence of fire, and are even attracted to fires and smoking or burned landscapes....The greatest arrays of higher animal species, and the largest numbers per unit area, are associated with fire-dependant, fire-maintained, and fire-initiated ecosystems.

TABLE 3.6
Environmental effects of burning

(a) CHANGE IN NUMBER OF SPECIES OF BREEDING BIRDS AND SMALL MAMMALS AFTER FIRE

	Foraging zone	*Before fire*	*After fire*	*Gained (%)*	*Lost (%)*
BIRDS	Grassland and shrub	48	62	38	8
	Tree trunk	25	26	20	16
	Tree	63	58	10	17
	TOTALS	136	146	21	14
SMALL MAMMALS	Grassland and shrub	42	45	17	10
	Forest	16	14	13	25
	TOTALS	58	59	16	14

(b) CHANGE IN DENSITY AND TREND OF POPULATION OF BREEDING BIRDS AND SMALL MAMMALS AFTER FIRE

	Foraging zone	*Density (%)*			*Trend (%)*		
		Increase	*Decrease*	*No change*	*Increase*	*Decrease*	*No change*
BIRDS	Grassland and shrub	50	9	41	24	10	66
	Tree trunk	28	16	56	4	8	88
	Tree	24	19	57	6	6	88
	TOTALS	35	15	50	12	8	80
SMALL MAMMALS	Grassland and shrub	24	13	63	20	5	75
	Forest	23	42	35	0	11	89
	TOTALS	23	25	52	14	1	80

Purposeful hunting, particularly when it involves modern fire-arms, means that the distribution of many animal species has become smaller very rapidly. This is very clearly illustrated by a study of the North American bison (figure 3.9), which on the eve of European colonization still had a population of some 60 million in spite of the presence of a small Indian population. By 1850 only a few dozen examples of bison still survived though conscious protective and conservation measures have saved it from extinction.

Animals native to remote ocean islands have been especially vulnerable since many have no flight instinct. They also provided a convenient source of provisions for seafarers. Thus the last example of the dodo (*Raphus cucullatus*) was slaughtered on Mauritius in 1681 and the last Steller's sea-cow (*Hydrodamalis gigas*) was killed on Bering Island in 1768 (Illies, 1974: 96). The land-birds which are such a feature of coral atoll ecosystems rapidly become extinct when cats, dogs, and rats are introduced. The endemic flightless rail of Wake Island, *Rallus wakensis*, became extinct during the prolonged siege of the island in the Second World War, and

17
The Moa is an extinct land bird from New Zealand. This reconstructed version was placed in the Dunedin Public Gardens. The 'hunters' are from left: Te Rangihiroa (Sir Peter Buck), Hemi Papakakura, and Tutere Wirepa

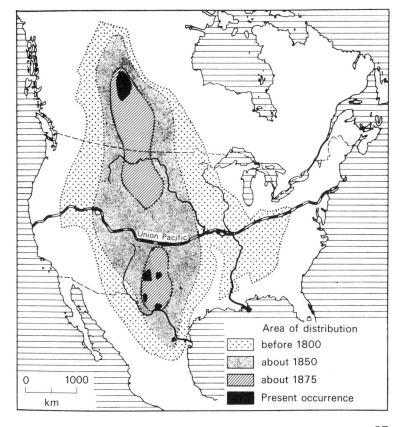

Area of distribution
before 1800
about 1850
about 1875
Present occurrence

0   1000
km

FIG. 3.9
The former and present distribution of the bison in North America (after Ziswiler in Illies, 1974, fig. 31)

18
The Dodo. Top: the skin and skull remains. Bottom: its reconstructed form. The last example disappeared three hundred years ago in Mauritius

the flightless rail of Laysan, *Porzanula palmeri*, is also now extinct. Sea-birds are more numerous on the atolls, but many colonies of terns, noddies, and boobies have been drastically reduced by vegetation clearance and by introduced rats and cats in recent times (Stoddart, 1968). Other atoll birds, including the albatross, have been culled because of the threat they pose to aircraft using military airfields on the islands. Some birds, including the sulids, have declined because they are large, vulnerable, and edible (Feare, 1978).

The fish resources of the oceans are still basically exploited by hunting and gathering techniques, and about 70 million tonnes of fish are caught in the world each year. There are countless examples of fish decline brought about by reckless over-exploitation. Overall (see Ehrlich *et al.*, 1977: 358) it has been estimated, for instance, that whale stocks have been reduced by at least half through uncontrolled hunting during the past half-century. Populations of the large varieties, those that have been most heavily exploited, have been cut

19
*The Japanese and the Soviets
continue to slaughter large
numbers of whales and if
reckless over-exploitation
continues some species will
become extinct*

to a tiny fraction of their former sizes, and the hunting, especially by the Soviets and the Japanese, still goes on. As Fisher *et al.* (1969) have put it, 'It may not be long before the blue whale joins the dinosaurs in the museum of oblivion.'

The introduction of a new animal species can cause the decline of another, whether by predation, competition, or by hybridization. This last mechanism has been found to be a major problem with fish in California, where many species have been introduced by man (see p. 71). Hybridization results when fish are transferred from one basin to a neighbouring basin, since closely related species of the type likely to hybridize usually exist in adjacent basins. One species can eliminate another closely related to it through genetic swamping (Moyle, 1976).

The expansion of animal populations under man's influence

Although most attention tends to be directed towards the decline in animal numbers and distribution brought about by man, there are many circumstances where man's alteration of the environment and modification of competition has favoured the expansion of some species. Such expansion is not always welcome or expected, as Marsh (1864: 34) appreciated:

> Insects increase whenever the birds which feed upon them disappear. Hence in the wanton destruction of the robin and other insectivorous birds, the *bipes implumis*, the featherless biped, man, is not only exchanging the vocal orchestra which greets the rising sun for the drowsy beetle's evening drone, and depriving his groves and his fields of their fairest ornament, but he is waging a treacherous warfare on his natural allies.

The acts of man, however, are not invariably detrimental, and even great cities may have effects on animal life which can be considered as desirable or tolerable. This has been brought out in the studies of bird populations in several urban areas. For example, Nuorteva (in Jacobs, 1975) studied the bird fauna in the city of Helsinki (Finland) in agricultural areas near rural houses, and in uninhabited forests (see table 3.7). The city supported by far the highest biomass and the highest number of birds, but exhibited the lowest number of species and the lowest diversity. In the man-made rural areas the number of species, and hence diversity, were much higher than in the uninhabited forest, and so was biomass. Altogether, human civilization appeared to have brought about a very significant increase of diversity in the whole area: there were 37 species in city and rural areas that were not found in the forest. Similarly, after a detailed study of suburban neighbourhoods in west-central California, Vale and Vale (1976) found that in suburban areas the number of bird species and the numbers of individuals increased with time. Moreover, when compared to the pre-suburban habitats adjacent to the suburbs, the residential areas were found to support larger numbers of both species and individuals. Horticultural activities appear to provide more luxuriant and more diverse habitats than do pre-suburban environments.

Some beasts other than the examples of birds given here are also favoured by urban expansion (Schmid, 1974). Animals that can tolerate disturbance, are adaptable, utilize patches of open or woodland-edge habitat, creep about inside buildings, tap man's food supply surreptitiously, avoid

	City (Helsinki)	Near rural houses	Uninhabited forest
Biomass (kg/km^2)	213	30	22
No. of birds/km^2	1089	371	297
Number of species	21	80	54
Diversity	1.13	3.40	3.19

TABLE 3.7
Dependence of bird biomass and diversity on urbanization

Source: data from Nuorteva, 1971, modified after Jacobs, 1975, table 2

recognizable competition with man, or attract human appreciation and esteem, may increase in the urban milieu. For these sorts of reasons the north-east megalopolis of the United States hosts thriving populations of squirrels, rabbits, raccoons, skunks, and opossums, while some African cities are now frequently blessed with the scavenging attention of hyaenas.

Jacobs (1975) provides another apposite example of how man can increase species diversity inadvertently. The saline Lake Nakuru in Kenya prior to 1961 was not a very diverse ecosystem. There were essentially one or two species of algae, one copopod, one rotifer, corrixids, notonectids and some 500 000 flamingoes belonging virtually to one species. In 1962, however, a fish *Tilapia grahami* was introduced in order to check mosquitoes. In the event it established itself as a major consumer of algae, and its numbers increased greatly. As a consequence, some thirty species of fish-eating birds (pelicans, anhingas, cormorants, herons, egrets, grebes, terns, and fish-eagles) have colonized the area to make Lake Nakuru a much more diverse system. Nonetheless, such fish introductions are not without their potential ecological costs. In Lake Atitlán in Central America the introduction of the game fish *Microperus salmoides* (largemouth bass) and *Pomoxis nigromaculatus* (black crappie), both voracious eaters, led to the decimation of local fish and crab populations. Similarly, the introduction to the Gatun Lake in the Panama Canal Zone in 1967 of the cichlid fish *Cichla ocellaris* (a native of the Amazon River) led to the elimination of six of the eight previously common fish species in 5 years, and the tertiary consumer populations such as the birds that were formerly dependent on the small fishes for food, appear less frequently (Zaret and Paine, 1973).

Economic activities may lead to an expansion in the number of examples of a particular habitat which can lead to an expansion in the distribution of certain species, though often man has led to a contraction in the range of a particular species because of the removal or modification of its preferred habitat. In the case of the little ringed plover (*Charadrius dubius*), a species virtually dependent on man-made habitats, principally wet gravel and sandpits, its range has greatly expanded as mineral extraction has been accelerated in recent decades (see figure 3.10).

Very often man's activities do not lead to species diversity but they may lead to great increases in numbers of individuals, by creating new and favourable environments. Two especially serious examples of this from the viewpoint of man are the explosions in the prevalence of both mosquitoes and bilharzia snails as a result of the extension of irrigation. Table 3.8 indicates the increased catch of mosquitoes on irrigated areas of the Kano Plains, Kenya, in comparison with the non-irrigated area. The increase is approximately five-fold although the number of species and the degree of diversity were both decreased. Table 3.9 indicates the massive incidence of bilharzia (*Schistosoma mansoni*) that has resulted from the spread of the host snails through the irrigation canals of the Gezira Scheme in the Sudan. Comparable explosions of birds have occurred as a result of agricultural

FIG. 3.10
The changing range of the little ringed plover Charadrius dubius.
(a) The increase in the number of pairs of little ringed plovers summering in Britain (after Murton, 1971, figure 6)
(b) The increase in the range related to habitat change, especially as a result of the increasing number of gravel pits (after Nature Conservancy Council, 1977, figure 11)

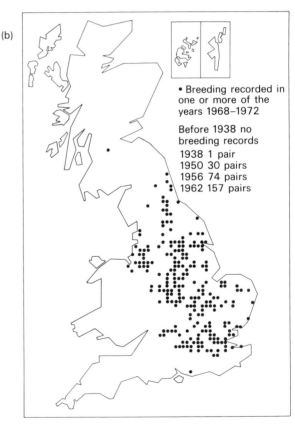

(b)

• Breeding recorded in one or more of the years 1968–1972

Before 1938 no breeding records
1938 1 pair
1950 30 pairs
1956 74 pairs
1962 157 pairs

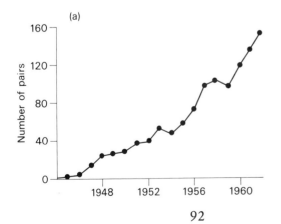

(a)

Species	Irrigated (83 trap nights)	Non-irrigated (86 trap nights)
An. gambiae s.l.	12 734	457
An. funestus	1 309	210
An. ziemanni	122	37
An. pharoensis	16	5
M. uniformis	73	1 462
M. africana	14	447
M. fuscopennata	3	2
M. karandalaensis	—	2
M. metallica	—	1
C. antennatus	73	47
C.p. fatigans	128	—
C. poicilipes	2	17
C. univittatus	12	79
C. tigripes	2	—
C. rima group	—	6
C. ethiopicus	1	—
C. aurantapex	—	1
Ae. lineatopennis	—	2
Ae. circumluteolus	6	21
Ae. ochraceous	—	3
Ae. sudanensis	2	—
Ae. africana	3	1
Others	—	31
TOTAL	14 500	2 831
Total species	16	20
Index of diversity	1.74	2.6

Note: An. = Anopheles C. = Culex
M. = Mansonia Ae. = Aedes

Source: Hill et al., 1977, table 1, p. 309

TABLE 3.8
Showing total catch of all mosquito species in light traps operated in irrigated and non-irrigated areas of the Kano Plains, Kenya, January—December 1973

Age group (years)	Percentage of human males infected	Percentage of human females infected
0—4	8.3	2.3
5—9	45.4	45.2
10—14	76.3	79.6
15—19	82.2	79.3
20—24	68.0	51.9
25—29	55.6	45.8
30—34	64.0	44.8
35—39	51.7	48.2
40—44	32.3	21.1

Source: after Amin, 1977

TABLE 3.9
Prevalence of Schistosoma mansoni infection in the Gezira irrigated area, Sudan, 1972

extension, whether it be the plagues of *Quelea* in West Africa or the bird pests of British agriculture (Jones, 1972).

One of the most remarkable examples of the consequences of the creation of new environments is provided by the European rabbit. Introduced into Britain in early Mediaeval times, and originally an inhabitant of the western Mediterranean lands, it was kept for food and fur in carefully tended warrens. Agricultural improvements, especially to grassland, together with the increasing decline in the numbers of predators such as hawks and foxes, brought about by game-guarding landlords (Sheail, 1971), enabled the rabbit to become one of the most numerous beasts in the British countryside. By the early 1950s there were 60—100 million rabbits in Britain. Frequently, as many contemporary reports demonstrate, it grazed the land so close that in areas of light soils, like the Breckland of East Anglia or in coastal dune areas, wind erosion became a serious problem. Similarly, the rabbit flourished in Australia, especially after the introduction of the merino sheep which created pasture-lands favourable to the rabbit. Erosion in susceptible lands like the Mallee was severe. Both in England and Australia an effective strategy that man developed to control the rabbit was the introduction of a South American virus, *Myxomatosis*.

Some of our most familiar British birds have benefited from agricultural expansion. As long as Britain was an intensively wooded country the starling was a rare bird. The lapwing is yet another component of the grassland fauna of central Europe which has benefited from agriculture and the creation of open country with relatively sparse vegetation (Murton, 1971). There is also a large class of beasts which so benefit from environmental conditions wrought by man that they become very closely linked to him. Such animals are often referred to as synanthropes. Pigeons and sparrows now form permanent and numerous populations in almost all the large cities of the world; human food supplies are the food supplies for many synanthropic rodents (rats and mice); a once shy forest-bird, the blackbird (*Turuds merula*) has in the course of a few generations become a regular and bold inhabitant of many gardens; and the squirrel (*Sciurus vulgaris*) in many places now occurs more frequently in parks than in forests (Illies, 1974: 101). The English sparrow (*Passer domesticus*), a familiar bird in towns and cities, currently occupies approximately one-quarter of the earth's surface, and over the past hundred years it has doubled the area that it inhabits as settlers, immigrants, and others have carried it from one continent to another (figure 3.11). It is found around settlements both in Amazonia and the Arctic Circle

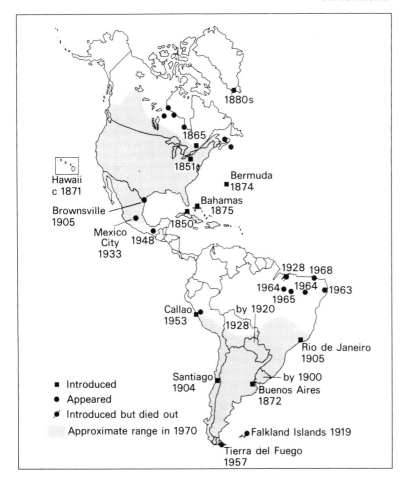

FIG. 3.11
The spread of the English sparrow in the New World (after Doughty, 1978: 4)

(Doughty, 1978). The marked increase in many species of gulls in temperate regions over recent decades is largely attributable to their increasing utilization of food scraps on refuse tips. This is, however, something of a mixed blessing, for most of the gull species which feed on urban rubbish dumps breed in coastal areas, and there is now good evidence to show that their greatly increased numbers are having harmful effects on other less common species, especially the terns (*Sterna* spp.). It may seem incongruous that the niches for scavenging birds which exploit rubbish tips should have been filled by sea-birds (Murton, 1971), but the gulls have proved ideal replacements for the kites which man had removed, as they have the same ability to watch out for likely food sources from aloft and then to hover and plunge when they spy suitable sources of sustenance.

Most of the examples which we have given so far, to illustrate how man can lead to expansion in the numbers and

95

distributions of certain animal species, have been used to make the point that such expansion frequently occurs as an incidental consequence of man's activities. There are, of course, many ways in which man has deliberately and effectively promoted the expansion of particular species (table 3.10 presents data for some introduced mammals in Britain). This may sometimes be done deliberately to reduce the numbers of a species which has expanded as an unwanted consequence of human actions. Perhaps the best known exemplification of this is biological control using introduced predators and parasites. Thus an Australian insect, the cottony-cushion scale, *Icerya purchasi*, was found in California in 1868. By the mid-1880s it was effectively destroying the citrus industry, but its ravages were quickly controlled by a parasitic fly and a predatory beetle (the Australian ladybird) being introduced deliberately from Australia. Because of the uncertain ecological effects of

TABLE 3.10
Introduced mammals in
Great Britain

Species	Date of introduction of present stock	Reason for introduction
House mouse *Mus musculus*	Neolithic?	Accidental
Wild goat *Capra hircus*	Neolithic?	Food
Fallow deer *Dama dama*	Roman or earlier	Food, sport
Domestic cat *Felis catus*	Early Middle Ages	Ornament, pest control
Rabbit *Oryctolagus cuniculus*	Mid to late twelfth century	Food, sport
Black rat *Rattus rattus*	Thirteenth century?	Accidental
Brown rat *Rattus norvegicus*	Early eighteenth century (1728–29)	Accidental
Sika deer *Cervus nippon*	1860	Ornament
Grey squirrel *Sciurus carolinensis*	1876	Ornament
Indian muntjak *Muntiacus muntjak*	1890	Ornament
Chinese muntjak *Muntiacus reevesi*	1900	Ornament
Chinese water deer *Hydropetes inermis*	1900	Ornament
Edible dormouse *Glis glis*	1902	Ornament
Musk rat *Ondatra zibethica*	1929 (−1937)	Fur
Coypu *Myocastor coypus*	1929	Fur
Mink *Mustela vison*	1929	Fur
Reindeer *Rangifer tarandus*	1952	Herding, ornament
Bennett's wallaby *Macropus rufogriseus bennetti*	1939 or 1940	Ornament
Himalayan (Hodgson's) porcupine *Hystrix hodgsoni*	1969	Ornament
Crested porcupine *Hystrix cristata*	1972	Ornament
Mongolian gerbil *Meriones unguiculatus*	1973	Ornament

Source: from Jarvis (1979), table 1, p. 188

synthetic pesticides such biological control has its attraction but the importation of natural enemies is not without its own risks. For example, the introduction into Jamaica of mongooses to control rats led to the undesirable decimation of many native birds and small land mammals.

One further deliberate method of increasing the numbers of wild animals, of conserving them, and of gaining an economic return from them, is game cropping. In some circumstances, because they are better adapted to, and utilize more components of, the environment, wild ungulates provide an alternative means of land use to domestic stock. The exploitation of the saiga antelope (*Saiga tatarica*) in the USSR is the most successful story of this kind (Edington and Edington, 1977). Previously, hunting (much overdone because of the imagined medical properties of its horns) had led to its near demise, but this was banned in the 1920s and a system of controlled cropping was instituted. Under this regime (which produces appreciable quantities of meat and leather) total numbers have risen from about 1000 to over 2 million, and in the process the herds have reoccupied most of their original range.

Animal extinctions

As the size of human populations has increased, and his technology has developed, man has been responsible for the extinction of many species of both birds and mammals. There appears to be a close correlation, for example, between the curve of population growth since the mid-seventeenth century and the curve of the number of species that have become extinct (figure 3.12).

20
The Saiga, *populations of which were decimated by ruthless hunting, has now become more numerous in the USSR because of a System of Controlled Cropping*

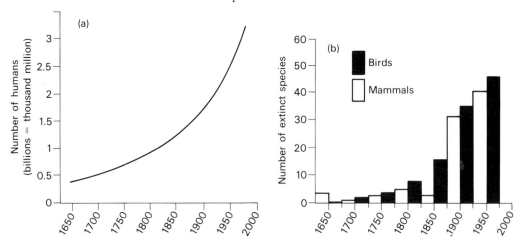

FIG. 3.12
Geometric increase in the human population (a), paralleled by increasing numbers of extinction in birds and mammals (b), suggesting that as man's numbers increase more and more living species become exterminated (after Ziswiler, in National Academy of Sciences, 1972, figure 3.2)

Some workers, notably Martin (1967 and 1974), believe, however, that man's role in animal extinctions goes back to the Stone Age and to the Late Pleistocene. They believe that extinction closely follows the chronology of prehistoric man's spread and his development as a big-game hunter. They would also maintain that there are no known continents or islands in which accelerated extinction definitely predates man's arrival. An alternative interpretation, however, is that the Late Pleistocene extinctions of big mammals was brought about by the rapid and substantial changes of climate at the termination of the last Glacial (Martin and Wright, 1967).

The dates of the major episodes of Pleistocene extinction are crucial to the discussion (table 3.11). Martin (1967: 111−15) writes:

Radiocarbon dates, pollen profiles associated with extinct animal remains, and new stratigraphic and archaeological evidence show that, depending on the region involved, late-Pleistocene extinction occurred

TABLE. 3.11
Dates of major episodes of generic extinction in the Late Pleistocene

Area	Date (years BP)
North America	11 000
South America	10 000
West Indies	Mid-post Glacial
Australia	13 000
New Zealand	900
Madagascar	800
Northern Eurasia	13 000−11 000
Africa and south-east Asia (?)	40 000−50 000

Source: data in Martin, 1967: 111

either after, during or somewhat before worldwide climatic cooling of the last maximum...of glaciation....Outside continental Africa and South East Asia, massive extinction is unknown before the earliest known arrival of prehistoric man. In the case of Africa, massive extinction coincides with the final development of Acheulean hunting cultures which are widespread throughout the continent....The thought that prehistoric hunters ten to fifteen thousand years ago (and in Africa over forty thousand years ago) exterminated far more large animals than has modern man with modern weapons and advanced technology is certainly provocative and perhaps even deeply disturbing.

The arguments that have been used in favour of anthropogenic interpretation can be summarised thus. First, massive extinction in North America seems to coincide in time with the arrival of man in sufficient quantity and with sufficient technological skill in making suitable artefacts (the bifacial Clovis blades) to be able to kill large numbers of animals (Krantz, 1970). Second, in Europe the efficiency of Upper Palaeolithic hunters is attested by such sites as Solutré in France, where a Late-Perigordian level is estimated to contain the remains of over 100 000 horses. Third, many beasts which have not known man are remarkably tame and stupid in his presence, and it would have taken them a considerable time to learn to flee or seek concealment at the sight or scent of man. Fourth, man the big-game hunter, in addition to hunting animals to death, may also have competed with them for particular food or water supplies.

Moreover, certain objections have been levelled against the climatic change model and these tend to support the anthropogenic model. It has been suggested, for instance, that changes in climatic zones are generally sufficiently gradual for beasts to be able to shift with the shifting vegetation and climatic zones of their choice. Similar environments are available in North America today as were present, in different locations and in different proportions, during Late Pleistocene times. Secondly, it can be argued that the climatic changes associated with the multiple glaciations, interglacials, pluvials and interpluvials do not seem to have caused the same abrupt degree of elimination as those in the Late Pleistocene.

This is not to say, however, that the climatic hypothesis is without foundation or support. The migration of animals in response to rapid climatic change could be halted by geographical barriers such as high mountain ranges or seas. The relatively rich state of the African big mammalian fauna is due, according to this point of view, to the fact that the African biota is not, or was not, as greatly restricted by any insuperable geographical barrier. Another possible way in which climatic change could cause extinction is through its influence on disease transmission. It has been suggested that during glacials animals would be split into discrete groups cut off by ice sheets, but that as the ice melted (before 11 000 BP in many areas), contacts between groups would once again be opened up and diseases to which immunity might have been lost because of isolation could spread rapidly. Large mammals, because of their lower reproduction rates, would recover their numbers much more slowly, and it was large mammals (according to Martin) that were the main sufferers from the Late-Pleistocene extinctions.

The detailed dating of the European megafauna's demise lends further credence to the climatic model (Reed, 1970). The Eurasiatic boreal mammals such as mammoth, woolly rhinoceros, musk ox, and steppe bison, were associated with and adapted to the cold steppe which was the dominant environment in northern Europe during the glacial phases of the last Glaciation. Each of these forms, especially the mammoth and the steppe bison, had been hunted by man for several tens of thousands of years, yet managed to survive through the last Glacial. They appear to have disappeared, according to Reed, within the space of a few hundred years when warm conditions associated with the Allerød inter-stadial led to the restriction and near disappearance of their habitat.

Grayson (1977) has added to the doubts expressed about the anthropogenic overkill hypothesis. He suggests that the overkill theory, because it states that the end of the North American Pleistocene was marked by extraordinarily high rates of extinction of mammalian genera, requires terminal Pleistocene mammalian generic extinctions to have been relatively greater than generic extinctions within other classes of vertebrates at this time. When he examined the extinction of birds he found that an almost exactly compar-able proportion became extinct at the end of the Pleistocene as one finds for the megafauna. Moreover, as the radiocarbon dates for early man in countries like Australia are pushed back it becomes increasingly clear that humans and several species of megafauna were living together for quite long periods, thereby undermining the notion of rapid overkill (Gillespie *et al.*, 1978).

There are further arguments that can be marshalled against the view that man the predator played a critical role in the Late Pleistocene extinctions in North America (Butzer, 1972; 509–10). There are, for example, relatively few Palaeo-Indian sites over an immense area, and the majority of these have a very limited cultural inventory. In addition there is no clear evidence that Palaeo-Indian subsistence was necessarily based, in the main part, in big-game hunting, and if it was, only two genera were hunted intensively: mammoth and bison. A final point that militates against the argument that man was primarily responsible for the waves of extinction is the survival of many big-game species well into the nineteenth century, despite a much larger and more efficient Indian population.

Thus the role of man in the great Late Pleistocene extinction is still a matter of debate. The problem is complicated because certain major cultural changes in man may have occurred in response to climatic change. The cultural changes may have assisted in the extinction process, and increasing numbers of technologically competent humans may have delivered the final *coup de grace* to isolated remnants already doomed by rapid post-Glacial environmental changes (Guilday, 1967).

When it comes to a consideration of modern-day extinctions the role of man is much less surrounded by controversy. Nonetheless, some modern extinctions of species are natural. Extinction is a biological reality: it is part of the process of evolution. In any period, including the present, there are naturally doomed species, which are bound to disappear either through over-specialization, or an incapacity to adapt themselves to climatic change and the competition of others, or because of natural cataclysms such as earthquakes, eruptions and floods. Fisher *et al.* (1969) believe that probably one-quarter of the species of birds and mammals that have become extinct since 1600 may have died out naturally. In spite of this, however, the rate of animal extinction brought about by man in the last 400 years is of a very high order when compared to the norm of geological time. In 1600 there were approximately 4226 living species of mammals: since then 36 (0.85%) have become extinct; and at least 120 of them (2.84%) are presently believed to be in some (or great) danger of extinction. A similar picture applies to birds. In 1600 there were about 8 684 living species: since then 94 (1.09%) have become extinct; and at least 187 of them (2.16%) are presently, or have very lately been, in danger of extinction (Fisher *et al.*, 1969).

Some beasts appear to be more prone to extinction than others, and a distinction is now often drawn between *r*-selected species and *k*-selected species. These are two ends of a spectrum. The former have a high rate of increase, short gestation periods, quick maturation, and the advantage that they have the ability to react quickly either to new environmental opportunities or to make use of transient habitats

101

TABLE 3.12
Characteristics of species affecting survival

Endangered	Safe
Large size	Small size
Predator	Grazer, scavenger, insectivore
Narrow habitat tolerance	Wide habitat tolerance
Valuable fur, oil, hide, etc.	Not a source of natural products
Restricted distribution	Broad distribution
Lives largely in international waters	
Migrates across international boundaries	Lives largely in one country
Reproduction in one or two vast aggregates	Reproduction by solitary pairs or in many small aggregates
Long gestation period	Short gestation period
Small litters	Big litters and quick maturation
Behaviour idiosyncrasies that are non-adaptive today	Adaptive
Intolerance of the presence of man	Tolerance of man

(such as seasonal ponds). The life duration of individuals tends to be short, populations tend to be unstable, and the species may over-exploit their environment to their eventual detriment. Many pests come into this category. The other end of the spectrum, the *k*-selection species, are those which tend to be endangered or to become extinct. Their prime characteristics are that they are better adapted to physical changes in their environment (such as seasonal fluctuations in temperature and moisture) and live in a relatively stable environment (Miller and Botkin, 1974). These species tend to have much greater longevity, longer generation times, fewer offspring, but a higher probability of survival of young and adults. They have traded a high rate of increase and the ability to exploit transient environments for the ability to maintain more stable populations with low rates of increase, but correspondingly low rates of mortality and a closer adjustment to the long-term capacity of the environment to support their population.

Table 3.12, which is modified after Ehrenfield (1972), attempts to bring together some of the characteristics of species which affects their survival in man's world.

Possibly one of the most fundamental ways in which man is causing extinction is by reducing the *area* of natural habitat available to a species. Even wildlife reserves tend to be small 'islands' in an inhospitable sea of man-modified vegetation or urban sprawl. We know from many of the classic studies in true island biogeography that the number

102

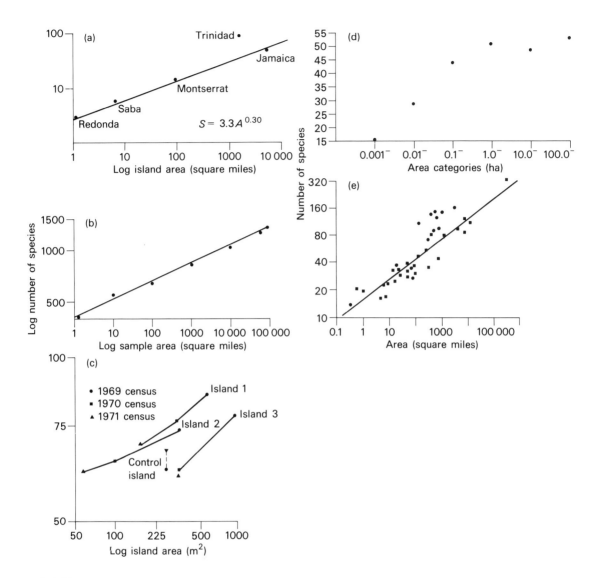

FIG. 3.13

Some relationships between the size of 'islands' and numbers of species (after Gorman, 1979, figures 3.1, 3.2, 8.1, and 8.2):

(a) *The number of amphibian and reptile species living on West Indian islands of various sizes. Note that Trinidad, joined to South America 10 000 years ago, lies well above the area–species curve of the other islands*

(b) *The area–species curve for the number of species of flowering plants found in a sample area of England*

(c) *The effect on the number of arthropod species of reducing the size of mangrove islands. Islands 1 and 2 were reduced after both the 1969 and the 1970 census. The control island was not reduced, the change in species number being attributable to random fluctuation*

(d) *The number of species of birds living in British woods of various size categories*

(e) *The number of species of land-birds living in the lowland rain forest on small islands of New Guinea, plotted as a function of island area. The squares represent islands which have not had a land connection to New Guinea and whose avifaunas are at equilibrium. The regression line is fitted through these points. The circles represent former land-bridge islands connected to New Guinea some 10 000 years ago. Note that the large ones have more species than one would expect for their size*

103

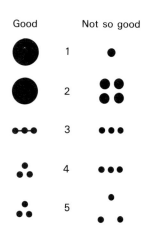

FIG. 3.14
*A set of general design rules for
nature reserves based on
theories of island biogeography.
The designs on the left are
preferable to those on the right
because they should enjoy
lower rates of species
extinction:*
*(1) A large reserve will hold
larger populations with
lower probabilities of going
extinct than will a small
reserve*
*(2) A single reserve is preferable
to a series of smaller
reserves of equal total area,
since these will support only
small populations with
relatively high probabilities
of going extinct*
*(3–5) If reserves must be
fragmented, then they
should be connected by
corridors of similar
vegetation or be placed
equidistant and as near to
each other as possible. In
this way immigration rates
between the fragments
will be increased, thereby
maximizing the chances of
extinct populations being
replaced from elsewhere in
the reserve complex*
(after Gorman, 1979, figure 8.4)

of species living at a particular location is related to area
(see figure 3.13 for some examples); islands support fewer
species than do similar areas of mainland, and small islands
have fewer species than do large ones. Thus it may well
follow that if man destroys the greater part of a vast belt
of natural forest, leaving just a small reserve, initially it
will be 'supersaturated' with species, containing more than
is appropriate to its area when at equilibrium (Gorman,
1979). Since the population sizes of the species living in
the forest will be now greatly reduced, the extinction rate
will increase and the number of species will decline towards
equilibrium. For this reason it may be a sound principal to
make reserves as large as is possible; a larger reserve will
support more species at equilibrium by allowing the existence
of larger populations with lower extinction rates. Several
small reserves will plainly be better than no reserves at all,
but they will tend towards holding fewer species at equilibrium than will a single reserve of the same area (figure
3.14). If it is necessary to have several small reserves, they
should be placed as close to each other as possible so that
each may act as a source area for the others. In this way
their equilibrial number of species will be raised due to
increased immigration rates.

There are situations when small reserves may have advantages over a single large reserve: they will be less prone to
total decimation by some natural catastrophe such as a fire,
they may allow the preservation of a range of rare and
scattered habitats; and they may allow the survival of a group
of competitors one of which would exclude the others from
a single reserve.

CHAPTER 4

The Impact of Man on the Soil

Introduction

Man lives close to and depends on the soil. It is one of the thinnest and most vulnerable of man's resources and is one upon which, both deliberately and inadvertently, he has had a very major impact.

Natural soil is the product of a whole range of factors and the classic expression of this is that of Jenny (1941):

$$S = f(cl, o, r, p, t, ...)$$

where S denotes any soil property, cl the regional climate, o the biota, r is the topography, p the parent material, t is the time (or period of soil formation), and the dots represent additional, unspecified factors. In reality soils are the product of highly complex interactions of many interdependent variables, and the soils themselves are not merely a passive and dependent factor in the environment. Nonetheless, by following Jenny's subdivision of the classic factors of soil formation one can see more clearly the influence that man has had on soil, be it detrimental or beneficial. This is brought out in summary form in table 4.1, adapted from the work of Bidwell and Hole (1965). Space precludes, however, that we can follow ass these aspects of anthropogenic soil modification or, to use the terminology of Yaalon and Yaron (1966), of *metapedogenesis*.

We will therefore concentrate on certain highly important changes which man has brought about, especially chemical changes (such as salinization and lateritization), various structural changes (such as compaction), some hydrological changes (including the effects of drainage and the factors leading to peat bog development), and, perhaps most important of all, soil erosion.

105

TABLE 4.1
*Suggested effects of the
influence of man on five classic
factors of soil formation*

(a) PARENT MATERIAL
  Beneficial: adding mineral fertilizers, accumulating shells and bones, accumulating ash locally, removing excess amounts of substances such as salts.
  Detrimental: removing through harvest more plant and animal nutrients than are replaced, adding materials in amounts toxic to plants or animals, altering soil constituents in a way to depress plant growth.

(b) TOPOGRAPHY
  Beneficial: checking erosion through surface roughening, land forming and structure building; raising land level by accumulation of material; land levelling.
  Detrimental: causing subsidence by drainage of wetlands and by mining; accelerating erosion; excavating.

(c) CLIMATE
  Beneficial: adding water by irrigation; rainmaking by seeding clouds; removing water by drainage; diverting winds, etc.
  Detrimental: subjecting soil to excessive insolation, to extended frost action, to wind, etc.

(d) ORGANISMS
  Beneficial: introducing and controlling populations of plants and animals; adding organic matter including 'nightsoil'; loosening soil by ploughing to admit more oxygen; fallowing; removing pathogenic organisms as by controlled burning.
  Detrimental: removing plants and animals; reducing organic matter content of soil through burning, ploughing, over-grazing, harvesting, etc; adding or fostering pathogenic organisms; adding radioactive substances.

(e) TIME
  Beneficial: rejuvenating the soil through adding of fresh parent material or through exposure of local parent material by soil erosion; reclaiming land from under water.
  Detrimental: degrading the soil by accelerated removal of nutrients from soil and vegetation cover; burying soil under solid fill or water.

Source: modified from Bidwell and Hole (1965)

Salinity: natural sources

Many semi-arid and arid areas are naturally salty. By definition they are areas of substantial water deficit where evapotranspiration exceeds precipitation. Thus whereas in humid areas there is sufficient water to percolate through the soil

TABLE 4.2
*Soluble salt content of rivers
in semi-arid areas*

River	Total dissolved solids (ppm)
Indus	250–300
Colorado	795
White Nile	174
Tigris–Euphrates	200–400
Niger	< 60–80

and to leach soluble materials from the soil and the rocks into the rivers and hence into the sea; in deserts this is not the case. Salts therefore tend to accumulate. This tendency is exacerbated by the fact that many desert areas are characterized by closed drainage basins (endoreic drainage) which act as terminal evaporative sumps for rivers.

The amount of natural salinity varies according to numerous factors, one of which is the source of salts. Some of the salts are brought in to the deserts by rivers (table 4.2) though it needs to be pointed out that most of these rivers do not have particularly high salt contents (generally less than 300 ppm). A second source of salts is the atmosphere – a source which in the past has often not been accorded sufficient importance. Rainfall, coastal fogs, and dust storms all transport significant quantities of soluble salts. This is shown by the data in table 4.4 for some forested catchments in southwestern Australia, where up to 130 kg ha^{-1} year^{-1} of chlorides are introduced in precipitation. Further soluble salts may be derived from the weathering and solution of bedrock. In the Middle East, for example, notably in Iran, there are extensive salt domes and evaporative beds within the bedrock which create locally high ground-water and surface-water salinity levels. In other areas such as the Rift Valley of southern Ethiopia and northern Kenya volcanic rocks may provide a large source of sodium carbonate (trona) to ground-waters, while elsewhere the rocks in which ground-water occurs may contain salt because they are themselves ancient desert sediments. Even in the absence of such localized sources of highly saline ground-water it needs to be remembered that over a period of time most rocks will provide soluble products to ground-water and in a closed hydrological system such salts will eventually accumulate to significant levels.

A further source of salinity may be marine transgressions. At times of higher sea-levels, it has sometimes been proposed (see, for example, Godbole, 1972) that salts would have been laid down by the sea. Likewise in coastal areas salts in ground-water aquifers may be contaminated by contact with sea-water (see p. 110).

Increased salinity brought about by man

It has already been stated that salinity is a normal characteristic of many desert areas. However, man has increased the extent and degree of salinity in many different ways.

The extension of irrigation and the use of a wide range of different techniques (see table 4.3) for water abstraction and application, can lead to a build-up of salt levels in the soil through the mechanism of raising ground-water so that it is near enough to the ground-surface for capillary rise and subsequent evaporative concentration to take place. In the case of the semi-arid northern plains of Victoria in Australia, for instance, the water-table has been rising at around 1.5 m/year so that now in many areas it is almost within 1 m of the surface (figure 4.1). When groundwater comes within 3 m of the surface in clay soils, but less for silty and sandy soils, capillary forces will bring moisture to the surface where evaporation will take place (Currey, 1977).

Secondly many irrigation schemes require the addition of large quantities of water over the soil surface. This is especially true for rice cultivation. Such spreads of surface water are readily evaporated and so salinity levels build up.

Thirdly the construction of large dams and barrages to control water flow and to give a head of water creates large reservoirs from which further evaporation can take place.

Fourthly, notably in areas of soils with high permeability, water seeps laterally and downwards from irrigation canals

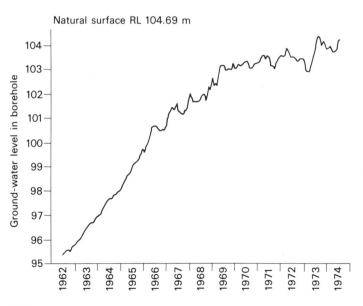

FIG. 4.1

Piezometer record to show ground-water level changes in the Murray Valley, Victoria, Australia, from 1962 to 1974 as a result of the extension of irrigation (after Currey, 1977, figure 2.13)

108

TABLE 4.3
Irrigation systems and methods

(a) IRRIGATION SYSTEMS
  i. *Sources of water supply*
    1. Rivers
    2. Springs, artesian wells
    3. Rainwater
    4. Ground-water

  ii. *Methods of raising water*
    1. Manual methods
      (*a*) Draw well, e.g. *shaduf* (Arabic), *cigonal* (Spanish)
    2. Worked by animals
      (*a*) Inclined plane, e.g. *gird* (Arabic)
      (*b*) Geared wheel, e.g *noria* (Spanish/Arabic), *nora* (Portuguese), *sakieh* (Arabic)
    3. Automatic devices
      (*a*) Impounding the flow of a river by a dam or weir
      (*b*) Kanat
      (*c*) Water wheels, e.g. *noria* (Spanish/Arabic), *naûra* (Arabic)
      (*d*) Windmill pumps
    4. Motorpumps
      (*a*) Diesel pumps
      (*b*) Electric pumps
      (*c*) Steam pumps

  iii. *Water storage*
    1. Reservoirs
    2. Ponds
    3. Cisterns
    4. Tanks
    5. Water towers

  iv. *Water distribution (supply and drainage)*
    1. Irrigation canals
      (*a*) Main canals
      (*b*) Secondary canals
      (*c*) Distributory canals
      (*d*) Furrows
    2. Drainage canals
      (*a*) Main drainage
      (*b*) Secondary drainage
      (*c*) Collector drains
    3. Levelling or terracing

(b) IRRIGATION METHODS
  i. *Surface irrigation*
    1. Dam or barrage
    2. Dam/barrage and channel irrigation
    3. Channel irrigation
    4. Spraying

  ii. *Underground irrigation*

Source: modified after Manshard, 1974, figure 5.3, p. 68

109

FIG. 4.2

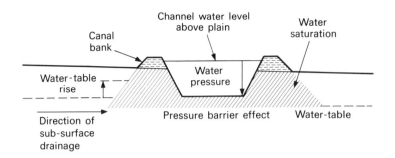

The effect of an irrigation channel in causing a local rise in the water-table, through the development of a pressure barrier which influences the movement of sub-surface drainage (after Currey, 1977, figure 2.12)

so that further evaporation takes place (figure 4.2). Many distribution channels in a gravity scheme are located on the elevated areas of a flood plain or riverine plain to make maximum use of gravity and the elevated landforms selected are natural levees, river bordering dunes and terraces all of which are composed of silt and sand which may be particularly prone to seepage loss.

In coastal areas salinity problems are created by sea water incursion brought about by over-pumping. This can be explained as follows. Fresh water has a lower density than salt water, such that a column of sea water can support a column of fresh water approximately 2.5% higher than itself (or a ratio of about 40:41). So where a body of fresh water has accumulated in a reservoir rock which is also open to penetration from the sea, it does not simply lie flat on top of the salt water but forms a lens, whose thickness is approximately forty-one times the elevation of the piezometric surface above sea level. This is called the Ghyben-Herzberg principle (see figure 4.3). The corollary of this rule is that if the hydrostatic pressure of the fresh water falls as a result of over-pumping in a well, then the underlying salt water will

21

The extension of irrigation in the Indus valley of Pakistan by means of large canals has caused widespread salination of the soils. Waterlogging is also prevalent. The white efflorescences of salt in the fields has been termed 'a Satanic mockery of snow'

110

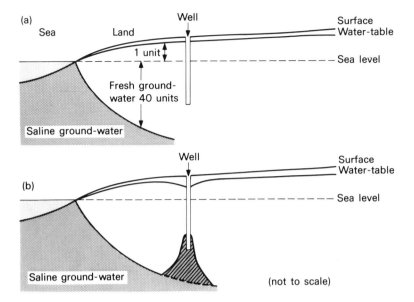

FIG. 4.3
(a) Illustrates the Ghyben–
Herzberg relationship
between fresh and saline
ground-water
(b) Illustrates the effect of
excessive pumping from
the well. The diagonal
hatching represents the
increasing incursion of
saline water (after Goudie
and Wilkinson, 1977,
figure 63)

rise by 40 units for every unit by which the fresh water table is lowered.

This problem presents itself on the coast of Israel, in California (Banks and Richter, 1953) on the island of Bahrain, and in some of the small coastal dune aquifers of the United Arab Emirates. A comparable situation arises in the case of the Nile Delta where, as a result of the construction of the Aswan Dam, ground-water levels have dropped downstream, leading to the intrusion of coastal salt water which has salinated the soil above, thus rendering it less suitable for cultivation. This is one of the costs which have to be paid for the undoubted gains brought about by rationalizing the flow of the Nile so that little of the water is wasted by draining out to sea.

The problem of sea water incursion as a result of over-pumping of aquifers is not, however, restricted to arid and semi-arid areas. It was noted as early as the middle of the last century in London and Liverpool, England, and there are now many records of this phenomenon in Germany, the Netherlands, Japan, and the eastern seaboard of the USA (Todd, 1959).

Increases in soil salinity are not restricted to irrigated areas. In certain parts of the world salinization has resulted from vegetation clearance (Peck, 1978). The removal of native forest vegetation allows a greater penetration of rainfall into deeper soil layers which causes ground-water levels to rise creating seepage of sometimes saline water in low-lying areas. Through this mechanism an estimated

111

2×10^5 ha of land in southern Australia which at the start of European settlement supported good crops or pasture is now suitable only for halophytic species. Similar problems exist also in North America, notably in Manitoba, Alberta, Montana, and North Dakota.

The clearance of the native evergreen forest (predominantly *Eucalyptus* forest) in southern Australia has led both to an increase in recharge rates of ground-water (table 4.4) and to an increase in the salinity of the streams.

TABLE 4.4

Hydrological and chemical data for south-western Australia, illustrating the effects of deforestation on ground-water recharge and river water chemistry

Catchment	Chloride input in precipitation $(kg ha^{-1} year^{-1})$	Chloride loss in streamflow $(kg ha^{-1} year^{-1})$	Recharge before clearing (mm/year)	Recharge with farming (mm/year)
(a) *Forested*				
Julimar	53	78	—	—
Seldom seen	120	160	—	—
More seldom seen	120	140	—	—
Waterfall gully	110	180	—	—
North Dandalup	130	180	—	—
Davies	130	140	—	—
Yarragil	97	130	—	—
Harris	84	130	—	—
(b) *Farmland*				
Brockman	80	340	8	73
Wooroloo	78	420	4	61
Dale	24	460	0.8	24
Hotham	48	370	2	26
Williams	31	650	1	37
Collie East	50	740	2	60
Brunswick	110	350	70	500

Source: from data in Peck, 1975

The spread of salinity

Man-induced salinity is not a new problem. Jacobsen and Adams (1958) have shown that it was a problem in Mesopotamian agriculture after about 2400 BC. Individual fields which at 2400 BC were recorded as salt-free can be shown through records of ancient temple surveyors to have developed conditions of sporadic salinity by 2100 BC. Further evidence is provided by crop choice, for the onset of salinization strongly favours the adoption of crops which are most salt-tolerant. Counts of grain impressions in excavated pottery from sites in southern Iraq dated to about 3500 BC suggest at that time the proportions of wheat and barley were nearly

112

equal. A little more than 1000 years later the less salt-tolerant wheat accounted for only one-sixth of the crop, while by about 2100 BC it accounted for less than 2% of the crop. By 1700 BC the cultivation of wheat had been abandoned completely in the southern part of the alluvial plain.

These changes in crop choice were accompanied by serious declines in yield which can also probably be put down to salinity effects. At 2400 BC the yield was 2537 litres/ha, by 2100 BC it was 1460, and by 1700 BC it was down to 897. It seems likely that this played an important part in the break-up of Sumerian civilization.

Another area where salination has been a severe problem is the Indus Plain of Pakistan, where Sir John Marshall, the archaeologist, described the salt as 'a Satanic mockery of snow'. Snelgrove (1967) reports that of the 25 million ha of arable land in the country, 4.6 million ha are now mostly waterlogged or poorly drained, 1.9 million ha are predominantly severely saline, 4.5 million have saline patches, and some 0.4 million ha are being lost yearly through the spread of these conditions. The problem has largely followed the rise of ground-water levels by 0.15–0.60 m/year brought about by the building of major irrigation systems in areas of somewhat sandy and silty and permeable soils during the last hundred or so years.

In summary, it has been estimated that the percentage of salt-affected and waterlogged soils amounts to 50% of the irrigated area in Iraq, 23% of all Pakistan, 50% in the Euphrates valley of Syria, 30% in Egypt and over 15% in Iran (Worthington, 1977, p. 30).

Consequences of salinity

One consequence of the evaporative concentration of salts, and the pumping of saline waters back into rivers and irrigation canals from tubewells and other sources, is that river waters leading from irrigation areas show higher levels of dissolved salts. These, particularly when they contain nitrates, can create problems in terms of human consumption. Table 4.5 illustrates the changes in total hardness levels that have been found for river waters in the USA.

A further problem is that as irrigation water is concentrated by evapotranspiration, the calcium and magnesium tend to precipitate as carbonates, leaving sodium ions dominant in the soil solution. The sodium ions tend to be adsorbed by colloidal clay particles, deflocculating them and leaving the resultant structureless soil almost impermeable to water and unfavourable to root development.

113

TABLE 4.5
*Changes in water hardness
brought about by irrigation*

Location	Total hardness above irrigation area	mg/l as $CaCO_3$ below irrigation area	Increase
Rio Grande, Texas	111	631	X 5.7
Yakima, Washington	33	134	X 4.1
Sunnyside, Washington	40	299	X 7.5
Arkansas River	212	890	X 4.2
Sutter Basin, California	72	480	X 6.7
		Mean X 5.6	

Source: Hotes and Pearson, 1977: 141

The death of vegetation in areas of saline patches, due both to poor soil structure and toxicity, creates bare ground which becomes a focal point for erosion by wind and water.

Probably the most serious impact of salination is on plant growth. This takes place partly through its effect on soil structure (see p. 119), but more significantly through its effects on osmotic pressures and through direct toxicity.

When a water solution containing large quantities of dissolved salts comes into contact with a plant cell it will cause a shrinkage of the protoplasmic lining. The phenomenon is due to the osmotic movement of the water, which passes from the cell towards the more concentrated soil solution. The cell then collapses and the plant succumbs.

The toxicity effect varies according to different plants and different salts. Sodium carbonate, by creating highly alkaline soil conditions may damage plants by a direct caustic effect; while high nitrate may promote undesirable vegetative growth in grapes or sugarbeets at the expense of sugar content. Likewise, boron is injurious to many crop plants at solution concentrations of more than 1 or 2 ppm.

The expected yield reduction from salinity build-up can be illustrated in table 4.6. The measure of soil salinity utilized is the electrical conductivity in μmho/cm of a saturated soil extract. The tolerances of different plants to salinity differ greatly but all suffer from increased salinity.

Reclamation of salt–affected lands

Because of the extent and seriousness of salinity, be it natural or man-induced, various reclamation techniques have been initiated. These can be divided into three main types: eradication, conversion and control.

Eradication predominantly involves the removal of salt

114

Crop	Percentage yield reduction		
	10	25	50
Barley	11.9	15.8	17.5
Sugarbeet	10.0	13.0	16.0
Cotton	9.9	11.9	16.0
Wheat	7.1	10.0	14.0
Rice	5.1	5.9	8.0
Maize	5.1	5.9	7.0
Alfalfa	3.0	4.9	8.2

TABLE 4.6
Yield reductions for selected agricultural crops at different salinity levels, expressed by the electrical conductivity (μmho/cm) of saturated soil extracts

Source: from data in Carter, 1975

either by improved drainage or by the addition of quantities of fresh water to leach the salt out of the soil. Both solutions involve considerable expense and pose severe technological problems in areas of low relief and limited fresh water availability. Improved drainage can either be provided by open drains or by the use of tubewells (as at Mohenjo Daro, Pakistan) to reduce ground-water levels and associated salinity and waterlogging. A minor eradication measure, which may have some potential, is the biotic treatment of salinity through the harvesting of salt-accumulating plants such as *Suaeda fruticosa*.

Conversion involves the use of chemical methods to convert harmful salts into less harmful ones. For example, gypsum is frequently added to sodic soils to convert caustic alkali carbonates to soluble sodium sulphate and relatively harmless calcium carbonate:

$$Na_2 CO_3 + CaSO_4 \leftrightarrows CaCO_3 + Na_2 SO_4 \downarrow \text{leachable}$$

Some of the most effective ways of reducing the salinity hazard involve miscellaneous control measures such as less wasteful and lavish application of water through the use of sprinklers rather than traditional irrigation methods, the lining of canals to reduce seepage, the realignment of canals through less permeable soils, and the use of more salt-tolerant plants. As salinity is a particularly serious threat at the time of germination and for seedlings, various strategies can be adopted during this critical phase of plant growth: plots can be irrigated lightly each day after seeding to prevent salt build-up, major leaching can be carried out just before planting, and areas to be seeded can be bedded in such a way that salts accumulate at the ridge tops whereas the seed is planted on the slope between the furrow bottom and the ridge top (Carter, 1975).

115

Lateritization

In some parts of the tropics there are extensive sheets of a material called laterite, an iron- and/or aluminium-rich duricrust (see Maignien, 1966 or Macfarlane, 1976). These iron-rich sheets result naturally, either because of a preferential removal of silica during the course of extensive weathering (leading to a *relative* accumulation of the sesquioxides of iron and aluminium) or because of an *absolute* accumulation of these compounds.

One of the properties of laterites is that they harden on exposure to air and through desiccation. Once hardened they are not favourable to plant growth. One particular way in which exposure may take place is by accelerated erosion, while forest removal may so cause a change in microclimate that desiccation of the laterite surface can take place. Indeed, one of the main consequences of the removal of the humid tropical rain forest (see p. 38) is that lateritization may occur. This tends to limit the extent of successful soil utilization and greatly retards the re-establishment of forest. Although Vine (1968: 90) and Sanchez and Buol (1975) have warned against exaggerating this problem as it applies to agricultural land use, there are records from many parts of the tropics of accelerated induration brought about by forest removal (Goudie, 1973). In the Cameroons, for example, around 2 m of complete induration can take place in less than a century. In India, foresters have for a long time been worried by the role that plantations of teak (*Tectona grandis*) can play in lateritization, for teak is deciduous, demands light, likes to be well spaced (to avoid crown friction), does not appreciate competition from undergrowth, and is shallow-rooted. These characteristics mean that teak plantations tend to create more exposure of the soil surface to erosive and desiccative forces than does the native vegetation cover.

One of the main exponents of the role that man has played in the lateritization process in the tropical world has been Gourou (1961: 21–2), and although he may be guilty of exaggerating the extent and significance of laterite, Gourou does give many examples from low latitudes of agricultural productivity having declined as a result of the onset of lateritization. It is worth quoting him at length:

On the whole, laterite is hostile to agriculture owing to its sterility and compactness. All tropical countries have not reached the same degree of lateritic 'suicide', but when the evolution has advanced a considerable way, man is placed in very strange conditions....Laterite is a pedological leprosy.

116

Man's activities aggravate the dangers of laterite and increase the rate of the process of lateritization. To begin with, erosion when started by negligent removal of the forest simply wears away the friable and relatively fertile soil which would otherwise cover the laterite and support forest or crops....The forest checks the formation of the laterite in various ways. The trees supply plenty of organic matter and maintain a good proportion of humus in the soil. The action of capillary attraction is checked by the loosening of the soil; and the bases are retained through the absorbent capacity of humus. The forest slows down evaporation from the soil...it reduces percolation and consequently leaching. Lastly the forest may improve the composition of the soil by fixing atmospheric dust.

Accelerated podzolization and acidification

There is an increasing amount of evidence that the introduction of agriculture, deforestation, and pastoralism to parts of upland western Europe promoted some major change in soil character, notably an increase in the development of acidic and podzolized conditions, associated with the development of peat bogs. Climatic changes of the type envisaged by Blyth and Sernander and later workers (see Goudie, 1977a, p. 94) may have played a role, as could progressive leaching of Devensian (last Glacial) drifts during the passage of the Holocene, but the association in time and space of human activities with soil deterioration is becoming increasingly clear (Evans *et al.*, 1975).

By replacing the natural forest vegetation with cultivation and pasture man set in train various related processes, especially on base-poor materials. First, the destruction of deep-rooting trees would curtail the enrichment of the surface of the soil by bases brought up from the deeper layers. Secondly, the use of fire to affect forest clearance may have released nutrients in the form of readily soluble salts, some of which would inevitably be lost in drainage, especially in soils poor in colloids (Dimbleby, 1974). Thirdly, the taking of crops and animal products would deplete the soil reserves to an extent probably greater than would be controlled by any manuring practices of prehistoric man. Fourthly, as the soil degraded, the vegetation which came in — especially bracken and heather — would itself tend to produce a more acidic humus type of soil than the original mixed deciduous forest, and so continue the process.

Various workers now attribute much of the podzolization in upland Britain to such processes, and Dimbleby has concluded that 'although a few soils have been podzols since the Atlantic period, the majority are secondary, having arisen as a result of man's assault on the landscape, particularly in the Bronze Age. (See also Bridges, 1978.)

The development of podzols, by impeding downward percolating waters, may have accelerated the formation of peats, which tend to develop where there is waterlogging brought about by impeded drainage. Many peat bogs in highland Britain appear to coincide broadly in age with the first major land-clearance episodes (P. D. Moore, 1973; Merryfield and P. D. Moore, 1974). Another mechanism which would have contributed to their development is that when a forest canopy is removed (as by deforestation) the transpiration demand of the vegetation is reduced, less rainfall is intercepted, and so the supply of ground-water is increased, aggravating any waterlogging tendencies.

The role of natural processes must not be totally forgotten, however, and Ball's assessment would seem judicious (Ball, 1975: 26):

It seems to be on balance that the highland trends in soil formation due to climate, geology and relief have been clearly running in the direction of leaching, acidity, podzolization, gleying and peat formation. For the British highlands generally, man has only intervened to hasten or slow the rate of these trends, rather than being in a position to alter the whole trend from one pedogenetic trend to another.

However, it would plainly be misleading to stress only the deleterious effects of man's actions on European soils. Traditional agricultural systems have often employed laborious techniques to augment soil fertility and to reduce such properties as undesirable acidity. In Britain, for example, the addition of chalk to light sandy land goes back at least to Roman times and the marl pits from which the chalk was dug are a striking feature of the Norfolk landscape, where Prince (1962) has identified at least 27 000 hollows. Similarly, in the Netherlands, Germany, and Belgium there are soils which for centuries (certainly more than a thousand years) have been built up (often over 50 cm) and fertilized with a mixture of manure, sods, litter, or sand. Such soils are called Plaggen soils (Pope, 1970). Plaggen soils also occur in Ireland, and the addition of sea-sand to peat was carried out in pre-Christian times. Likewise, prior to European settlement in New Zealand, the Maoris used thousands of tons of gravel and sand, carried in flax baskets, to improve soil structure (Cumberland, 1961).

Soil structure alteration

One of the most important features of a soil, both in terms of its suitability for plant growth and in terms of its inherent

118

erodibility, is its structure. There are many ways in which man can alter this, especially by compacting it by agricultural machinery, by the use of recreation vehicles and by changing its chemical character through irrigation (see p. 114). Soil compaction tends to increase the resistance of soil to penetration by roots and emerging seedlings, and limits oxygen and carbon dioxide exchange between the root zone and the atmosphere. Moreover, it reduces the rate of water infiltration into the soil which may change the soil moisture status and accelerate surface runoff and soil erosion (Chancellor, 1977). For example, the effects of the passage of vehicles on some soil structural properties are shown in table 4.7.

TABLE 4.7
Change to soil properties resulting from the passage of 100 motorcycles in New Zealand

Soil property	Total no. of sites	No. of sites with significant change *	Mean percentage at significant sites	No. of sites with significant increase	No. of sites with significant decrease	Main direction of change	Mean percentage change in direction
Infiltration capacity	16	16 (100%)	84.3	3	13	Decrease	78.1
Bearing capacity	21	10 (48%)	22.8	2	8	Decrease	18.6
Soil moisture	20	14 (70%)	15.5	5	9	Decrease	16.7
Dry bulk density	19	11 (58%)	13.6	9	2	Decrease	13.3

* Change is significant when greater than: 10% for infiltration capacity; 10% for bearing capacity; 5% for bulk density; 5% for soil moisture
Source: Crozier *et al.*, 1978, table I

Most notable of all is the reduction that is caused in soil infiltration capacity, which may explain why vehicle movements can often lead to gully development. Whether one is dealing with primitive sledges (as in Swaziland) or with the latest recreational toys of leisured Californian adolescents, the effects may be comparable. Grazing is another activity that can cause a deterioration of soil structure through the effects of trampling and compaction. Heavily grazed land tends to have infiltration capacities which are considerably lower than those found on ungrazed land. This is indicated for some American examples in table 4.8. The removal of vegetation cover and associated litter also leads to a change in infiltration capacity because it protects the soil from packing by raindrops and provides organic matter for binding soil particles together in open aggregates. Soil fauna that live on the organic matter assist this process by churning together the organic material and mineral particles. Table 4.9 is an attempt to rank the influence of different land use types of infiltration. In general, experiments show that re-afforestation leads to an improvement in soil structure, and especially in

TABLE 4.8
Rates of infiltration on grazed and ungrazed lands in America

Site	Rate of infiltration (mm/h)	
	Ungrazed	Heavily grazed
Montana	2.5–66.0	5.1–15.2
Oklahoma	134.6–309.9	40.6–83.8
Colorado	40.6–83.8	20.3–30.5
Montana	109.2–185.4	20.3–96.5
Wyoming	30.5–38.1	17.8–30.5
Louisiana	45.7	17.8
Kansas	33.0	20.3
Arizona	40.6	30.5

Source: processed by author from data in Gifford and Hawkins, 1978

TABLE 4.9
Relative influence of land use on the minimum rate of infiltration

Highest infiltration	Woods, good
	Meadows
	Woods, fair
	Pasture, good
	Woods, poor
	Pasture, fair
	Small grains, good rotation
	Small grains, poor rotation
	Legumes after row crops
	Pasture, poor
	Row crops, good rotation (more than one quarter in hay or sod)
	Row crops, poor rotation (one quarter or less in hay or sod)
Lowest infiltration	Fallow

Source: from Dunne and Leopold (1978), table 6.2 after US Soil Conservation Service

the pore volume of the soils (see, for example, Challinor, 1968). Ploughing is also known to produce a compacted layer at the base of the zone of ploughing (Baver *et al.*, 1972). This layer has been termed the 'plough sole'. The normal action of the plough is to leave behind a loose surface layer and a dense subsoil where the soil aggregates have been pressed together by the sole of the plough. The compacting action can be especially injurious when the depth of ploughing is both constant and long-continued, and when heavy machinery is used on wet ground (Greenland, 1977).

On the other hand farmers have for many centuries achieved improvements in soil structure by deliberate practices, particularly with a view to developing the all-important crumb structure. In pre-Roman times people in Britain and France

added lime to heavy clay soils, while the agricultural im-
provers of the eighteenth and nineteenth centuries improved
the structure of sandy heath soils by adding clay, and clay
with calcium carbonate (marl). They also compacted such
soils and added binding organic matter by breeding sheep and
feeding them with turnips and other fodder plants (Russell,
1961).

In the Modern era attempts have been made to reduce soil
crusting by applying municipal and animal wastes on farm
land, by adding chemicals such as phosphoric acid, and by
adopting a cultivation system of the no-tillage type. This is
based on the idea that the use of herbicides has eliminated
much of the need for tillage and cultivation in row crops;
seeds are planted directly into the soil without ploughing,
and weeds are controlled by the herbicides. With this method
less bare soil is exposed and heavy farm machinery is less
likely to create soil compaction problems (see Carlson,
1978, for some of these methods).

Soil structures may also be modified to induce greater
runoff of water, particularly in arid zones where the runoff
thus obtained can augment the meagre water supply for
crops, livestock, industrial and urban reservoirs, and ground-
water-recharge projects. In the Negev farming was practised
using such runoff, especially in the Nabatean and the Romano-
Byzantine periods (about 300 BC to AD 630), and attempts
were made to induce runoff by clearing the surface gravel of
the soil and heaping it into thousands of mounds. This
exposed the finer silty soil beneath, thereby facilitating soil
crust formation by raindrop impact, decreasing the infiltration capacity and reducing surface roughness, so that runoff
increased (Evenari *et al.*, 1971). Today a greater range of techniques are available for the same end: soils can be smoothed
and compacted by heavy machinery, soil crusting can be
promoted by dispersion of soil colloids with sodium salts,
the wettability of the soil surface can be reduced by applying
water-repellent materials, and soil pores can be filled with
binders (Hillel, 1971).

Soil drainage and its impact

Soil drainage 'has been a gradual process and the environmental changes to which it has led have, by reason of that
gradualness, often passed unnoticed' (Green, 1978: 171).
To be true, the most spectacular feats of drainage — arterial
drainage — involving the construction of veritable rivers and
large dike systems such as are epitomised by the Netherlands
and the Fenlands of eastern England, have received attention.

121

However, more widespread than arterial drinage, and sometimes independent of it, is the drainage of individual fields, either by surface ditching or by underdrainage with tile pipes and the like. Green (1978) has attempted to map the areas of drained agricultural land. In Finland, Denmark, Great Britain, the Netherlands, and Hungary the majority of agricultural land is drained (figure 4.4). The drainage conditions of the soil have also frequently been altered by the development of ridge and furrow patterns created by ploughing. Such patterns are a characteristic feature of many of the heavy soils of lowland England (figure 4.5).

Soil drainage has been one of the most successful ways in which man has striven to increase agricultural productivity and it was practised by Etruscans, Greeks, and Romans (N. Smith, 1976). Large areas of marshland and floodplain have been drained to man's advantage. Thus by leading water away the water-table will be lowered and stabilized, providing

FIG. 4.4

Percentage of drained agricultural land in Europe. There are no data for the blank areas (after Green, 1978, figure 1)

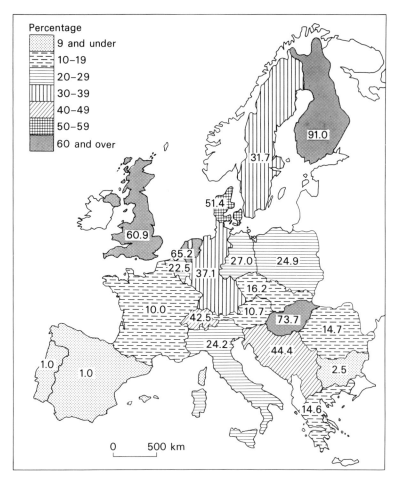

122

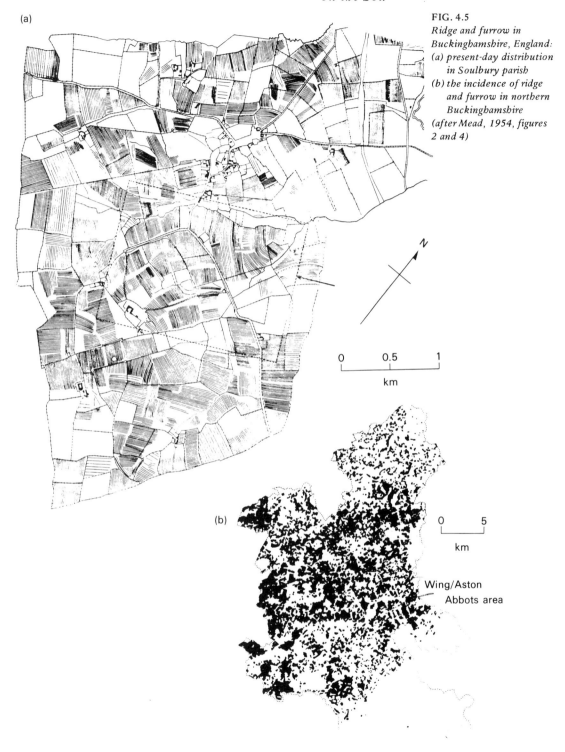

(a)

FIG. 4.5
*Ridge and furrow in
Buckinghamshire, England:
(a) present-day distribution
in Soulbury parish
(b) the incidence of ridge
and furrow in northern
Buckinghamshire
(after Mead, 1954, figures
2 and 4)*

0   0.5   1
km

(b)

0   5
km

Wing/Aston
Abbots area

a greater depth for the root zone. Moreover, well-drained soils warm up earlier in the spring and thus permit earlier planting and germination of crops. Farm work will be made easier if the soil is not too wet, the damage to crops produced by winter freezing may be minimized, undesirable salts may be carried away, and the general physical condition of the soil may be improved. In addition, drained land may have certain inherent virtues: tending to be flat it is less prone to erosion and is more amenable to mechanical cultivation. It will also be less prone to drought risk than certain other types of land (Karnes, 1971). Paradoxically, by reducing the area of saturated ground, drainage may alleviate flood risk in some situations by limiting the extent of a drainage basin that generates saturation excess overland flow.

Conversely, soil drainage can have some effects which are either undesirable or unplanned. For example some drainage systems, by raising drainage densities, can increase flood risk by reducing the distance over which unconcentrated overland flow (which is relatively slow) has to travel before reaching a channel (down which flow is relatively fast). In central Wales, for instance, the establishment of drainage ditches in peaty areas to enable afforestation, has tended to increase flood peaks in the rivers Wye and Severn (Howe *et al.*, 1966).

Soil quality can also be reduced in the long term because of drainage. The fall in water level in organic soils can lead to the oxidation and eventual disappearance of peaty materials which in the early stages of post-drainage use may be highly productive. This has been the case in the English Fenland, and in the Everglades of Florida, where drainage of peat soils has led to a subsidence in the soil of 32 mm per year (Stephens, 1956).

The soil climate of neighbouring areas may also be modified when the water-tables of drained land are lowered. This has been known to create problems for forestry in areas of marginal water availability.

Some of the most contentious problems caused by drainage are those associated with the reduction of wetland wildlife habitats.

Soil fertilization

The chemistry of soils has been changed deliberately by the addition of chemical fertilizers. Sometimes these may create environmental problems such as water pollution (see p. 168), while the substitution of chemical fertilizers for more traditional applications of organic materials may accelerate soil structure deterioration and soil erosion (see p. 131).

On the other hand, the use of synthetic fertilizers has greatly increased agricultural productivity in many parts of the world, and remarkable increases in yields have been achieved.

The employment of chemical fertilizers on a large scale is little more than 150 years old. In the early nineteenth century nitrates were imported from Chile and sulphate of ammonia was attained after the 1820s as a by-product of coal gas manufacture. In 1843 the first fertilizer factory was established at Deptford Creek, but for a long time super-phosphates were the only manufactured fertilizers in use. In the twentieth century synthetic fertilizers, particularly nitrates, were developed, notably by Scandinavian countries which used their vast resources of water power. Potassic fertilizers came into use much later than the phosphatic and nitrogenous; nineteenth-century farmers hardly knew them (Russell, 1961). The rapid development in the use of the three main fertilizers — nitrates, phosphates, and potash — in the first half of the twentieth century is shown in table 4.10.

Date	Nitrogen (N)	Phosphoric acid (P_2O_5)	Potash (K_2O)
1900	16	110	7
1913	29	180	23
1929	48	198	52
1939	60	170	75
1946	165	358	120
1956	291	386	305

Source: from Russell, 1961, table 14, p. 185

TABLE 4.10
Quantities of fertilizers used by farmers in the UK, expressed in thousands of tons of plant food

Fires and soil

The importance and antiquity of fire as an agency through which transformation of man's environment is attained (see p. 26), requires that some attention be given to the effects of fire on soil characteristics and on soil erosion (see p. 134).

Fire has often been used intentionally to change soil characteristics, and both the release of nutrients by fire and the value of ash have for long been recognized, notably by those involved in shifting agriculture (see p. 39) based on slash-and-burn techniques. Following on from cultivation, the loss of nutrients by leaching and erosion is very rapid (Nye and Greenland, 1964), and this is why after only a few years the shifting cultivators have to move on to new plots. Fire rapidly alters the amount, form, and distribution of plant nutrients in ecosystems, and compared to normal biological decay of plant remains, burning rapidly releases some nutrients into a plant-available form. Indeed, the amounts of P, Mg, K, and Ca released by burning forest and scrub vegetation are high in relation to both the total and available quantities of these elements in soils (Raison, 1979). In forests burning often causes the pH of the soil to rise by three units or more, creating alkaline conditions where primarily there was acidity. Burning also leads to some direct nutrient loss by volatilization and corrective transfer of ash, or by loss of ash to water erosion or wind deflation. The removal of the forest causes soil temperatures to increase because of the absence of shade, and humus is therefore often lost at a faster rate than it is formed (Grigg, 1970).

Soil erosion: general considerations

In the late 1930s, towards the end of the so-called Dust Bowl years, Sauer conducted a campaign against what he called the 'destructive exploitation in modern colonial expansion' (Sauer, 1938: 497), and placed soil erosion squarely into the context of geography:

We may well consider whether the theme of soil erosion should not be moved up to the first category of problems before the geographers of the world. It is very important for the future of mankind. It has critical significance for certain chapters of historical geography. The physical processes involved are poorly observed and generalized and their study will undoubtedly shake somewhat the rather lethargic present position of geomorphology...best of all the subject is suited to a 'hologeographic' approach in which the development of surface conditions of specific localization is examined as an interaction of identified physical and economic (i.e. Wirtschaft) processes.

That soil erosion is a major and serious aspect of man's role in changing his own environment is not to be doubted. There is a long history of weighty books and papers on the subject (see for example, Marsh, 1864; H. H. Bennett, 1938; Jacks and White, 1939; Morgan, 1979). Although there are many techniques available for attempting to reduce the intensity of the problem (see Hudson, 1971) it still appears to remain intractable. As L. J. Carter (1977: 409) has reported in the context of the USA:

...although nearly $15 billion has been spent on soil conservation since the mid-1930s, the erosion of croplands by wind and water... remain one of the biggest, most pervasive environmental problems the nation faces. The problem's surprising persistence apparently can be attributed at least in part to the fact that, in the calculation of many farmers, the hope of maximizing short-term crop yields and profits has taken precedence over the longer term advantages of conserving the soil. For even where the loss of topsoil has begun to reduce the land's natural fertility and productivity, the effect is often masked by the positive response to heavy application of fertilizer and pesticides, which keep crop yields relatively high.

Although construction, urbanization, war, mining and other such activities are often significant in accelerating erosion of the soil, the prime cases are deforestation and agriculture. Pimentel (1976) has estimated that in the USA soil erosion on agricultural land operates at a rate of about $30 t\,ha^{-1}\,year^{-1}$, which is approximately eight times quicker than topsoil is formed. They calculate that water runoff delivers around 4 billion tonnes of soil to the rivers of the forty-eight contiguous states and that three-quarters of this comes from agricultural land. They estimate that another billion tonnes of soil is eroded by the wind, a process which created the Dust Bowl of the 1930s.

One serious consequence of accelerated erosion is the sedimentation that takes place in reservoirs, thereby shortening their lives and reducing their capacity. Many small reservoirs, especially in semi-arid areas, appear to have an expected life of only 30 years or even less (see for example, Rapp *et al.*, 1972).

Soil erosion associated with deforestation and agriculture

Forests protect the underlying soil from the direct effects of rainfall, runoff is generally reduced, tree roots bind the soil, and the litter layer protects the ground from rain-splash. It is thus to be anticipated that with the removal of forest for agriculture or for other reasons rates of soil loss will increase, and mass movements will increase in magnitude and frequency. The rates of erosion that result will be particularly high if the ground is left bare, though under crops the increase will be less marked. Furthermore, the method of ploughing, the time of planting, the nature of the crop, and the size of fields will all have an influence on the severity of erosion.

It is seldom that we have reliable records of rates of erosion over a sufficiently long time-span to show just how much human activities have led to an acceleration of rates. Recently, however, techniques have been developed which enable the rate of erosion on slopes to be gauged over a lengthy time-span by means of using dendrochronological techniques to date the time of root exposure for suitable species of tree. In Colorado, USA, Carrara and Carroll (1979) found that rates over the last 100 years have been about 1.8 mm/year, whereas in the previous 300 years the rate was between around 0.2 and 0.5 mm/year, indicating an acceleration of about six-fold. This great jump has been attributed to the introduction of large numbers of cattle to the area about a century ago.

Table 4.11, which is based on data from tropical Africa, shows the comparative rates of erosion for three main types of land use: trees, crops, and barren soil. It is very evident from these data that under crops, but more especially when ground is left bare, or under fallow, soil erosion rates are greatly magnified. At the same time, and causally related, the percentage of the rainfall that becomes runoff is increased.

In some cases the erosion produced by forest removal will be in the form of widespread surface stripping. In other cases the erosion will occur as more spectacular forms of mass movement, such as mudflows, landslides and debris avalanches. Some detailed data on debris avalanche production in North American catchments as a result of deforestation and forest road construction are presented in table 4.12, and they illustrate the substantial effects created by clear-cutting and by the construction of logging roads. It is indeed probable that a large proportion of the erosion associated with forestry operations is caused by road construction, and care needs to be exercised to minimize this effect. The digging of drainage ditches in upland

TABLE 4.11
Runoff and erosion under various covers of vegetation in parts of Africa

Locality	Average annual rainfall (mm)	Slope (%)	Annual runoff (%)			Erosion (t ha^{-1} year^{-1})		
			A	B	C	A	B	C
Ouagadougou (Upper Volta)	850	0.5	2.5	2–32	40–60	0.1	0.6–0.8	10–20
Sefa (Senegal)	1300	1.2	1.0	21.2	39.5	0.2	7.3	21.3
Bouake (Ivory Coast)	1200	4.0	0.3	0.1–26	15–30	0.1	1–26	18–30
Abidjan (Ivory Coast)	2100	7.0	0.1	0.5–20	38	0.03	0.1–90	108–170
Mpwapwa* (Tanzania)	c 570	6.0	0.4	26.0	50.4	0	78	146

Source: after Charreau, table 5.5 p. 153 in Greenland and Lal, 1977
Note: A = forest or ungrazed thicket
         B = crop
         C = barren soil
*From Rapp, *et al.*, 1972, figure 5, p. 259

128

pastures and peat moors to permit tree-planting in central Wales has also been found to cause accelerated erosion (Clarke and McCulloch, 1979).

In general the greater the proportion of a river basin that is deforested the greater the sediment yield per unit area will be. In the USA the rate of sediment yield appears to double for every 20% loss in forest cover.

Soil erosion resulting from deforestation and agricultural practice is often regarded as being especially serious in tropical areas or semi-arid areas (see T. R. Moore, 1979, for a good case-study). However, recent measurements by Morgan (1977) on sandy soils in the English East Midlands near Bedford indicate that rates of soil loss under bare soil on steep slopes can reach $17.69 \, t \, ha^{-1} \, year^{-1}$, compared with 2.39 under grass and nothing under woodland (table 4.13). Water is not the only active process creating accelerated erosion in eastern England though it is important (Evans and Nortcliff, 1978). Ever since the 1920s dust storms

TABLE 4.12

Debris-avalanche erosion in forest, clear-cut and roaded areas

Site	Period of record (years)	Area (%)	Area (km²)	No. of slides	Debris-avalanche erosion (m³ km⁻² year⁻¹)	Rate of debris-avalanche erosion relative to forested areas
Stequaleho Creek, Olympic Peninsula						
Forest	84	79	19.3	25	71.8	X 1.0
Clear-cut	6	18	4.4	0	0	0
Road R/W	6	3	0.7	83	11 825	X 165
			24.4	108		
Alder Creek, western Cascade Range, Oregon						
Forest	25	70.5	12.3	7	45.3	X 1.0
Clear-cut	15	26.0	4.5	18	117.1	X 2.6
Road R/W	15	3.5	0.6	75	15 565	X 344
			17.4	100		
Selected Drainages, Coast Mountains, south-west British Columbia						
Forest	32	88.9	246.1	29	11.2	X 1.0
Clear-cut	32	9.5	26.4	18	24.5	X 2.2
Road R/W	32	1.5	4.2	11	282.5	X 25.2
			276.7	58		
H. J. Andrews Experimental Forest, western Cascade Range, Oregon						
Forest	25	77.5	49.8	31	35.9	X 1.0
Clear cut	25	19.3	12.4	30	132.2	X 3.7
Road R/W	25	3.2	2.0	69	1 772	X 49
			64.2	130		

Source: after D. N. Swanston and F. J. Swanson, 1976, table 4

22
The removal of vegetation in Swaziland creates spectacular gulley systems, which in southern Africa are called dongas. The smelting of local iron ores in the early nineteenth century required the use of a great deal of fire wood which may have contributed to the formation of this example

	Plot	Splash	Overland flow	Rill	Total
1	*Bare soil*				
	Top slope	0.33	6.67	0.10	7.10
	Mid-slope	0.82	16.48	0.39	17.69
	Lower slope	0.62	14.34	0.06	15.02
2	*Bare soil*				
	Top slope	0.60	1.11	—	1.71
	Mid-slope	0.43	7.78	—	8.21
	Lower slope	0.37	3.01	—	3.38
3	*Grass*				
	Top slope	0.09	0.09	—	0.18
	Mid-slope	0.09	0.57	—	0.68
	Lower slope	0.12	0.05	—	0.17
5	*Woodland*				
	Top slope	—	—	—	0.00
	Mid slope	—	—	—	0.012
	Lower slope	—	0.012	—	0.008

TABLE 4.13
Annual rates of soil loss (t/ha) under different land use types in eastern England

Source: from Morgan, 1977

have been recorded in the Fenlands, the Brecklands, East Yorkshire (Radley and Sims, 1967) and in Lincolnshire (see, for example, Arber, 1946) and they seem to be occurring with increased frequency. This results from changing agricultural practices, including the substitution of artificial fertilizers for farmyard manure, a reduction in the process of 'claying' whereby clay was added to the peat to stabilize it, the removal of hedgerows to facilitate the use of bigger farm machinery, and, perhaps most importantly, the increased cultivation of sugar beet. This crop requires a fine tilth and tends to leave the soil relatively bare in the early summer compared with other crops (Pollard and Miller, 1968).

However, perhaps the most famous case of soil erosion by deflation was the so-called Dust Bowl of the 1930s in the USA (see figure 4.6). In part this was caused by a series of hot, dry years which depleted the vegetation cover and made the soils dry enough to be susceptible to wind erosion. However, the situation created by this drought was gravely exacerbated by years of over-grazing and unsatisfactory farming techniques. Perhaps the prime cause of this event was the rapid expansion of wheat cultivation in the Great Plains. The number of cultivated hectares doubled during the First World War as tractors (for the first time) rolled out onto the plains by the thousands. In Kansas alone wheat hectarage increased from under 2 million ha in 1910 to almost 5 million ha in 1919. After the war the wheat cultivation went on apace, helped by the development of the combine harvester, and government assistance. The farmer, busy sowing wheat and reaping gold, could foresee no end to his land of milk and honey, but the years of favourable climate were not to last and over large areas the tough sod

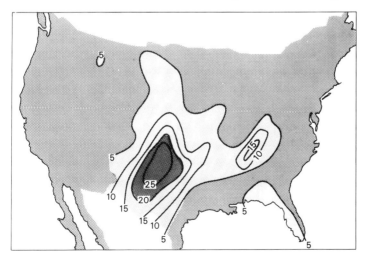

FIG. 4.6

During the 1930s overgrazing and unwise cultivation in the Great Plains of the USA caused serious dust storms during the late spring and early summer. The map shows the number of days with dusty conditions or dust storms in the so-called 'Dust Bowl' in April 1935 (after D. H. Davis, 1942, figure 60)

23
The Dust Bowl created in the 1930s caused severe problems for the inhabitants of Cimarron County, Oklahoma

which exasperated the earlier homesteaders had given way to friable soils of high erosion potential. Drought, acting on damaged soils, created the 'black blizzards' which have been so graphically described by Coffey (1978: 79–80):

...there was something fantastic about a dust cloud that covered 1.35 m. square miles, stood three miles high and stretched from Canada to Texas, from Montana to Ohio – a cloud so colossal it obliterated the sky...a four-day storm in May 1934...transported some 300 million tons of dirt 1500 miles, darkened New York, Baltimore and Washington for five hours, and dropped dust not only on the President's desk in the White House, but also on the decks of ships some 300 miles out in the Atlantic...masses of dust began to billow into huge tumbling clouds ebony black at the base and muddy tan at the top, some so saturated with dust particles that ducks and geese caught in flight, suffocated; some turning the sky so black that chickens, thinking it night, would roost. Oklahoma counted 102 storms in the span of one year; North Dakota reported 300 in eight months...

Dust storms are still a serious problem in various parts of the United States: the Dust Bowl was not solely a feature of the 1930s. Thus, for example, in the San Joaquin Valley area of California in 1977 a dust storm caused extensive damage and erosion over an area of about 2000 km². More than 25 million tonnes of soil were stripped from grazing land within a 24 h period. While a combination of drought and a very high wind (as much as 300 km/h) provided the predisposing natural conditions for the stripping to occur,

132

Location	Forest cover	Years of record	Annual rainfall (mm)	Soil loss (ta ha^{-1} year^{-1})
Holly Spring (Missouri	Burned	2	1 595	0.825
	Protected	2	1 677	0.262
Guthrie (Oklahoma)	Burned	10	765	0.28
	Protected	10	765	0.025
Statesulleo (North Carolina)	Burned	9	1 162	7.7
	Protected	9	1 162	0.05
Tyler (Texas)	Burned	9	1 022	0.9
	Protected	9	1 022	0.125
East Texas	Burned	1.5	–	0.512
	Protected	1.5	–	0.25
North Missouri (A)	Burned	Year 1	1 627	1.27
		Year 2	1 010	0.5
		Year 3	1 262	0.125
North Missouri (B)	Burned	Year 1	1 627	0.512
		Year 2	1 010	0.255
		Year 3	1 262	0.075

Source: after data by Ralston and Hatchell, 1971, in Foster, 1976

TABLE 4.14
Soil losses from burned and protected woodlands in the USA

over-grazing and the general lack of windbreaks in the agricultural land played a major role. In addition broad areas of land had recently been stripped of vegetation, levelled or ploughed up prior to planting. Other quantitatively less important contributing factors included stripping of vegetation for urban expansion, extensive denudation of land in the vicinity of oilfields, and local denudation of land by vehicular recreation (Wilshire *et al.*, in press). One interesting observation made in the months after the dust storm was that in subsequent rain storms runoff occurred at an accelerated rate from those areas that had been stripped by the wind,

24
In the High Plains near Lubbock in Texas the effect of soil erosion and drifting was very evident in 1977. Note the vast fields and absence of windbreaks

133

exacerbating problems of flooding and initiating numerous gullies. Elsewhere in California dust yield has been considerably increased by mining operations in dry lake beds (Wilshire, 1980).

Soil erosion produced by fire

Many fires are set by man, either deliberately or non-deliberately (see p. 28), and because they remove vegetation and expose the ground they tend to lead to increased rates of soil erosion.

The burning of forests, for example, can, especially in the first years after the fire event, lead to high rates of soil loss (see table 4.14). Burnt forest tends to have rates a whole order of magnitude higher than those in protected areas. Comparably large changes in soil erosion rates have been observed to result from the burning of heather in the Yorkshire moors, northern England, and the effects of burning may be felt for the six years or more that may be required to get regeneration of the heather (*Calluna*) (see table 4.15). In the Australian Alps fire in experimental catchments has been found to lead to a greatly increased flow in the streams (see p. 156) together with a marked surge in the delivery of suspended load. Combining these two effects of increased flow-rate and sediment yield it was found that after fire the total sediment load was increased 1000 times (Pereira, 1973). Likewise, watershed experiments in the chaparral scrub of Arizona, involving denudation by a destructive fire, indicated that whereas erosion losses prior to the fire were only 43

TABLE 4.15

Soil erosion associated with Calluna *(heather) burning on the North Yorkshire moors*

Condition of Calluna or ground surface	Mean rate of litter accumulation (+) or erosion (−) (mm/year)	No. of observations
(a) *Calluna* 30–40 cm high. Complete canopy	+ 3.81	60
(b) *Calluna* 20–30 cm high. Complete canopy	+ 0.25	20
(c) *Calluna* 15–20 cm high. 40–100% cover	− 0.74	20
(d) *Calluna* 5–15 cm high. 10–100% cover	− 6.4	20
(e) Bare ground. Surface of burnt *Calluna*	− 9.5	19
(f) Bare ground. Surface of peaty or mineral subsoil	− 45.3	25

Source: data in Imeson, 1971

t km^{-2} year^{-1} after the fire they were between 50 000 and 150 000 t km^{-2} year^{-1}. The causes of the marked erosion associated with chaparral burning are interesting. There is normally a distinctive 'non-wettable' layer in the soils supporting chaparral. This layer, composed of soil particles coated by hydrophobic substances leached from the shrubs or their litter, is normally associated with the upper part of the soil profile (Mooney and Parsons, 1973), and builds up through time in the unburned chaparral. The high temperatures which accompany chaparral fires (see p. 31) cause these hydrophobic substances to be distilled and they condense on lower soil layers. This process results in a shallow layer of wettable soil overlying a non-wettable layer. Such a condition, especially on steep slopes, can result in severe surface erosion.

Soil erosion associated with construction and urbanization

There are now a number of studies which illustrate clearly that urbanization can create significant changes in erosion rates.

The highest rates of erosion are produced in the construction phase when there is much bare ground and much disturbance produced by vehicle movements and exvacations. M. G. Wolman and Schick (1967) and M. G. Wolman (1967) have shown that the equivalent of many decades of natural or even agricultural erosion may take place during a single year from areas cleared for construction. In Maryland they found that sediment yields during construction reached 55 000 t km^{-2} year^{-1} while in the same area rates under forest were around 80–200 t km^{-2} year^{-1}, and those under farming 400 t km^{-2} year^{-1}. New road cuttings in Georgia were found to have sediment yields up to 20 000–50 000 t km^{-2} year^{-1}. Likewise, in Devon, England, Walling and Gregory (1970) found that suspended sediment concentrations in streams draining construction areas were ×2 to ×10 (occasionally up to ×100) those from undisturbed areas. In Virginia, USA, Vice *et al.* (1969) found equally high rates of erosion during construction and reported that they were ×10 those from agricultural land, ×200 those from grassland and ×2000 those from forest in the same area.

However, construction does not go on for ever, and once the disturbance ceases, roads are surfaced, and gardens and lawns are created. The rates of erosion go down massively and may be of the same order as those under natural or pre-agricultural conditions (table 4.16).

135

The Human Impact

Attempts at soil conservation

Because of the adverse effects of accelerated erosion a whole array of techniques has now been widely adopted to conserve soil resources, (table 4.17) though some of the techniques such as hill-slope terracing may have some antiquity. There are some parts of the world where such devices are one of the most prominent components of the landscape. This applies to many wine-growing areas, to some arid zone regions (such as Yemen and Peru), and to a wide selection of localities in the more humid tropics (Luzon, Java, Sumatra, Assam, Ceylon, Uganda, Cameroons, etc.). In areas subject to wind erosion other strategies may be necessary. Since soil only blows when it is dry, anything which conserves soil moisture is beneficial. Another approach to wind erosion is to slow down the wind by physical barriers, either in the form of an increased roughness of the soil surface brought about by careful ploughing, or by planted vegetative barriers, such as windbreaks and shelter-belts (see p. 268).

Attempts at soil conservation have not always been without drawbacks. For example, the establishment of a ground cover in dry areas to reduce erosion may so reduce soil moisture because of accelerated evapotranspiration that the growth of the main crop may be adversely affected. On a

TABLE 4.16

Rates of erosion associated with construction and urbanization

	Location	Land use	Source	Rate $(t\ km^{-2}\ year^{-1})$
1	Maryland, USA	Forest	Wolman (1967)	39
		Agriculture		116–309
		Construction		38 610
		Urbanized		19–39
2	Virginia, USA	Forest	Vice *et al.* (1969)	9
		Grassland		94
		Cultivation		1 876
		Construction		18 764
3	Detroit, USA	General non-urban	Thompson (1970)	642
		Construction		17 000
		Urban		741
4	Maryland, USA	Rural	Fox (1976)	22
		Construction		337
		Urban		37
5	Maryland, USA	Forest and grassland	Yorke and Herb (1978)	7–45
		Cultivated land		150–960
		Construction		1 600–22 400
		Urban		830
6	Wisconsin, USA	Agricultural	Daniel *et al.* (1979)	<1
		Construction		19.2

TABLE 4.17
Methods used to combat soil erosion

1 *Revegetation*
   (a) Deliberate planting
   (b) Suppression of fire, grazing, etc., to allow regeneration

2 *Measures to stop stream bank erosion*

3 *Measures to stop gully enlargement*
   (a) Planting of trailing plants, etc.
   (b) Weirs, dams, gabions, etc.

4 *Crop management*
   (a) Maintaining cover at critical times of year
   (b) Rotation
   (c) Cover crops

5 *Slope runoff control*
   (a) Terracing
   (b) Deep tillage and application of humus
   (c) Transverse hillside ditches to interrupt runoff
   (d) Contour ploughing
   (e) Preservation of vegetation strips (to limit field width)

6 *Prevention of erosion from point sources like roads, feedlots*
   (a) Intelligent geomorphic location
   (b) Channelling of drainage water to non-susceptible areas
   (c) Covering of banks, cuttings, etc., with vegetation

7 *Suppression of wind erosion*
   (a) Soil moisture preservation
   (b) Increase in surface roughness through ploughing up clods or by planting of windbreaks

25
The loess lands of China have been particularly susceptible to the development of large ravines. However, these conservation terraces, built by a production bridgade have effectively reduced the problem and allowed the land to become rehabilitated

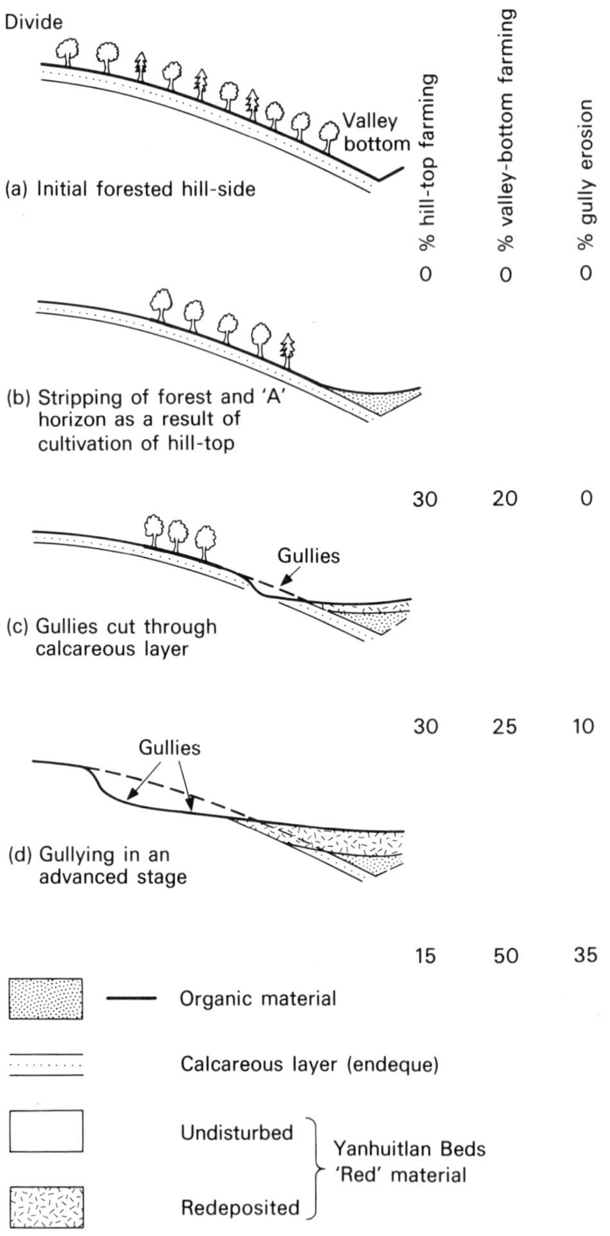

FIG. 4.7
Beneficial effect of gullying on production of agricultural land in Nochixtlan, Mexico (after Kirkby in Whyte, 1977, figure 1)

wider scale major afforestation schemes may cause substantial runoff depletion in river catchments (see p. 158). Likewise, the provision of mulching can sometimes be detrimental: in cool climates, the reduction in soil temperature shortens the growing season whilst in wet areas, higher soil moisture may induce gleying and anerobic conditions (Morgan, 1979: 60). Some terrace schemes also have not lacked in shortcomings. They have been known to hold

back so much water on hillsides that the soils become saturated and landsliding is induced. Similarly strip cropping,
because it requires the farming of small areas, is not compat-
ible with highly mechanized agricultural systems, and insect
infestation and weed control are additional problems which
it has posed.

Soil conservation measures may not always be appropriate
for soil erosion itself is not always a totally unsatisfactory
phenomenon. Sanchez and Buol (1975), for instance, have
pointed out that in recent volcanic areas, soil erosion can
be the mechanism for removing the more weathered base-
depleted material from the soil surface and exposing the
more fertile, less weathered, base-rich material beneath.
Likewise, in the Nochixtlan area of south Mexico, soil
erosion has been utilized by local farmers to *produce* agricultural land. Severe gullies have cut in to steep valley side
slopes (figure 4.7) and since the Spanish Conquest an average
depth of 5 m has been stripped from the entire surface area.
The local Mixtec farmers, far from seeing this high rate of
erosion as a hazard to be feared, direct the flow of the eroded
material to feed their fields with fertile soil and to extend
their area of fields. Over the past 1000 years (see Whyte,
1977), the Mixtec cultivators have managed to use the gully
erosion to double the width of the main valley floors from
1.5 to 3 km and to infill the narrow tributary valley floors
with flights of terraces. Judicious use of the phenomenon of
gully erosion has enabled them to convert poor hill-top
fields into the rich alluvial farmland below.

Nonetheless it is undoubtedly true that manipulation of
the soil is one of the most significant ways in which man
changes his environment, and one in which he has had some
of the most detrimental effects. Soil deterioration has led to
many cases of what W. C. Lowdermilk once termed 'regional
suicide', and the overall situation is at least as bleak as it was
in the post Dust-Bowl years when Jacks commented:

The organization of civilized societies is founded upon the measures
taken to wrest control of the soil from wild Nature, and not until
complete control has passed into human hands can a stable super-
structure of what we call civilization be erected on the land (in Jacks
and Whyte, 1939: 17).

CHAPTER 5

The Human Impact on the Waters

Man's deliberate modification of rivers

Although there are many ways through which man influences water quantity and quality in rivers and streams (for example, by direct channel manipulation, modification of watershed characteristics, urbanization, and pollution), the first of these is of particularly great importance (Mrowka, 1974). Indeed, there are a great variety of methods for direct channel manipulation and many of them have a long history. Perhaps the most widespread of these is the construction of dams and reservoirs. The first recorded dam was probably constructed in Egypt some 5000 years ago, but since that time the adoption of this technique has spread, whether to improve agriculture, to prevent floods, to generate power, or to provide a reliable source of water. The construction of dams has increased markedly, especially between 1945 and 1971 (see Beaumont, 1978; and figure 5.1). Table 5.1 shows an estimate of the amount of stable runoff which is regulated by

TABLE 5.1
Stable river runoff (km^3) *of the continents of the world*

Continent	Of under- ground origin	Regulated by lakes	Regulated by reservoirs	Total	Regulated by reservoirs as percentage of total	Total stable runoff as percentage of total runoff
Europe	1 065	60	200	1 325	15.1	43
Asia	3 410	35	560	4 005	14.0	30
Africa	1 465	40	400	1 905	21.0	45
North America	1 740	150	490	2 380	20.6	40
South America	3 740	—	160	3 900	4.1	38
Australasia	465	—	30	495	6.1	25

Source: after Beaumont, 1978

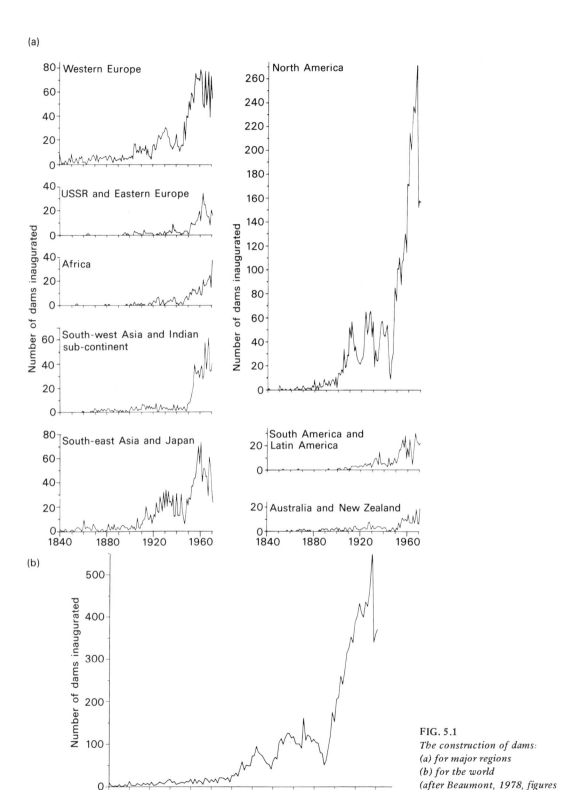

(a)

FIG. 5.1
The construction of dams:
(a) for major regions
(b) for the world
(after Beaumont, 1978, figures
1 and 2)

141

water reservoirs in the continents of the world. The impact of man's activities is especially marked in Africa and North America where about 20% of the total runoff is now regulated by them. Stable runoff in this context is defined as river flow resulting largely from ground-water discharge.

One of the most apparent features of man-made dams and reservoirs is that they are becoming increasingly large. In the 1930s the Hoover or Boulder Dam in the USA (221 m) was by far the tallest in the world. By the early 1970s it was exceeded in height by at least thirteen others. Of the eleven barrages over 5 km long only one, Fort Peck, USA, is more than 40 years old. A barrage at Kiev in the USSR is to be 41 km in length. Moreover, whereas Lake Mead, behind the Hoover Dam, was the largest in the world in 1936 with 38 billion m^3 of water, by the 1970s it was dwarfed. Kariba covered 160 billion m^3, Aswan's Lake Nasser covered 157 billion m^3, and Ghana's Akosombo, 148 billion m^3 (Beckinsale, 1969).

Such large dams are capable of causing almost total regulation of the streams they impound, but in general the degree to which peak flows are reduced depends on the size of the dam and the impounded lake in relation to catchment characteristics. In Britain, as table 5.2 shows, peak flow reduction downstream from selected reservoirs varies considerably, with some tendency for the greatest degree of reduction to occur in those catchments where the reservoirs cover the largest percentage of the area. When one considers the magnitude of floods of different recurrence intervals before and after dam construction one finds that dams have

TABLE 5.2
*Peak flow reduction
downstream from selected
British reservoirs*

Reservoir	Percentage of catchment inundated	Percentage peak flow reduction
Avon, Dartmoor	1.38	16
Fernworthy, Dartmoor	2.80	28
Meldon, Dartmoor	1.30	9
Vyrnwy, Mid-Wales	6.13	69
Sutton Bingham, Somerset	1.90	35
Blagdon, Mendip	6.84	51
Stocks, Forest of Bowland	3.70	70
Daer, Southern Uplands	4.33	56
Camps, Southern Uplands	3.13	41
Catcleugh, Cheviots	2.72	71
Ladybower, Peak District	1.60	42
Chew Magna, Mendips	8.33	73

Source: after Petts and Lewin, 1979, table 1, p. 82

much less effect on rare events of high magnitude (Petts and Lewin, 1979), and this is brought out in table 5.3. Nonetheless, most dams achieve their aim: to regulate river discharge, and they have been highly successful in achieving what they were constructed for: millions of people depend upon them for survival, welfare, and employment.

Reservoir	*Recurrence interval* (years)			
	1.5	2.3	5.0	10.0
Avon, R. Avon	0.90	0.89	0.93	1.02
Stocks, R. Hodder	0.83	0.86	0.84	0.95
Sutton Bingham, R. Yeo	0.52	0.61	0.69	0.79

TABLE 5.3
The ratios of post- to pre-dam discharges for flood magnitudes of selected frequency

Source: after Petts and Lewin, 1979, table 2, p. 84

However, dams may have a whole series of environmental consequences that may or may not have been anticipated (figure 5.2 and Makkaveyev, 1972). Some of these are dealt with in greater detail elsewhere, such as subsidence (p. 206), earthquake triggering (p. 235), the transmission and expansion in the range of organisms (p. 92), the build-up of soil salinity (p. 108), changes in ground-water levels creating slope instability (see p. 213) and waterlogging (p. 110). Certain of these processes may in turn affect the viability of the scheme for which the dam was created.

A particularly important consequence of the impoundment of a reservoir behind a dam is the reduction in the sediment load of the river downstream. A clear demonstration of this effect has been given for the South Saskatchewan River in Canada (table 5.4) by Rasid (1979). During the pre-dam period, as typified by 1962, the total annual suspended loads at Saskatoon and Lemsford Ferry were remarkably similar. As soon as the reservoir began to fill late in 1963, however, some of the suspended sediment began to be trapped, and the transitional period was marked by a progressive reduction in the proportion of sediment which reached Saskatoon. In the 4 years after the dam was fully operational the mean annual sediment load at Saskatoon was only 9% that at Lemsford Ferry.

Such sediment retention is also well illustrated by the Nile (table 5.5) both before and after the construction of the great Aswan High Dam. Until its construction the late summer and autumn period of high flow was characterized by high silt concentrations, but since it has been finished the silt load is rendered lower through the year as a whole and the seasonal peak is removed.

143

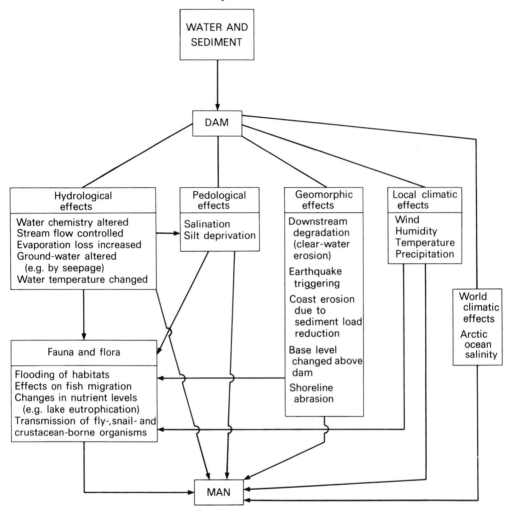

FIG. 5.2
Generalized representation of the possible effects of dam construction on man and various components of his environment

This sediment removal in turn has various possible consequences, including a reduction in flood deposited nutrients on fields, less nutrients for fish in the south-east Mediterranean Sea, accelerated erosion of the Nile Delta, and accelerated riverbed erosion because less sediment is available to cause bed aggradation. This last process is often called 'clear-water-erosion' (see Beckinsale, 1972) and in the case of the Hoover Dam it affected the river channel of the Colorado for 150 km downstream by causing incision. In turn such channel incision may initiate a rejuvenation of headward erosion in tributaries and may cause the lowering of ground-water tables and the undermining of bridge piers and other structures downstream of the dam. On the other hand, in regions such as North China, where modern dams trap silt, the incision of the river channel downstream may alleviate the

Period of record	Lemsford Ferry	Saskatoon	Difference at Saskatoon (%)
Pre-dam			
1962	1 813 305	1 873 278	+ 3
Transitional			
1963	4 892 159	446 788	− 8
1964	7 711 006	4 145 553	− 46
1965	9 731 837	2 721 021	− 72
1966	5 228 474	1 675 142	− 68
MEAN	6 890 869	3 254 626	− 53
Post-dam			
1967	12 618 814	445 967	− 96
1968	2 660 643	101 412	− 96
1969	10 562 413	2 146 496	− 80
1970	5 643 278	117 847	− 98
MEAN	7 871 287	702 930	− 91

TABLE 5.4
Total yearly suspended load (tons) of the South Saskatchewan River at Lemsford Ferry and Saskatoon, 1962–70

Source: Rasid, 1979, table 1

strain on levées and lessen the expenses of levée strengthening or heightening. However, clear-water erosion does not always follow from silt retention in reservoirs. There are examples of rivers where, before impoundment, floods carried away the sediment brought in to the main stream by steep tributaries. Reduction of the peak discharge after the completion of the dam leaves some rivers unable to scour away the sediment that accumulates as large fans of sand or gravel below each tributary mouth (Dunne and Leopold, 1978). The bed of the main stream is raised and if water-intakes, towns, or other structures lie alongside the river they can be threatened again by flooding or channel shifting across the accumulating wedge of sediment.

There are some landscapes of the world which are dominated by dams, canals, and reservoirs. Probably the most striking

TABLE 5.5
Silt concentrations (in parts per million) in the Nile at Gaafra before and after the construction of the Aswan High Dam

BEFORE (averages for the period 1958–63)											
Jan.											Dec.
64	50	45	42	43	85	674	2702	2422	925	124	77
AFTER											
44	47	45	50	51	49	48	45	41	43	48	47
RATIO											
1.5	1.1	1.0	0.8	0.8	1.7	14.0	60.0	59.1	21.5	2.58	1.63

Source: Abul-Atta, 1978: 199

26
*The Aswan High Dam in Egypt
will largely control the flow of
the Nile, providing protection
both against floods and water
shortage in years of drought.
The massive structure does,
however, have some
undesirable consequences
including the trapping of
fertile silts (table 5.5)*

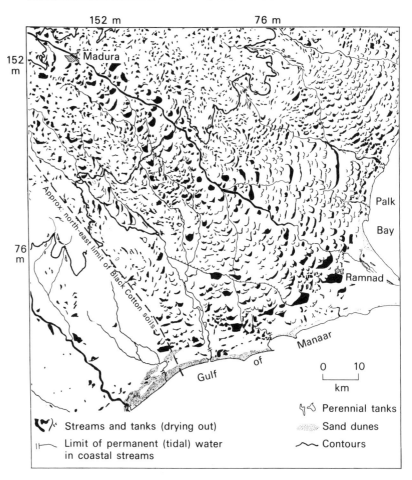

FIG. 5.3
*The Madurai–
Ramanathapuram tank
country in south India
(after Spate and Learmonth,
1967, figure 25.12)*

146

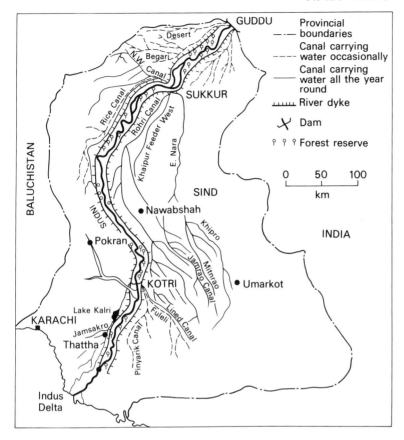

FIG. 5.4
*The irrigated areas in Sind
(Pakistan) along the Indus
Valley (after Manshard, 1974,
figure 5.7)*

example of this (figure 5.3), is the 'tank' landscape of south-east India where myriads of little streams and areas of overland flow have been dammed by small earth structures to give what Spate (Spate and Learmonth, 1967: 778) has likened to 'a surface of vast overlapping fish-scales'.

In the northern part of the subcontinent, in Sind, the landscape changes wrought by the hydrological hand of man are no less striking, with the mighty snow-fed Indus being controlled by great embankments (*bunds*) and interrupted by great barrages. Its waters are distributed over thousands of square kilometres by a canal network that has evolved over the past 4000 years (figure 5.4).

Another landscape where equally far-reaching changes have been wrought by man is the Netherlands. Coates (1976) has calculated that in the reclamation of that country from the sea, and in the extension of drainage lines, man, prior to 1860, moved 1 000 million m^3 of material. The area is dominated by man-made canals, rivers, drains, and lakes. As C. T. Smith (1978: 506) has put it:

147

The Human Impact

It can be said of the Netherlands with more truth than of any other country that it is a creation of man, for it owes its existence to the long continued struggle to drain and reclaim new land and to protect existing lands from the invasion of the sea.

Particularly in the sixteenth, seventeenth, and eighteenth centuries the Dutch applied their remarkable expertise in hydrological management to countries other than their own and drained many areas both on coasts and inland (figure 5.5), creating major river networks in the process.

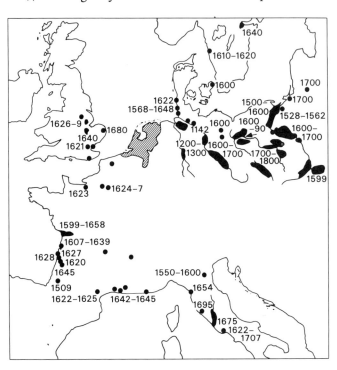

FIG. 5.5
Areas where the great Dutch engineers were involved in wetland reclamation schemes (after Van Veen in C. T. Smith, 1978, figure 9.12)

Another direct means of river manipulation is channelization. This involves the construction of embankments, dikes, levées and floodwalls to confine floodwaters; and the improvement of channels with respect to their ability to transmit floods by enlarging their capacity through straightening, widening, deepening, or smoothing.

Some of the great rivers of the world are now lined by great embankment systems such as those that run for more than 1 000 km alongside the Nile, 700 km along the Hwang Ho, 1 400 km by the Red River in Vietnam, and over 4 500 km in the Mississippi Valley (Ward, 1978). Like dams, such embankments and related structures often achieve what they are meant to achieve but they may also create some environmental problems, and they may also have some disadvantages.

148

For example, they reduce natural storage for floodwaters both by preventing water from spilling on to much of the floodplain, and by stopping bank storage in cases where impermeable floodwalls are used. Likewise flow of water in tributaries may be constrained. In addition, embankments may on occasions exacerbate the flood problem they were designed to reduce by preventing floodwaters downstream of a breach from draining back into the channel once the peak has passed.

Channel improvement, designed to improve water flow, may also have effects that were not necessarily envisaged or which are not necessarily desirable. For example, the more rapid movement of water along improved channel sections can aggravate flood peaks further downstream and cause excessive erosion. The lowering of water-tables in the 'improved' reach may cause over-drainage of adjacent agricultural land so that sluices must be constructed in the channel to maintain levels. On the other hand, lined channels may obstruct interflow and shallow ground-water and so cause surface saturation.

Channelization may also have miscellaneous effects on fauna through the increased velocities, reductions in the extent of shelter in the channel bed, and by reduced nutrient imputs due to the destruction of overhanging bank vegetation (see Keller, 1976 and figure 5.6). In the case of large swamps, like those of the Sudd in Sudan or the Okavango in Botswana, the channelization of rivers could completely transform the whole character of the swamp environment. Figure 5.6 illustrates some of the differences that exist between natural and man-made channels.

A third direct modification of channels is produced by the construction of bypass and diversion channels to carry excess floodwater or to enable irrigation to take place. Such channels may be as old as irrigation itself. They may contribute to the salinity problems encountered in many irrigated areas (see p. 108).

Other deliberate modifications of river regimes may be achieved by inter-basin water transfers (for water supply), by the addition of urban waste water (from sewerage plants) and by water abstraction (for water supply, ground-water recharge, etc.). In advanced industrialized societies water uses of this type are increasing. Wolman (1965), for example, revealed that 1400 billion litres per day of water were required for all purposes in the USA out of a total surface water runoff of 4540 billion litres per day.

When one turns to the coastal portions of rivers, to the estuaries, the possible effects of another human impact,

NATURAL CHANNEL

MAN-MADE CHANNEL

Suitable water temperatures:
  adequate shading; good cover for fish
  life; minimal variation in temperatures;
  abundant leaf material input

Increased water temperatures:
  no shading; no cover for fish life;
  rapid daily and seasonal fluctuations
  in temperatures; reduced leaf material
  input

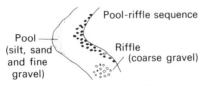

Pool-riffle sequence

Pool
(silt, sand
and fine
gravel)

Riffle
(coarse gravel)

Mostly riffle

Sorted gravels provide diversified habitats
  for many stream organisms

Unsorted gravels:
  reduction in habitats; few organisms

POOL ENVIRONMENT

High flow

High flow

Diversity of water velocities:
  high in pools, lower in riffles. Resting areas
  abundant beneath undercut banks or behind
  large rocks, etc.

May have stream velocity higher than
  some aquatic life can withstand. Few
  or no resting places

Low flow

Low flow

Sufficient water depth to support fish and
other aquatic life during dry season

Insufficient depth of flow during dry
seasons to support diversity of fish
and aquatic life. Few if any pools
(all riffle)

FIG. 5.6

Comparison of the natural channel morphology and hydrology with that of a channelized stream, suggesting some possible ecological consequences (after Keller, 1976, figure 4)

dredging, may be as complex as the effects of dams and reservoirs upstream, (La Roe, 1977). Dredging and filling are certainly widespread and often desirable. Dredging may be performed to create and maintain canals, navigation channels, turning basins, harbours and marinas; to lay pipelines; and to obtain a source of material for fill or construction. Filling is the deposition of dredged materials to create new land. There are miscellaneous ecological effects of such actions. In the first place, direct disruption of habitats will take place. Secondly, the generation of large quantities of suspended silt will tend physically to smother bottom-dwelling plants and animals; will tend to smother fish by

150

clogging their gill structures; will, through the effect of turbility, reduce photosynthesis, and will tend to lead to eutrophication by an increased nutrient release. Likewise, the destruction of marshes, mangroves, and sea grasses by dredge and fill might result in the loss of these natural purifying systems. The removal of vegetation might also cause erosion. Moreoever, as silt deposits stirred up by dredging accumulate elsewhere in the estuary they would tend to create 'false bottom'. Characterized by shifting, unstable sediments the dredged bottom, fill deposits, or spoil areas would be slowly − if at all − recolonized by fauna and flora. Furthermore, dredging would tend to change the configuration of currents, the rate of freshwater drainage, and might provide avenues for salt water intrusion.

Urbanization and its effects on river flow

The process of urbanization has a considerable hydrological impact both in terms of controlling rates of erosion (see p. 135), the delivery of pollutants to rivers (see p. 174) and in terms of influencing the nature of runoff and other hydrological characteristics. An attempt to generalize some of these impacts in terms of an historical model of urbanization is summarized usefully by Savini and Kammerer (1961) and reproduced here in table 5.6.

One of the most important of these impacts is the way in which urbanization affects flood runoff. Research both in the United States and in Britain has shown that because urbanization leads to a great extension of impermeable surfaces of tarmac, tiles, and concrete, so there is a tendency for flood runoff to increase in comparison with rural sites. City drainage densities may be greater than in the natural condition (Graf, 1977) and the installation of sewers and storm drains accelerates runoff, as illustrated in figure 5.7. The greater the area that is sewered the greater is the discharge for a particular recurrence level. Peak discharges are higher and occur sooner after runoff starts in basins that have been affected by urbanization and the installation of sewers (figure 5.8). Some runoff may be generated in urban areas because low vegetation densities mean that evapotranspiration is limited.

However, in many cases the effect of urbanization is greater for small floods, and as the size of the flood and its recurrence interval increase, so the effect of urbanization diminishes (Martens, 1968; Hollis, 1975). A probable explanation for this is that during a severe and prolonged storm event a non-urbanized catchment may become so saturated

151

TABLE 5.6
*Stages of urban growth and
their miscellaneous hydrological
impacts*

Stage	Impact
1 Transition from pre-urban to early-urban stage:	
(a) Removal of trees or vegetation	Decrease in transpiration and increase in storm flow
(b) Construction of scattered houses with limited sewerage and water facilities	
(c) Drilling of wells	Some lowering of water-table
(d) Construction of septic tanks, etc.	Some increase in soil moisture and perhaps some contamination
2 Transition from early-urban to middle-urban stage:	
(a) Bulldozing of land	Accelerated land erosion
(b) Mass construction of houses, etc.	Decreased infiltration
(c) Discontinued use and abandonment of some shallower wells	Rise in water-table
(d) Diversion of nearby streams for public supply	Decrease in runoff between points of diversion and disposal
(e) Untreated or inadequately treated sewerage into streams and wells	Pollution of streams and wells
3 Transition from middle-urban to late-urban stage:	
(a) Urbanization of area completed by addition of more buildings	Reduced infiltration and lowered water-table, higher flood peaks and lower low flows
(b) Larger quantities of untreated waste into local streams	Increased pollution
(c) Abandonment of remaining shallow wells because of pollution	Rise in water-table
(d) Increase in population requiring establishment of new water supply and distribution systems	Increase in local stream-flow if supply is from outside basin
(e) Channels of streams restricted at least in part to artificial channels and tunnels	Higher stage for a given flow (therefore increased flood damage); changes in channel geometry and sediment load
4 Transition from middle-urban to late-urban stage:	
(a) Construction of sanitary drainage system system and treatment plant for sewage	Removal of additional water from area
(b) Improvement of storm drainage system	
(c) Drilling of deeper, large-capacity industrial wells	Lowered water pressure, some subsidence, salt water encroachment
(d) Increased use of water for air conditioning	Overloading of sewers and other drainage facilities
(e) Drilling of recharge wells	
(f) Waste-water reclamation and utilization	Recharge to ground-water aquifers; more efficient use of water resources

Source: modified after Savini and Kammerer, 1961

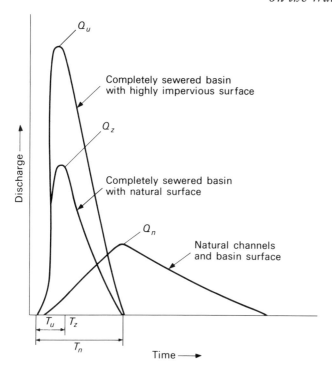

FIG. 5.7
Effect of urban development on flood hydrographs. Peak discharges (Q) are higher and occur sooner after runoff starts (T) in basins after they have been developed or sewered (after Fox, 1976, figure 3)

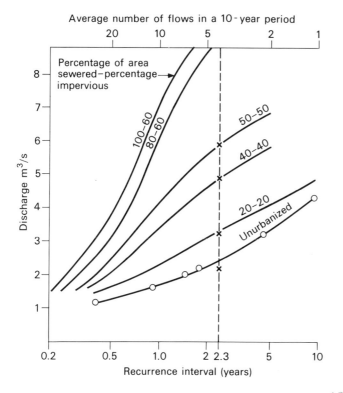

FIG. 5.8
Flood frequency curves for a 1 square mile basin in various states of urbanization (after US Geological Society, in Viessman, et al., 1977, figure 11.33)

153

and its channel network so extended that it begins to behave hydrologically as if it were an impervious catchment with a dense surface-water drain network. Hence, under these conditions, a rural catchment produces floods of a type and size similar to those of its urban counterpart. Moreover, a further mechanism probably operates in the same direction, for in an urban catchment it seems probable that some throttling of flow takes place in surface-water drains during intense storms, thereby tending to attenuate the very highest discharges. Thus, Hollis believes, whilst small frequent floods are increased many times by urbanization, large rare floods (the ones likely to cause extreme damage) are not significantly affected by the construction of suburban areas within a catchment area (figure 5.9). Nonetheless, a whole series of techniques have been developed in an attempt to reduce and delay urban storm runoff (table 5.7) for Hollis's findings may not be universally applicable. For example, K. V. Wilson (1967) working in Jackson, Mississippi, found that the 50-year flood for an urbanized catchment was three times higher than that of a rural one.

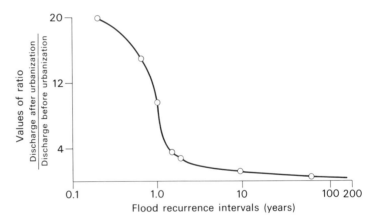

FIG. 5.9
Effects on flood magnitude of paving 20% of a basin (after Hollis, 1975)

Water transfers for industrial and municipal purposes are having an increasing impact on river regimes in urbanized societies (Richards and Wood, 1977). Under dry weather flow conditions, stream-flow in urban catchments in the Midlands and south-east England is mainly imported water. This is illustrated by the River Tame which contains about 90% effluent in its 95% duration flow. This proportion is increasing as more water is imported (figure 5.10), reduced in quality and added to low natural base-flows reduced by lack of recharge.

154

Area	Reducing runoff	Delaying runoff

Large flat roof	Cistern storage
	Rooftop gardens
	Pool storage or
	  fountain storage
	Sod roof cover
		Ponding on roof by con-
		  stricted drainpipes
		Increasing rough roughness
		(1) rippled roof
		(2) gravelled roof

Car parks	Porous pavement
	(1) gravel car parks
	(2) porous or
	    punctured asphalt
	Concrete vaults and
	  cisterns beneath car
	  parks in high value
	  areas
	Vegetated ponding areas
	  around car parks
	Gravel trenches
		Grassy strips on car parks
		Grassed waterways draining
		  car parks
		Ponding and detention
		  measures for impervious
		  areas
		(1) rippled pavement
		(2) depressions
		(3) basins

Residential	Cisterns for individual
	  homes or groups
	  of homes
	Gravel drives (porous)
	Contoured landscape
	Ground-water recharge
	(1) perforated pipe
	(2) gravel (sand)
	(3) trench
	(4) porous pipe
	(5) dry wells
	Vegetated depressions
		Reservoir or detention
		  basin
		Planting a high-delaying
		  grass (high roughness)
		Grassy gutters or channels
		Increased length of travel
		  of runoff by means of
		  gutters, diversions and
		  so on

General	Gravel alleys Porous pavements	Gravel alleys

TABLE 5.7
Measures for reducing and delaying urban storm runoff

Source: after US Department of Agriculture, Soil Conservation Service, 1972; Viessman *et al.*, 1977: 569

Deforestation and its effect on river flow

As we have already noted (see p. 2) one of the first major indications that man could inadvertently adversely affect his environment was the observation that deforestation could create torrents and floods. The deforestation that gives rise to such flows can be produced both by felling and by fire.

The first experimental study in which a planned land-use change was executed to enable observation of the effects of stream-flow began at Wagon Wheel Gap, Colorado, in 1910

FIG. 5.10

Trends in 25-month moving averages of runoff as a percentage of 25-month moving averages of rainfall for the River Tame, Lee Marston, England, 1957–74. The trend reflects increasing amounts of imported 'runoff' (after K. S. Richards and Wood, 1977, figure 24.6)

$$Y = 67.75 + 0.027X$$

$$\frac{\text{25-month moving averages of runoff}}{\text{25-month moving averages of rainfall}} = Y$$

27

Flood risk in rivers like the Mississippi may be increased by man's activities. Among major causes are deforestation and urbanization

(Pereira, 1973). Here stream-flow from two similar watersheds of about 80 ha each were compared for 8 years. One valley was then clear-felled and the records were continued. After the clear-felling the annual water yield was increased 17% above that predicted from the flows of the unchanged control valley. Peak flows are also increased. Studies on two small basins in the Australian Alps (Wallace's Creek — 4l km² and Yarrango Billy River — 224 km²) which were burned over showed that rainstorms, which from previous records would have been expected to give rise to flows of 60–80 m³/s produced a peak of 370 m³/s (a five- or six-fold increase). Likewise catchment experiments in Arizona have shown that when chaparral scrub is burned there is a ten-fold increase in water yield.

As regeneration of vegetation takes place after forest has been cut or burned so stream-flow tends to revert towards normal, though the process may take some decades. This is

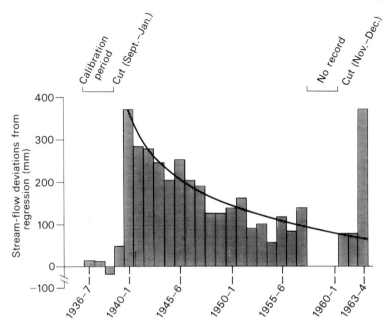

FIG. 5.11
The increase of water yield after clear-felling a forest: a unique confirmation from the Coweeta catchment in North Carolina, USA (after Pereira, 1973, figure 8)

illustrated in figure 5.11 which shows the dramatic effects produced on the Coweeta catchments in North Carolina by two spasms of clear felling together with the gradual return to normality in between.

The substitution of one forest type for another may also have effects on stream-flow. This can also be exemplified from the Coweeta catchments, where two experimental catchments were converted from a mature deciduous hardwood forest cover to a cover of white pine (*Pinus strobus*). Fifteen years after the conversion took place annual streamflow was found to be reduced by about 20% (Swank and Douglass, 1974). The reason for this notable change is that the interception and subsequent evaporation of rainfall is greater for pine that it is for hardwoods during the dormant season.

Additional data for the effects of land-use change on annual runoff levels are presented for tropical areas in table 4.10.

The reasons why the removal of a forest cover and its replacement with pasture, crops or bare ground have such important effects on stream-flow are many. A mature forest probably has a higher rainfall interception rate, probably has a tendency to reduce rates of overland flow, and probably generates soils with a higher infiltration capacity and better general structure. All these factors will tend to lead both to a reduction in overall runoff levels and to less extreme flood peaks. However, with careful management the replacement of forest by other land-use types need not be

detrimental either in terms of sediment loss or flood generation. In Kenya, for example, the tea plantations with shade
trees, protective grass covers, and carefully designed culverts
were found to be 'a hydrologically effective substitute' for
natural forest (Pereira, 1973: 127).

I In many studies the runoff from clean tilled land tends to
be greater than that from areas under a dense crop cover,
but tilling of the soil surface does not in every case increase
runoff (Gregory and Walling, 1973, p. 345). There are reports
from the USSR suggesting that the reverse may be the case,
and that autumn ploughing can cause a decrease in surface
runoff, presumably because of its effect on surface detention
and on soil structure.

Grazing practices also influence runoff, for heavy grazing
tends both to compact the soil and to cause vegetation
removal. In general it tends to lead to an increase in runoff.

Changes in river bank vegetation may have a particularly
strong influence on river-flow. In the south-west USA, for
instance, many streams are lined by the salt cedar (*Tamarix
pentandra*). With roots either in the water-table or freely
supplied by the capillary fringe these shrubs have full potential transpiration opportunity. The removal of such vegetation
can cause large increases in stream-flow. It is interesting to
note that the salt cedar itself is an alien, native to Eurasia,
which was introduced by man. It has spread explosively in
the south-west USA, increasing from about 4 000 ha in 1920
to almost 400 000 ha in the early 1960s (Harris, 1966). In
the Upper Rio Grande valley in New Mexico, the salt cedar
was introduced to try and combat anthropogenic soil erosion,
but it spread so explosively that it came to consume approximately 45% of the area's total available water (Hay, 1973).

Reforestation of abandoned farmlands accomplishes the
opposite results to deforestation: increased interception and
evapotranspiration can cause a decline in water yield. In parts
of the eastern USA farm abandonment and recolonization of
the land by pines, spruce, and cedar has been occurring
throughout the twentieth century and this has reduced
stream-flow by important amounts at a time when water
supplies for some eastern cities are becoming critically short
(Dunne and Leopold, 1978).

A process which is often associated with afforestation is
peat drainage. The hydrological effects of this are the subject
of controversy since there are cases of both increased and
decreased flood peaks after drainage. It has been suggested
that differences in peat type alone might be capable of
accounting for the different effects. Thus it is conceivable
that the drainage of a *Sphagnum* catchment would lead to

increased flooding since *Sphagnum* compacts with drainage, reducing its storage volume and its permeability. On the other hand, in the case of non-*Sphagnum* peat there would be relatively less change in structure, but there would be a reduction in moisture content and an increase in storage capacity, thereby tending to reduce flood flows. The nature of the peat is, however, but one feature to consider (Robinson, 1979), and the intensity of the drainage works (depth, spacing, etc.) may be important. In any case, there may be two (sometimes conflicting) processes operating as a result of peat drainage: the increased drainage network will facilitate rapid runoff, and the drier soil conditions will provide greater storage for rainfall. Which of these two tendencies is dominant will depend on local catchment conditions.

Changes in lake levels brought about by man

One of the results of human modification of river regimes is that lake levels have suffered some change, though it is not always possible to sort out the human influence from that of natural climate changes.

A lake basin for which there are particularly long records of change is the Valencia Basin in Venezuela (Böckh, 1973). It was the declining level of the waters in this lake which so struck the great German geographer, von Humboldt, in 1800, see p. 2). He recorded its level as being about 422 m above sea-level, and some previous observations on its level were made by Manzano in 1727, which established it has been at 426 m. The 1968 level was about 405 m, representing a fall of no less than 21 m in about 240 years (figure 5.12). It was believed by Humboldt that the cause of the declining level

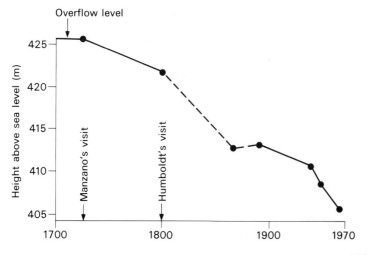

FIG. 5.12
Variations in the level of Lake Valencia, Venezuela, to 1968 (after Böckh, 1973, figure 18.2)

159

was the deforestation brought about by man, and this has been supported by Böckh, who points also to the abstraction of water for irrigation. This remarkable fall in level meant that the lake ceased to have an overflow into the River Orinoco. It has as a consequence become subject to a build-up in salinity, and is now eight times more saline than it was two and a half centuries ago.

Even the world's largest lake, the Caspian, has been modified by human activities. The most important change has been the fall of 3 m in its level since 1929 (see figure 5.13).

FIG. 5.13
Falling level of the Caspian Sea, illustrating the rapid post-revolutionary downward trend (after Goudie, 1977a, figure 5.15)

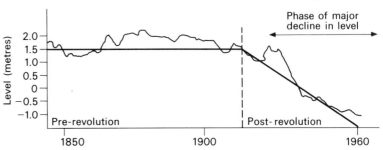

Some of this decline is undoubtedly the product of climatic change (Micklin, 1972) for winter precipitation in the northern Volga basin, the chief flow-generating area of the Caspian, has been generally below normal since 1930 because of a reduction in the number of moist cyclones penetrating into the Volga basin from the Atlantic. Nonetheless, man has contributed to this fall, particularly since the 1950s because of reservoir formation, irrigation, municipal and industrial withdrawals, and agricultural practices. In addition to the fall of level, salinity in the northern Caspian has increased by 30% since the early 1930s. A secondary effect of the changes in level has been a decline in fish numbers due to the disappearance of the shallows which are the biologically most productive zones of the lake, providing a food base for the more valuable types of fish and also serving as spawning grounds for some species. There are plans to divert some water from northward-flowing rivers in Siberia towards the Volga to correct the decline in Caspian levels but the possible climatic impacts of such action have caused some concern (see p. 253).

Similar declines in inflow to those evident from the Caspian apply to the Sea of Azov (Mote and Zumbrunne, 1977). The reduction of fresh water inputs from inflowing rivers has permitted an increase in the ingress of saline water from the Black Sea. Salinity has increased at the rate of 30–40% in 5 years (figure 5.14). As a consequence the valuable sturgeon and carp fisheries have declined, while the

160

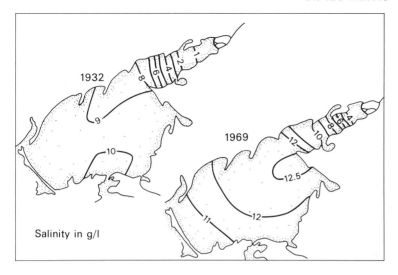

Salinity in g/l

FIG. 5.14
The changing salinity of the Sea of Azov (after Mote and Zumbrunnen, 1977, figure 2)

numbers of unwelcome stinging Black Sea jellyfish have multiplied.

Water abstraction from the Jordan River for irrigation purposes has caused a decline in the level of the Dead Sea. Under natural conditions fresh water from the Jordan constantly fed the less salty layer of the sea which occupied roughly the top 40 m of the 320 m deep body of water. Because the amount of water entering the lake via the Jordan was more or less equal to the quantity lost by evaporation, the lake maintained its stable, stratified state, with less salty water resting on the waters of higher salinity. However, with the recent man-induced diminution in Jordan discharge the sea's upper layer has receded because of the intense levels of evaporation. Its salinity has approached that of the older and deeper waters. It has now been established that as a consequence the layered structure has gone, creating a situation where there is increased precipitation of salts. Moreover, now that circulating waters carry oxygen to the bottom the characteristic hydrogen sulphide smell has largely disappeared (Maugh, 1979).

Changes in ground-water conditions

In many parts of the world man obtains his water supplies by pumping from ground-water (see, for example, Drennan, 1979). This has two main effects: the reduction in the levels of water-tables and the replacement, in coastal areas, of fresh water by salt water (see p. 110). Environmental consequences of these two phenomena include ground subsidence (see p. 201) and soil salinization. Increasing population

161

levels and the adoption of new exploitation techniques (for example, the replacement of irrigation methods involving animal or human power by electric and diesel pumps) has increased these problems.

Some of the reductions in ground-water levels that have been caused by abstraction are considerable. Figure 5.15a shows the rapid increase in the number of wells tapping ground-water in the London area from 1850 until the Second World War, while figures 5.15b and c illustrate the widespread and substantial changes in ground-water conditions that resulted. The piezometric surface in the confined chalk aquifer has fallen by more than 60 m over hundreds of square kilometres. Likewise, beneath Chicago, Illinois, pumping since the late nineteenth century has lowered the piezometric head by some 200 m.

The chemical changes in ground-water quality brought about by sea-water incursion may also be considerable. An example from the Salinas Valley of California is shown in figure 5.16. The most notable feature, apart from the general overall increase in the total dissolved solids content by approximately ten-fold, is the change in the ratio of chloride to bicarbonate. As the coast is approached, as one might expect, the quantity of chloride relative to bicarbonate rises from a ratio of 0.5 to around 200.

However, there are situations where man deliberately attempts to increase the natural supply of ground-water by attempting artificial recharge of ground-water basins (figure 5.17). Where the materials containing the aquifer are permeable (as in some alluvial fans, coastal sand dunes or glacial deposits) the technique of water-spreading is much used. In relatively flat areas river water may be diverted to spread evenly over the ground so that infiltration takes place. Alternative water-spreading methods may involve releasing water into basins which are formed by excavation, or by construction of dikes or small dams. On alluvial plains water can also be encouraged to percolate down to the water-table by distributing it to a series of ditches or furrows. In some situations natural channel infiltration can be promoted by building small check-dams down a stream course. In irrigated areas surplus water can be spread by irrigating with excess water during the dormant season. When artificial ground-water recharge is required in sediments with impermeable layers such water-spreading techniques are not effective and the appropriate technology may then be to pump water into deep pits or into wells. This latter technique is used in the coastal plain of Israel, both to replenish the ground-water reservoirs when surplus irrigation water is available, and to

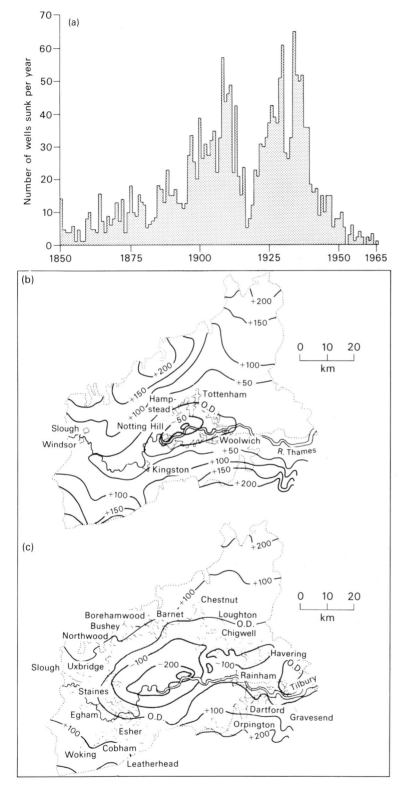

FIG. 5.15
*Changing ground-water
conditions in the London area
(modified after Porter, 1978):*
*(a) construction of wells tapping
    the confined aquifer below
    London (1850–1965)*
(b) ground-water contours in 1875
(c) ground-water contours in 1965

163

28
In Nebraska, America, fields are irrigated by centre-pivot irrigation schemes which use groundwater. Ground-water levels have fallen rapidly in many areas because of the adoption of this type of irrigation technology

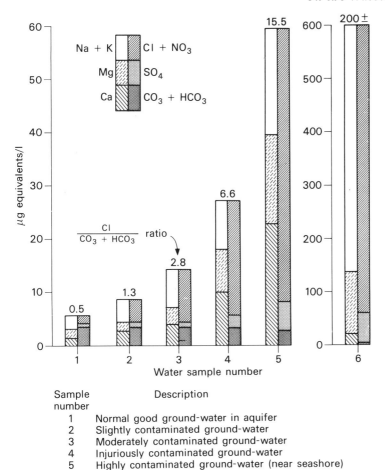

FIG. 5.16

Evidence of salt water intrusion exemplified by chemical analyses of a line of well-waters from the Salinas valley, California, extending from the centre of the aquifer to the coast. Chloride—bircarbonate ratios are shown above each quality diagram (after Simpson, in Todd, 1959, figure 12.14)

Sample number	Description
1	Normal good ground-water in aquifer
2	Slightly contaminated ground-water
3	Moderately contaminated ground-water
4	Injuriously contaminated ground-water
5	Highly contaminated ground-water (near seashore)
6	Sea water

attempt to diminish the problems associated with salt water intrusion.

As figure 5.18 shows, ground-water extraction in the Tel Aviv area greatly exceeded the sustained yield of the aquifer during the 1950s and water levels declined below sea level over about 60 km^2. Sea water intrusion became a problem. Completion of a new inter-basin water transfer scheme in the mid-1960s allowed injection of fresh water into a line of wells 8 km long in an attempt to provide a fresh water 'barrier' along the coast. Other boreholes were injected to the landward of this 'barrier' to help fill the aquifer that had been depressed by over-pumping. This operation proved to be effective almost immediately (Mandel, 1977) and by 1969 the situation was definitely stabilized.

(a)

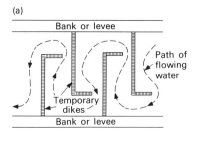

(c) Plan view

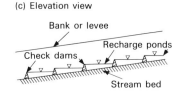

(b)

(c) Elevation view

FIG. 5.17
Examples of means of
recharging ground-water by
means of water-spreading
devices:
(a) temporary earth dikes
(b) ditch networks
(c) check-dams and ponds
(d) connected recharge basins
    adjoining a stream channel
(after Todd, 1964, figures
13.48 and 13.46)

(d)

FIG. 5.18
Profiles of the water-table in
the Tel Aviv area, Israel,
perpendicular to the sea coast
showing its natural state, its
state after over-pumping, and
its state after the aquifer had
been injected with fresh water
brought in by inter-basin water
transfer. (After Bachmat in
Mandel, 1977, figure 3.3, from
Arid Zone Development, ed.
Mundlak and Singer. Copyright
© 1977, the American Academy
of Arts and Sciences. Reprinted
by permission of the Ballinger
Publishing Company)

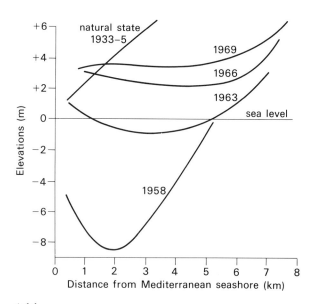

Water pollution

Water pollution is not new. During the reign of King George III a Member of Parliament reportedly wrote a letter to the Prime Minister complaining about the odour and the appearance of the Thames. He wrote the letter, it is said, not with ink but with water from the Thames itself (Strandberg, 1971).

Water pollution is frequently undesirable: it causes disease transmission through infection; it may poison men and animals; it may create objectionable odours and unsightliness; it may be the cause of the unsatisfactory quality even of treated water; and it may affect economic activities like shellfish culture.

The causes and forms of water pollution created by man are many and can be classified into the groups shown in table 5.8. Moreover, many of man's activities can contribute to changes in water quality, including agriculture, fire, urbanization, industry, mining, irrigation, and many others. Of these it is probably agriculture that is the most important. Some pollutants merely have local effects while others such as acid rain (see p. 271) or DDT may have continental or planetary implications.

It is not a simple matter to recognize trends in pollution. In general long-term records are sparse, gauging stations have often been moved, analytical methods change, and some trends in water chemistry may be due to natural factors (including climatic change) rather than to man. However, where long-term data are available some of the changes in water chemistry are striking. In their study of the information collated on Lake Michigan, the Mississippi river, the Ohio River and the Illinois River, Ackerman *et al.* (1970) found that since the start of the twentieth century dissolved solids concentrations had risen markedly. For chlorides the increase has varied from 100% in 52 years to 300% in 70 years while for sulphates it has increased from 80% in 43 years to 155% in 62 years.

It is also plainly not a simple matter to try and estimate the global figure for the extent of water pollution that man

1	Sewage and other oxygen-demanding wastes	
2	Infectious agents	
3	Organic chemical	
4	Other chemical and mineral substances	
5	Sediments (turbidity)	
6	Radioactive substances	
7	Heat (thermal pollution)	

TABLE 5.8
Classification of water pollutants

Source: after Strandberg (1971)

167

has caused. For one thing we know insufficient about the natural long-term levels of dissolved materials in the world's rivers. Nonetheless, some recent studies do give some general indication of the likely impact. Meybeck (1979), for instance, has calculated that about 500 million tonnes of dissolved salts reach the oceans each year as a result of man's activities. These inputs have increased by more than 30% the natural values for sodium, chloride, and sulphate, and have created an overall global augmentation of river mineralization by about 12%.

Chemical pollution by agriculture

As has already been stated, agriculture may be one, if not the most, important cause of pollution, either by the production of sediments or by the generation of chemical wastes (Ministry of Agriculture, Fisheries and Food, 1976). With regard to the latter it has been suggested that denitrification processes in the environment are not capable of keeping pace with the rate at which atmospheric nitrogen was being mobilized through industrial fixation processes and was being introduced into the biosphere in the form of commercial fertilizers (Manners, 1978). Nitrogen, with phosphorus, tends to regulate the growth of aquatic plants and therefore the eutrophication of inland waters. Excess nitrates can also cause health hazards to men and beasts, including methaemoglobinaemia in enfants.

Eutrophication is the enrichment of waters by nutrients. The process occurs naturally during, for example, the slow aging of lakes, but it has been accelerated both by runoff from fertilized agricultural land and by the discharge of domestic sewage and industrial effluents (Lund, 1972). This process commonly leads to excessive growths of algae followed in some cases by a serious depletion of dissolved oxygen as the algae decay after death. Changes in diatom assemblages can occur (see, particularly, Batterbee, 1977).

Increases in the application of nitrogenous fertilizers have almost amounted to a revolution (Green, 1976). Thus in America the use of nitrogen fertilizer increased thirty-fold in the 23 years up to 1969 (Sanders, 1972). In western Europe the increase in rates of application is also impressive, especially in the Low Countries (see table 5.9 and figure 5.19).

When one examines the evidence to see whether increasing nitrate fertilizer applications are indeed leading to widespread upward trends in nitrate concentrations in river and groundwaters, it is often conflicting (Manners, 1978; Rodda *et al.*,

168

Country	1964/5	1971/2
Netherlands	124	175
Belgium	69	105
Norway	57	82
Denmark	56	113
West Germany	56	84
United Kingdom	43	73
Finland	40	66
Sweden	38	76
France	30	50
Austria	29	50
Switzerland	25	40
Italy	23	31
Republic of Ireland	7	25

TABLE 5.9
Nitrogen fertilizer consumption in 1964/5 and 1971/2 in West European countries in kg N/ha of cultivated land

Source: from data in Stikstof presented by Green, 1976

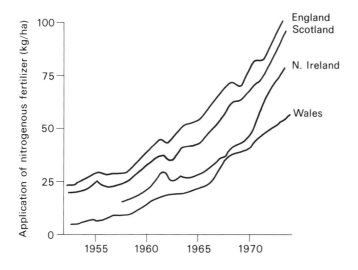

FIG. 5.19
Application of nitrogenous fertilizer in relation to total area under crops and grass (excluding hill grazing) in the United Kingdom (after Green, 1976, figure 12)

1976). This may be because soil and vegetation have a large storage capacity for nitrogen, while a great deal probably depends on local soil, climate, and land-management conditions. Further problems are presented by the inadequacy of long-term data. This complexity in the evidence is brought out strongly in Tomlinson's analysis of trends of nitrate concentrations in English rivers (Tomlinson, 1970) summarised in table 5.10. In six of his rivers nitrate concentrations increased significantly with time, in eight the correlation co-efficients were positive but not significant, in three cases the correlations were negative and not significant, while in one case the correlation was negative and significant.

TABLE 5.10
Trends in nitrate concentrations in English rivers in relation to fertilizer use

River	Place	Period	Correlation coefficient with time
Dee	Chester	1961−67	− 0.77
Great Ouse	Bedford	1953−67	− 0.22
Kennett	Reading	1953−67	+ 0.34
Rother	Horsham	1957−67	+ 0.90
Severn	Tewkesbury	1953−67	+ 0.78
Stour	Langham	1953−67	+ 0.73
Tees	Darlington	1958−67	− 0.34
Thames	Hampton	1953−64	+ 0.22
Blithe	Newton	1953−67	+ 0.56
Derwent	Hathersage	1953−67	+ 0.26
Devon	Hawton	1953−67	+ 0.47
Dove	Monks Bridge	1953−67	+ 0.68
Dove	Stratton	1961−67	+ 0.47
Leen	Newstead Abbey	1957−63	− 0.16
Manifold	Iham	1956−67	+ 0.25
Poulter	Elkesley	1953−67	+ 0.41
Tyne	Wylam	1956−67	+ 0.08
Wensum	Norwich	1953−67	+ 0.05

Source: from data in Tomlinson, 1970.

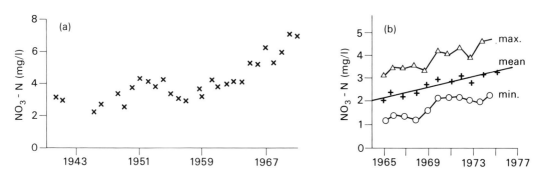

FIG. 5.20
(a) Mean annual nitrate nitrogen concentration and runoff, River Stour, Essex, England (after Edwards, 1975, figure 10.1)
(b) Yearly maximum (△), minimum (o) and mean (+) nitrate concentrations for the River Frome, Dorset, England (after Casey and Clarke, 1979)

However, even if an increase in nitrate levels is evident as in the River Stour, East Anglia (see figure 5.20a) or the Frome in Dorset (see figure 5.20b) this may not necessarily be because of the application of fertilizers. Some nitrate pollution may be derived from organic wastes. There has also been some concern in Britain that there has been a decline in the amount of organic matter present in the soil, and this could lead to a lowering of its ability to assimilate nitrogen. Moreover, the pattern of tillage may affect the liberation of nitrogen. The increased area and depth of modern ploughing accelerates the decay of residues and may change the pattern of water movement in the soil. Finally, tile drainage has also expanded in area very greatly in recent

170

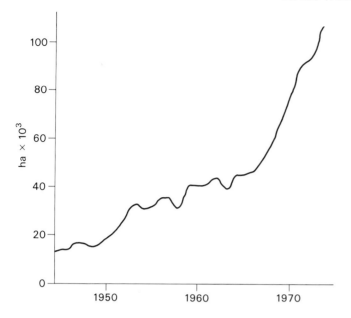

FIG. 5.21
Annual total area of field drainage by tile drains in England and Wales (after Green, 1976, figure 3)

decades in England (figure 5.21). This will affect the movement of water through the soil and hence the degree of leaching of nitrates and other materials (Edwards, 1975).

Given the uncertainties surrounding the question of nitrate pollution, and bearing in mind the major advances in agricultural productivity that they have permitted, attempts at controlling their use have not been received with complete favour. Indeed, as Viets (1971) has pointed out, if fertilizer use were to be curtailed it might lead to less vegetation cover and increased erosion and sediment delivery to rivers. Furthermore he suggests that it would necessitate an increase in land hectarage to maintain production and that this would also cause greater erosion and that the increased ploughing would lead to greater nitrate loss from grasslands. Nevertheless some farmers are inefficient and wasteful in their use of fertilizers and there is scope for economizing (Cooke, 1977).

Pesticides are another source of chemical pollution brought about by agriculture. There is now a tremendous array of pesticides and they differ greatly in their mode of action, in the length of time they remain in the biosphere, and in their toxicity.

Much of the most adverse criticism of pesticides has been directed against the chlorinated hydrocarbon group of insecticides, which includes DDT, Dieldrin and various others. These insecticides are toxic not only to the target organism but also to other insects (that is, they are non-specific) and

171

they are also highly persistent. Appreciable quantities of the original application may survive in the environment in unaltered form for years. This can lead to two severe impacts: global dispersal, and the 'biological magnification' of these toxic substances in food chains (Manners, 1978). This latter problem is well illustrated for DDT in figure 5.22.

Additional to the influence of nitrate fertilizers, the confining of animals on feedlots results in tremendously concentrated sources of nutrients and pollutants. Animal wastes in the USA are estimated to be as much as 1.6 billion tonnes per year, with 50% of this amount originating from feedlots. It needs to be remembered that 1000 head of beef produce the equivalent organic load of 6000 people (Sanders, 1972). The number of cattle fed on feedlots in the USA is rapidly increasing (see figure 5.23), partly because *per capita* consumption of meat has moved sharply upward, and partly because the confinement of cattle on small lots on which they are fed a controlled selection of feeds leads to the greatest possible weight gains with the least possible cost and time (Bussing, 1972). Cattle feedlot runoff is a high-strength organic waste, high in oxygen-demanding material, and has caused many fish-kills in rivers in states such as Kansas.

Other sources of chemical pollution

The importance of nitrates in causing eutrophication is paralleled by the role of phosphorus (Schindler, 1974).

FIG. 5.22
Biological concentration occurs when relatively indestructible substances (DDT for example) are ingested by lesser organisms at the base of the food pyramid. An estimated 1000 kg of plant plankton are needed to produce 100 kg of animal plankton. These, in turn, are consumed by 10 kg of fish, the amount needed by a man to gain 1 kg. The ultimate consumer (man) then, takes in the DDT taken in by 1000 kg of the lesser creatures at the base of the food pyramid, when he ingests enough fish to gain 1 kg (after Strandberg, 1971, figure 2)

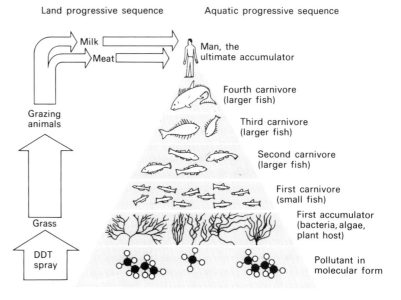

172

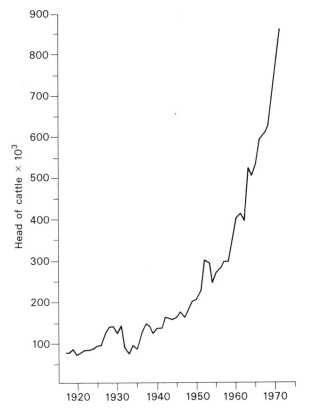

FIG. 5.23
Cattle on feed in feedlots in Colorado, 1917–71 (after Bussing, 1972, figure 2)

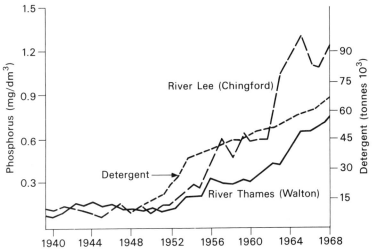

FIG. 5.24
Comparison of the increasing phosphate content of the rivers Thames and Lee with the annual consumption of detergents (after Royal Commission on Environmental Pollution in Rodda et al., 1976, figure 7.11)

There has been a marked increase in Britain in the phosphorus content of some rivers since the early 1950s, an increase related to the use of detergents (figure 5.24).

Other changes in surface water chemistry may be produced by the washing out of acid materials derived from

173

air pollution in precipitation. This is particularly clear in the heavily industrialized area of north-western Europe (figure 5.25) where there is a marked zonation of acid rain with pH values that often fall below 4 or 5. A broadly comparable situation exists in North America (Johnson, 1979).

Mining can also create serious chemical pollution. In the strip-mining area of Kentucky, for example, Collier (1964) found that oxidation of the iron sulphide in the soil banks and other parts of the mining area provided an excess of hydrogen ions. The ions then reacted with the mineral matter of the spoil bank, releasing soluble products at a rate ten to fifteen times greater than in the non-mined area. Such pollution was not entirely undesirable in its effects. Collier found that this release of minerals was good for tree growth and increased their rate of development.

In Britain coal seams and mudstones in the coal measures contain pyrite and marcasite (ferrous sulphide). In the course of mining the water-table is lowered, air gains access to these minerals and they are oxidized. Sulphuric acid may be produced.

As a consequence mine-drainage waters may have pH values as low as 2 or 3. They have high sulphate and iron concentrations, they may contain toxic metals, and because of the reaction of the acid on clay and silicates in the rocks, they may also contain appreciable amounts of calcium, magnesium, aluminium, and manganese. Following reactions with sediments or mixing with alkaline river waters, or when chemical or bacterial oxidation of ferrous compounds occurs, the iron may precipitate as ferric hydroxide. This may discolour the water and leave unsightly deposits (Rodda *et al.*, 1976: 299). Some of the reactions involved in the development of acid mine drainage are shown in table 5.11.

The use of salt for de-icing roads has increased the chloride content of runoff in some areas. For example, the chloride content of Lough Neagh, Northern Ireland, almost doubled between 1958 and 1969 because of salt application to roads in its catchment. In the USA some 6 million tonnes of salt are applied to the roads each year, and in those states where it is applied the quantities amount to some 32 tonnes/km. Sugar maples seem susceptible to such levels of salt and ancient specimens are dying along rural roads all over New England (Wagner, 1974: 99).

Similarly, storm-water runoff from urban areas may contain large amounts of contaminants, derived from litrer, garbage, carwashings, horticultural treatments, vehicle drippings, industry, construction, animal droppings, and

174

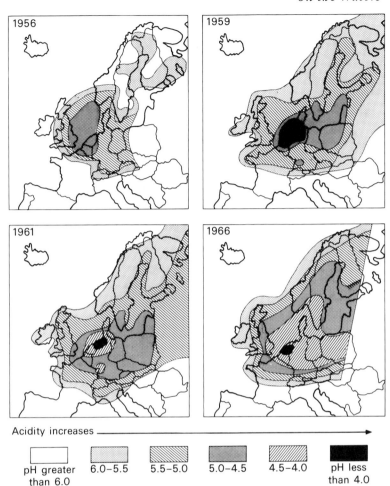

FIG. 5.25
The distribution of acid precipitation in Europe between 1956 and 1966 (after Oden, 1971, cited by Murdoch, 1975, figure 10)

Acidity increases

| pH greater than 6.0 | 6.0–5.5 | 5.5–5.0 | 5.0–4.5 | 4.5–4.0 | pH less than 4.0 |

1   Oxidation of the sulphide (usually FeS_2) in a wet environment producing ferrous sulphate and sulphuric acid

$$2FeS_2 + 2H_2O + 7O_2 = 2FeSO_4 + 2H_2SO_4$$

2   Ferrous sulphate, in the presence of sulphuric acid and oxygen, can oxidize to produce ferric sulphate, especially in the presence of the bacterium, *Thiobacillus ferro-oxidous*

$$4FeSO_4 + 2H_2SO_4 + O_2 = 2Fe_2(SO_4)_3 + 2H_2O$$

3   The ferric iron so produced combines with the hydroxyl $(OH)^-$ ions of water to form ferric hydroxide, which is insoluble in acid and precipitates

$$Fe_2(SO_4)_3 + 6H_2O = 2Fe(OH)_3 + 3H_2SO_4$$

Source: Down and Stocks, 1977: 110–11

TABLE 5.11
Acid mine drainage: stages of development

the chemicals used for snow and ice clearance. Comparison of contaminant profiles for urban runoff and raw domestic sewage, based on surveys throughout the USA, indicates the importance of pollution from urban runoff sources (table 5.12). Further data for a variety of world cities are listed in table 5.13.

In New York City some half million dogs leave up to 20 000 tonnes of pollutant faeces and up to 3.8 million litres of urine in the city streets each year, all of which is flushed by gutters to storm-water sewers.

The nuclear industry has also caused some water pollution (see figure 5.26), and its effects may be compounded by the process of biological concentration and magnification effects to which we have already referred in the context of DDT (see p. 72). This is illustrated by the case of Perch Lake, Ontario, which is fed by a stream that contains radio-active material seeping from a nearby liquid disposal area. Strontium 90 is one of these polluting radionuclides and it becomes concentrated in its movement up the food chain into the muskrat and perch.

Sewage is still a major pollutant. The New York Metro-politan area alone produces 6.8 billion litres of sewage per day of which about 16% is raw, and enters the Hudson and East Rivers around New York. In addition the city produces many tons of sewage sludge, fly ash and dredge waste per day, and 8.6 million tonnes of waste are dumped each year, into the New York bight, off the mouth of the Hudson River. In an area of about 100 km² there is a black toxic sludge

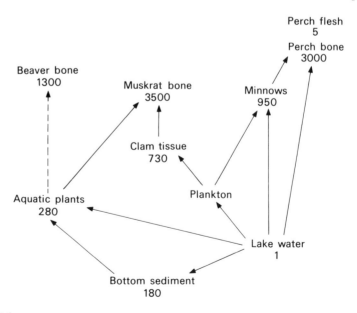

FIG. 5.26
The biological concentration of strontium 90 in the Perch Lake food web (after Ophel, cited in Murdoch, 1975, figure 4)

TABLE 5.12
*Comparison of containment
profiles for urban surface
runoff and raw domestic
sewage, based on surveys
throughout the USA*

Constituent*	Urban surface runoff	Raw domestic sewage
Suspended solids	250–300	150–250
BOD †	10–250	300–350
Nutrients		
(a) Total nitrogen	0.5–5.0	25–85
(b) Total phosphorus	0.5–5.0	2–15
Coliform bacteria (MPW/100 ml)	10^4–10^6	10^6 or greater
Chlorides	20–200	15–75
Miscallaneous substances		
(a) Oil and grease	yes	yes
(b) Heavy metals	(10–100) times sewage conc.	traces
(c) Pesticides	yes	seldom
(d) Other toxins	potential exists	seldom

* All concentrations are expressed in mg unless stated
† Biochemical oxygen demand
Source: Burke, 1972, table 7.36.1

TABLE 5.13
*Comparison of storm-water
quality from various sources
for selected parameters*

Study location	BOD (mg/l)	Total solids (mg/l)	Suspended solids (mg/l)	Phosphate (mg/l)	Chloride (mg/l)	Faecal coliforms (MPN/100 ml)
Durham, North Carolina	2–232	194–8 860	27–7 340	0.15–2.5	3–390	7 000–86 000
Cincinatti, Ohio	1–173	–	5–1 200	0.02–7.3	5–705	500–76 000
Coshocton, Ohio	0.5–23	–	5–2 074	0.08	–	2–56 000
Detroit, Michigan	96–234	310–914	–	–	–	25 000–930 000
Seattle, Washington	10	–	–	4.3	–	16 000
Stockholm, Sweden	18–80	300–3 000	–	–	–	4 000–200 000
Pretoria, South Africa	30	–	–	–	–	240 000
Oxhey, Herts, UK	100	–	2045	–	–	–
Moscow, USSR	18–285	–	100–3 500	–	–	–
Morristown, New Jersey	3–17	–	56–550	0.02–4.3	–	–
Ann Arbor, Michigan	28	–	2080	0.8	–	100

Source: Ellis, 1975

which smothers all forms of marine life (Southwick, 1976: 16).

The world's oceans are becoming increasingly prone to contamination by oil as world production, transport, and utilization of this material expands. The effects of this pollution on animals (see p. 76) have been widely studied. The sources of pollution include tanker collisions with other ships, the explosion of individual tankers because of the build-up of unsafe gas levels, the wrecking of tankers on coasts because of navigational or mechanical failure, seepage from offshore oil installations, and the flushing of tanker holds. There is no doubt that the great bulk of the oil and related materials polluting the oceans results from the action of man (Blumer, 1972), though man should not be attributed with all the blame, for natural seepages are reasonably common (Landes, 1973). Paradoxically, the actions of man mean that many natural seepages now cause less pollution than formerly, for they have diminished as wells have drawn down the levels of hydrocarbons in the oil-bearing rocks. Likewise, the flow of asphalt that once poured from the Trinidad Pitch Lake into the Gulf of Paria has also ceased because mining of the asphalt has lowered the lake below its outlet.

Of the various serious causes of oil pollution a more important mechanism than the much-publicized role of tanker accidents is the discharge of the ballast water taken into empty tankers to provide stability on the return voyage to the loading terminal (Pitt, 1979). It is in this field, however, that technical developments have led to most amelioration. For example, the quantity of oil in tanker ballast water has been drastically reduced by the LOT (load on top— system, in which the ballast water is allowed to settle so that the oil rises to the surface. The tank is then drained until only the surface oil in the tank remains, and this forms part of the new cargo. In the future large tankers will be fitted with separate ballast tanks not used for oil cargoes, called segregated or clean ballast systems. Given such advances it appears likely that an increasing proportion of oil pollution will be derived from accidents involving tankers of ever-increasing size, such as the spillage of 300 million litres, which came from the wreck of the *Amoco Cadiz* in 1978. It is to this problem that more attention needs to be directed.

Nonetheless, it would be unbalanced to create the impression that water pollution is either a totally insoluble problem or that levels of pollution must inevitably increase. It is true that some components on the hydrological system — for example, lakes, because they may act as sumps — will prove relatively intractable to improvement, but in many rivers and estuaries striking developments have occurred in water quality in recent decades. This is brought out in the case of the River Thames which suffered a serious decline in its quality and in its fish life as London's pollution, and industries expanded. However (see figure 5.27) after about 1950, because of more stringent controls on effluent discharge, the downward trend in quality has been reversed and many fish, long absent from the Thames in London, are now returning (Gameson and Wheeler, 1977).

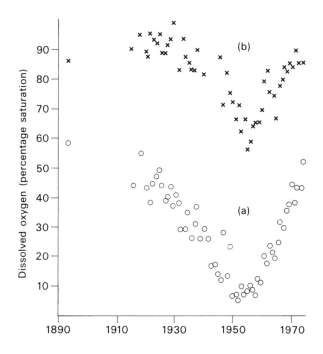

FIG. 5.27
The average dissolved-oxygen content of the River Thames at half-tide in the July–September quarter since 1890: (a) 79 km below Teddington weir (b) 95 km below Teddington weir (after Gameson and Wheeler, 1977, figure 4)

A similar picture emerges if one considers the trends in the state of Lake Washington near Seattle, USA. Studies there in 1933, 1950, and 1952 showed steady increases in the nutrient content and in associated growth of phytoplankton (algae). These resulted from the increasing levels of untreated sewage pumped into the lake from the Seattle area. A sewage diversion project started in 1963 and completed in 1968 (see figure 5.28) resulted in a great decrease in the sewage input to the lake and was reflected in a rapid decline in phosphates, phytoplankton, and turbidity, and a less marked decline in nitrate levels. Likewise, a long-term study of the levels of many heavy metals in sea water off the British Isles suggests that levels are generally low and that concentrations do not seem to be increasing (Preston, 1973).

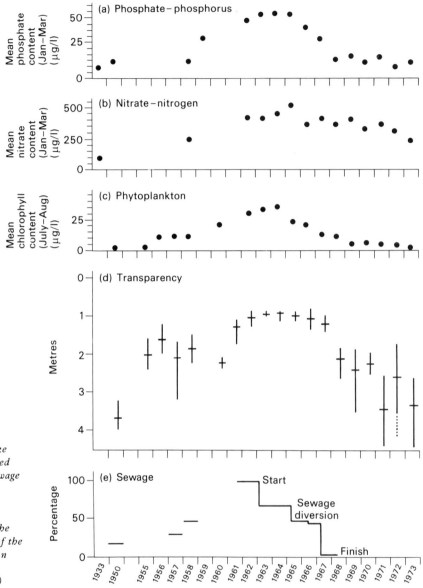

FIG. 5.28
Changes in the state of Lake Washington, USA, associated with levels of untreated sewage from 1933 to 1973. The relative amount of treated sewage entering the lake is shown as a percentage of the maximum rated capacity of the treatment plants, 76 million litres per day (after Edmonson, 1975, figure 3)

Deforestation and its effects on water quality

The removal of a tree cover not only may affect river flow (see p. 155) and stream water temperature (see p. 185) but may also cause changes in stream water chemistry. The reason for this is that in many forests large quantities of nutrients are cycled through the vegetation and in some cases (notably in humid tropical rain forest) the trees are a

180

great store of the nutrients. If the trees are destroyed the cycle of nutrients is broken and a major store is disrupted. The nutrients thus released may become available for crops, and shifting cultivators, for example, may utilize this fact and gain good crop yields in the first years after burning and felling of forest. Some of the nutrients may, however, be leached out of the soils and thereby appear as dissolved load in streams. Large increases in dissolved load may have undesirable effects, including eutrophication (Hutchinson, 1973), soil salination (see p. 112) and a deterioration in public water supply (Conacher, 1979).

A classic, but it must be added, extreme exemplification of this, is the experiment that was carried out in the Hubbard Brook catchments in New Hampshire (Bormann *et al.*, 1968). These workers monitored the effects of a 'savage' treatment of the forest on the chemical budgets of the streams. The treatment was to fell the trees, leave them in place, and to kill lesser vegetation and to prevent regrowth by the application of herbicide. The effects were dramatic: the total dissolved inorganic material exported from the basin was about 15 times larger after treatment and, in particular, there was a very substantial increase in stream nitrate levels (see table 5.14). Their concentration increased by an average of 50 times.

It has been argued, however, that the Hubbard Brook results are atypical (Sopper, 1975) because of the severity of the treatment. Most other forest clear-cutting experiments in the USA (table 5.15) indicate that nitrate/nitrogen additions to stream water are not so greatly increased. Under conventional clear-cutting the trees are harvested rather than left, all saleable material is removed, and encouragement is given to the establishment of a new stand of trees. Aubertin and Patric (1974), using such conventional clear-cutting rather than the drastic measures employed in Hubbard Brook, found that clear-cutting in their catchments in West Virginia had a negligible effect on stream temperatures (they left a forest strip along the stream), pH, and the concentrations of most dissolved solids.

Even if clear-cutting is practised, there is some evidence of a rapid return to steady-state nutrient cycling because of quick regeneration. As Marks and Borman (1972) have put it:

Because terrestrial plant communities have always been subjected to various forms of natural disturbances, such as wind storms, fires, and insect outbreaks, it is only reasonable to consider recovery from disturbance as a normal part of community maintenance and repair.

181

TABLE 5.14
Chemical budgets for forested (watershed 6) and cleared (watershed 2) basins on the Hubbard Brook experimental forest (in kilograms per hectare for period 1 June to 31 May)

Ion	Water-year	Forested			Cleared		
		Input	Output	Net gain	Input	Output	Net gain
Ca^{2+}	1966–7	2.4	10.7	−8.3	2.3	77.5	−75.0
	1967–8	3.0	12.2	−9.2	2.7	93.1	−90.4
	1968–9	1.7	11.7	−10.0	1.6	69.8	−68.2
Mg^{2+}	1966–7	0.4	2.9	−2.5	0.5	16.2	−15.7
	1967–8	0.8	3.4	−2.6	0.7	18.6	−17.9
	1968–9	0.3	3.1	−2.8	0.3	13.5	−13.2
K^{+}	1966–7	0.6	1.7	−1.1	0.5	23.0	−22.5
	1967–8	0.8	2.4	−1.6	0.7	36.5	−35.8
	1968–9	0.6	2.3	−1.7	0.6	33.4	−32.8
Na^{+}	1966–7	1.3	6.8	−5.5	1.3	18.1	−16.8
	1967–8	1.8	8.8	−7.0	1.7	19.0	−17.3
	1968–9	1.1	6.9	−5.8	1.0	13.2	−12.2
Al^{3+}	1966–7	1.4	2.8	−1.4	1.3	18.2	−16.9
	1967–8	*	3.1	−3.1	*	24.5	−24.5
	1968–9	*	3.2	−3.2	*	20.6	−20.6
NH_4^{+}	1966–7	2.4	0.4	2.0	2.3	0.9	1.4
	1967–8	3.3	0.3	3.0	3.1	0.6	2.5
	1968–9	3.2	0.1	3.1	2.9	0.6	2.3
NO_3^{-}	1966–7	20.4	5.8	14.6	30.1	460.0	−429.9
	1967–8	23.0	12.4	10.6	21.7	650.0	−628.3
	1968–9	16.4	11.5	4.9	14.6	470.0	−455.4
SO_4^{2-}	1966–7	43.2	51.4	−8.2	40.8	45.9	−5.1
	1967–8	48.0	58.0	−10.0	45.5	45.5	0.0
	1968–9	32.4	51.4	−19.0	30.0	49.8	−19.8
Cl^{-}	1966–7	6.9	4.6	2.3	9.5†	10.6	−1.1
	1967–8	5.2	5.3	−0.1	5.5	9.2	−3.7
	1968–9	6.4	5.1	1.3	6.3	7.4	−1.1
HCO_3^{-}	1966–7	*	2.0	−2.0	*	1.0	−1.0
	1967–8	*	2.5	−2.5	*	0.0	0.0
	1968–9	*	–	–	*	0.0	0.0
SiO_2	1966–7	*	36.8	−36.8	*	67.0	−67.0
	1967–8	*	36.4	−36.4	*	69.8	−69.8
	1968–9	*	28.9	−28.9	*	59.3	−59.3

* Not determined, but very low
† Based on data for 9 months
Source: Pierce *et al.*, 1970 in Rodda, 1976

They point out that rapid growth of vegetation minimizes nutrient losses from the ecosystem by three main mechanisms. It channels water from runoff to evapotranspiration, thereby reducing erosion and nutrient loss; it reduces the rates of decomposition of organic matter through moderation of the microclimate so that the supply of soluble ions for loss in drainage water is reduced; and it causes the simultaneous

| Site | Nature of disturbance | Nitrate–nitrogen loss (kg ha^{-1} year^{-1}) | |
		Control	Disturbed
Hubbard Brook	Clear-cutting without vegetation removal, herbicide inhibition of re-growth	2.0	97
Gale River (New Hampshire)	Commercial clear-cutting	2.0	38
Fernow (West Virginia)	Commercial clear-cutting	0.6	3.0
Coweeta (North Carolina)	Complex	0.05	7.3 *
H. J. Andrews' Forest (Oregon)	Clear-cutting with slash burning	0.08	0.26
Alsea River (Oregon)	Clear-cutting with slash burning	3.9	15.4
MEAN		1.44	26.83

* This value represents the second year of recovery after a long-term disturbance. All of the other results for disturbed ecosystems reflect the first year after disturbance.
Source: modified after Vitousek *et al.*, 1979

TABLE 5.15
Nitrate–nitrogen losses from control and disturbed forest ecosystems

incorporation of nutrients into the rapidly developing biomass so that they are not lost from the system.

Thermal pollution

The pollution of water by increasing its temperature is called thermal pollution. Many fauna are affected by temperature so that this environmental impact has some significance (Langford, 1972).

In industrial countries probably the main source of thermal pollution is from condenser cooling water released from electricity generating stations. Water discharged from power stations has been heated some 6–9°C, but usually has a temperature of less than 30°C. The extent to which such water affects river temperatures depends very much on the state of flow. For example, below the Ironbridge power station in England, the Severn River undergoes a temperature increase of only 0.5°C during floods, compared with an 8°C increase at times of low flow (Rodda *et al.*, 1976).

Over the past two decades or more (see Royal Commission on Environmental Pollution, 1972) both the increase in the capacity of individual electricity power generating units, and the improvements in their thermal efficiency, have led to a diminution in the heat rejected in relation to the amount of cooling water per unit of production (table 5.16). Economic optimization of generating plant has cut down the flow of cooling water per unit of electricity, though it has raised its temperature. This increased temperature rise of

183

Year	Temperature rise (°C)	Specific water circulation per unit of power generation (m³)
(a) *Coal and oil-fired*		
1950	7	0.21
1960	9	0.15
1970	10	0.12
1980 (estimated)	12—14	0.08—0.09
(b) *Nuclear*		
1962	8	0.33
1967	9	0.24
1980 (estimated)	12—14	0.09—0.14

Source: Royal Commission on Environmental Pollution, 1972, p. 21, table 7

the cooling water is more than offset by the reduction achieved in the volume of water utilized. Nonetheless, the expansion of generating capacity has meant that the total quantity of heat discharged has increased, even though it is much less than would be expected on a simple proportional basis.

Thermal pollution of streams may also follow on from urbanization (Pluhowski, 1970). This results from various sources: changes in the temperature regime of streams brought about by reservoirs according to their size, their depth and the season; changes produced by the urban heat island effect; changes in the configuration of urban channels (e.g. their width/depth ratio); changes in the degree of shading of the channel, either by covering it over or by removing a natural vegetation cover; changes in the volume of storm runoff; and changes in the ground-water contribution. Pluhowski found that the basic effect of cities on river water temperatures on Long Island, New York, was to raise temperatures in summer (by as much as 5—8°C) and to lower them in winter (by as much as 1.5—3°C).

Reservoir construction can also affect stream-water temperatures. Crisp (1977) found, for example, that as a result of the construction of a reservoir at Cow Green (Upper Teesdale, northern England) the temperature of the river downstream was modified. He noted a reduction in the amplitude of annual water temperature fluctuations by 1—2°C, a marked reduction in diurnal fluctuations, and a delay in the spring rise of water temperature by 20—50 days, and of the autumn fall by up to 20 days.

184

TABLE 5.17
*Effect of forest cutting on mean
monthly maximum river water
temperature in the USA*

Location	Temperature increase (°C)
Coweeta (North Carolina)	4
Fernow (West Virginia)	5.5
Penn State (Pennsylvania)	6
Hubbard Brook (New Hampshire)	6
H. J. Andrews (Oregon)	6.7
Coastal Range (Oregon)	8
MEAN	6.03

Source: from data in Sopper, 1975, table 2.

In rural areas human activities can also cause significant modifications in river water temperature (table 5.17). Swift and Messer (1971), for example, examined stream temperature measurements during six forest-cutting measurements on small basins in the Southern Appalachians, USA. They found that with complete cutting, because of shade removal, the maximum stream temperatures in summer went up from 19°C to 23°C. They believed that such temperature increases were detrimental to temperature-sensitive fish like trout (see figure 5.29), while the temporary shutdown of power plants may create severe cold-shock ills of fish in discharge-receiving waters in winter (J. R. Clark, 1977). Moreover, an increase in water temperature causes a decrease in the solubility of oxygen which is needed for oxidation of biodegradable wastes. At the same time, the rate of oxidation is accelerated, imposing a faster oxygen demand on the smaller supply and thereby depleting the oxygen content of the water still

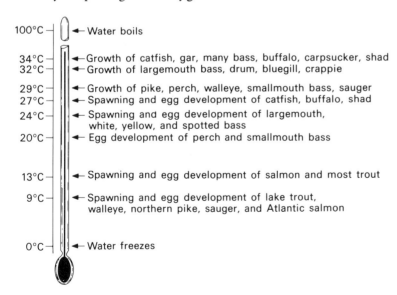

FIG. 5.29
Maximum temperatures for the spawning and growth of fish. Heated waste water may be up to 5–10°C warmer than receiving waters and consequently the local fish populations cannot reproduce or grow properly. (Figure 13-2 [after Giddings, Chemistry, Man and environmental change, Harper & Row] *from* Encounter with the Earth *by Leo F. Laporte. Copyright © 1975 by Leo F. Laporte. Reprinted by permission of Harper & Row, Publishers, Inc.)*

185

further. Temperature also affects the lower organisms, such as plankton and crustaceans. In general the more elevated the temperature is, the less desirable the types of algae in water. In cooler waters diatoms are the predominant phytoplankton in water that is not heavily eutrophic; with the same nutrient levels, green algae begin to become dominant at higher temperatures and diatoms decline; at the highest water temperatures, blue-green algae thrive and often develop into heavy blooms. One further ecological consequence of thermal pollution is that the spawning and migration of many fish are triggered by temperature and this behaviour can be disrupted by thermal change.

Pollution with suspended sediments

Probably the most important effect that man has had on water quality is his contribution to levels of suspended sediments in streams. This is a theme which is intimately tied up with that of soil erosion on the one hand (see p. 126) and with channel manipulation by means of such activities as reservoir construction (see p. 143) on the other. The clearance of forest, the introduction of ploughing and grazing by domestic animals, the construction of buildings, and the introduction of spoil materials into rivers by mineral extraction industries, have all led to very substantial increases in levels of stream turbidity. Frequently sediment levels are a whole order of magnitude greater than they would have been under natural conditions. However, the introduction of soil conservation measures, or a reduction in the intensity of land use, or the construction of reservoirs, can cause a relative (and sometimes absolute) reduction in sediment loads (see, for example, table 5.4). All three of these factors have contributed to the observed reduction in turbidity levels monitored in the rivers of the Piedmont Region of Georgia in the USA (figure 5.30).

FIG. 5.30
Decline of turbidity in the Chattahoochee Basin, Atlanta, Georgia, USA, 1931–52 (after Albert and Spector in Trimble, 1974, figure 27)

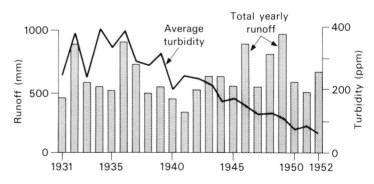

CHAPTER 6

Man as a Geomorphological Agent

Introduction

The role of man in creating landforms and modifying the operation of geomorphological processes such as weathering, erosion, and deposition is a theme of great importance though one that, particularly in the western world, has not received the attention that it deserves. Recently there have been some useful general surveys (see, for example, Brown, 1970; Jennings, 1966; Haigh, 1978) and, with the increasing concern for the relevance and application of geomorphological studies to human problems (see for example, Cooke and Doornkamp, 1974; Hails, 1977), the situation is likely to change. Moreover, the development of process studies in post-Second World War geomorphology has led to a relative reduction in the importance of evolutionary and historical geomorphology within the discipline. Examination of processes, and in particular of their rate of operation, has served to highlight the part played by man in modifying the physical landscape.

The range of impacts which man has achieved on both forms and process is considerable. For example in table 6.1 there is a list of some anthropogenic landforms together with some of the causes of their creation. There are very few spheres of human activity which do not create landforms. It is, however, useful to recognize that some features are produced by direct anthropogenic processes. The former tend to be more obvious in their form and origin and are frequently created deliberately and knowingly. They include (see table 6.2) landforms produced by constructional activity (such as

187

TABLE 6.1
Some anthropogenic landforms

Feature	Cause
Pits and ponds	Mining, marling
Broads	Peat extraction
Spoil heaps	Mining
Terracing, lynchets	Agriculture
Ridge and furrow	Agriculture
Cuttings	Transport
Embankments	Transport, river and coast management
Dikes	River and coast management
Mounds	Defence, memorials
Craters	War, *qanat* construction
City mounds (*tells*)	Human occupation
Canals	Transport, irrigation
Reservoirs	Water management
Subsidence depressions	Mineral and water extraction
Moats	Defence

tipping), excavation, by hydrological interference, and by farming (Spencer and Hale, 1961). Landforms produced by indirect anthropogenic processes are often less easy to recognize, not least because they do not so much involve the operation of a new process or processes as the acceleration of natural processes. They are the result of environmental changes brought about inadvertently by man's technology. Nonetheless, it is probably this indirect and inadvertent modification of process and form which is the most crucial aspect of anthropogeomorphology. By removing natural vegetation covers — through the agency of cutting, burning, and grazing — he has accelerated erosion (see p. 126) and sedimentation. Sometimes the results will be obvious, as when major gully systems rapidly develop; other results may have less immediate effect on landform but are nonetheless of great importance. By other indirect means man may create subsidence features and problems, trigger off mass movements like landslides, and even influence the operation of phenomena like earthquakes.

Finally there are situations where, through a lack of understanding of the operation of processes and the links between different processes and phenomena, man may deliberately and directly alter landforms and processes and thereby set in train a series of events which were not anticipated or desired. There are, for example, many records of man trying to reduce coast erosion by important and expensive engineering solutions, only to find that the erosion problems, far from being solved, were exacerbated (see p. 233).

TABLE 6.2
*Classification of anthropogenic
landforming processes*

1   *Direct anthropogenic processes*
    1.1   Constructional
           tipping: loose, compacted, molten
           graded: moulded, ploughed, terraced
    1.2   Excavational
           digging, cutting, mining, blasting of cohesive or
              non-cohesive materials
           cratered
           trampled, churned
    1.3   Hydrological interference
           flooding, damming, canal construction
           dredging, channel modification
           draining
           coastal protection

2   *Indirect anthropogenic processes*
    2.1   Acceleration of erosion and sedimentation
           agricultural activity and clearances of vegetation
           engineering, especially road construction and urbanization
           incidental modifications of hydrological regime
    2.2   Subsidence: collapse, settling
           mining
           hydraulic
           thermokarst
    2.3   Slope failure: landslide, flow, accelerated creep
           loading
           undercutting
           shaking
           lubrication
    2.4   Earthquake generation
           loading (reservoirs)
           lubrication (fault plane)

Source: Haigh, 1978

Landforms produced by excavation

Of the landforms produced by direct anthropogenic processes
those resulting from excavation are widespread, and may
have some antiquity. For example, Neolithic peoples in the
Breckland of East Anglia used antler picks and other means
to dig a remarkable cluster of deep pits in the chalk. The purpose of this was to obtain good-quality non-frost-shattered
flint to make stone tools. The cratered area, called Grimes
Graves, is well displayed on air photographs, and is illustrated
in figure 6.1. In many parts of Britain chalk has also been
excavated to provide marl for improving acidic, light, sandy
soils (see p. 118) and Prince (1962, 1964) has made a
meticulous study of the 27 000 pits and ponds in Norfolk
that have resulted mainly from this activity, an activity

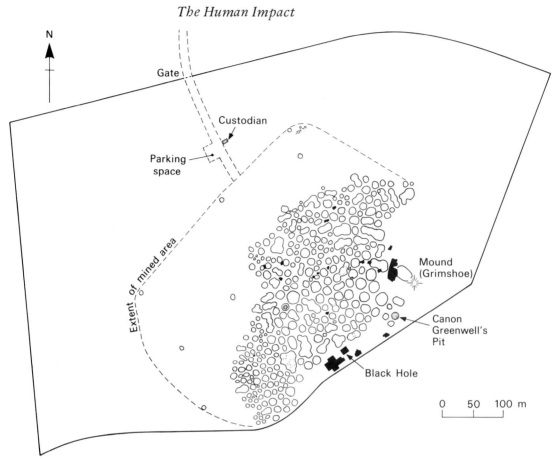

N

Gate

Custodian

Parking
space

Extent of mined area

Mound
(Grimshoe)

Canon
Greenwell's
Pit

Black Hole

0   50   100 m

FIG. 6.1

Flint mines at Grimes Graves,
Norfolk, England, dug during
Neolithic times (around 2000
BC) (after R. R. Clark, 1963)

particularly prevalent in the eighteenth century. It is often
difficult in individual cases to decide whether the depressions
are man-made, for in the same area solutional and periglacial
depressions are often evident, but man-made pits do tend to
have some distinctive features: irregular shape, a track going
into them, proximity to roads, etc. (see the debate between
Prince, and Sperling *et al.*, 1979).

Difficulties of identifying the true origin of excavational
features were also encountered in explaining the Broads, a
group of twenty-five freshwater lakes in the county of
Norfolk. They are of sufficient area, and depth, for early
workers to have precluded a human origin. It was proposed
instead that they were natural features caused by uneven
alluviation and siltation of river valleys which were flooded
by the rapidly rising sea level of the Holocene (Flandrian)
transgression. It was postulated by Jennings (1952) that the
Broads were initiated as a series of discontinuous natural
lakes, formed beyond the limits of a thick estuarine clay
wedge laid down in Romano-British times by a transgression

190

29
The Norfolk Broads were originally thought to be natural lakes. Recent researches by historical geographers have shown that for the most part they result from the activities of medieval peat diggers

of the sea over earlier valley peats. The waters of the Broads were thought to have been ponded back in natural peaty hollows between the flanges of the clay and the marginal valley slopes, or in tributary valleys whose mouths were blocked by the clay.

It is now clear, however, that the Broads are man-made (Lambert *et al.*, 1970). Some of them have rectilinear and steep boundaries, most of them are not mentioned in early topographic books, and archival records indicate that peat-cutting (turbary) was widely practised in the area. On these and other grounds it is believed that peat-diggers, prior to AD 1300, excavated 25.5 million cubic metres of peat and so created the depressions in which the lakes have formed. The flooding may have been aided by sea-level change. Comparably extensive peat excavation was also carried on in the Netherlands, notably in the fifteenth century.

Other excavational features result from war, especially craters resulting from bomb or shell impact. Regrettably the power of man to create such forms is increasing. It has been calculated (Westing and Pfeiffer, 1972) that between 1965 and 1971, 26 million craters, covering an area of 171 000 ha, were produced by bombing in Indochina. This represents a total displacement of no less than 2.6 billion cubic metres of earth, a figure much greater than that calculated as being involved in the peaceable creation of the Netherlands.

Some excavation is undertaken on a large scale for purely

aesthetic reasons, when Nature offends the eye. This can be illustrated by brief reference to the work of some English landscape gardeners. In 1676 at Cassiobury Park, Watford, Moses Cook the gardener says that he was 'forced to cut through one Hill, thirty rod, most of the hill two feet deep, into sharp gravel', to produce the landscape he desired. At nearby Moor Park in 1720 the intended view across the Vale of St Albans from a new house was found to be obscured by the brow of a hill, so that the hill-top was cut off to a depth of 10 m (Prince, 1959).

In many countries where land is scarce, whole hills are levelled and extensive areas stripped to provide fill for harbour reclamation. One of the most spectacular examples of this kind was the deliberate removal of steep-sided hills in the centre of Brazil's Rio de Janeiro, for housing development. In Bahrain, an island in the Arabian/Persian Gulf, a substantial part of the desert surface has been stripped to provide fill for land reclamation in the commercial and industrial area in the north of the island.

An excavational activity of a rather specialized type is the removal of limestone pavements — spreads of exposed limestone which were stripped by glaciers and then moulded into bizarre shapes by solutional activity — for ornamental rock gardens. These pavements, which consist of arid bare rock surfaces (clints) bounded by deep humid fissures (grikes) have both an aesthetic and a biological significance (S. D. Ward, 1979). They occur in northern England, notably in the Pennines and in the Morecambe Bay area, and provide a habitat for various rare plants (including *Actaea spicata*, *Ribes spicatum*, and *Dynopteris villarii*). A recent survey indicates that the pavements, which only cover about 2150 ha in Britain, have been severely damaged. At only 3% of 537 pavement units recorded could no damage be detected, while the proportion considered to be 95% or more intact was only 13%.

The most important cause of excavation is still mineral extraction, producing open-pit mines, strip mines, quarries for structural materials, borrow pits along roads, and similar features (Doerr and Guernsely, 1956). Of these 'without question, the environmental devastation produced by strip mining exceeds in quantity and intensity any of the other varied forms of man-made land destruction' (Strahler and Strahler, 1973: 284). This form of mining, which produced not far short of one-half of the total national coal production of the United States, is a particular environmental problem in the states of Pennsylvania, Ohio, West Virginia, Kentucky and Illinois. If, because of an increasing pressure on available

30 (opposite)
Strip mining for coal in Missouri, USA is a particularly unsightly example of the production of landforms by man

192

energy resources the production of coal is expanded then this particular geomorphological impact may also expand. The same applies to the probable exploitation of oil shales, a potential source of oil that at present is relatively un-exploited. This can be exploited by open-pit mining, by traditional room and pillar mining, and by underground *in situ* pyrolysis. Vast reserves exist but the amount of excavation required will probably be about three times the amount of oil produced (on a volume basis) suggesting that the extent of both the excavation and subsequent dumping of overburden and waste will be considerable (Routson *et al.*, 1979).

The world's largest excavation is the Bingham Canyon Copper Mine in Utah, USA. It has involved the removal of 3 355 million tonnes over an area of 7.21 km² to a depth of 774 m, seven times the amount of material moved to build the Panama Canal.

An attempt to provide a general picture of the importance of excavation in the creation of the landscape of Great Britain was given by Sherlock (1922). He estimated (see table 6.3) that up until the time in which he wrote, man had excavated around 31 billion cubic metres of material in the pursuit of his economic activities. That figure must now be a gross underestimate, partly because Sherlock himself was not in a position to appreciate the role of man in creating features like the Norfolk Broads, and partly because, since his time, the rate of excavation has greatly accelerated. Sherlock's 1922 study covers a period when earth-moving equipment was still ill-developed. Nonetheless, on the basis of his calculations, he was able to state (p. 333) that 'at the present time, in a densely peopled country like England,

TABLE 6.3
Total excavation of material by man in Great Britain until 1922

Activity	Approximate volume (m³)
Mines	15 147 000 000
Quarries and pits	11 920 000 000
Railways	2 331 000 000
Manchester Ship Canal	41 154 000
Other canals	153 800 000
Road cuttings	480 000 000
Docks and harbours	77 000 000
Foundations of buildings and street excavation	385 000 000
TOTAL	30 539 954 000

Source: Sherlock, 1922: 86

Man is many times more powerful, as an agent of denudation, than all the atmospheric denuding forces combined'.

Landforms produced by construction and dumping

The process of constructing mounds and embankments and the creation of dry land where none previously existed has great antiquity. In Britain the mound at Silbury Hill dates back to prehistoric times, and the pyramids of central America, Egypt, and the Far East are still more spectacular early feats of landform creation. Likewise hydrological

31
Early man made some striking constructional landforms:
Top: Silbury Hill, Wiltshire, England
Bottom: A tell in the Middle East, produced by the accumulation of the debris of years of human occupation

management has involved, over many centuries, the construction of massive banks and walls; the ultimate result being the landscape of the present-day Netherlands (figure 6.2). Transport developments have also required the creation of large constructional landmarks, but probably the most important features are those resulting from the dumping of waste materials, especially those derived from mining (see figure 6.3). It has been calculated that there are at least 2 000 million tonnes of shale lying in pit heaps in the coalfields of Britain (Richardson, 1976). In the Middle East and other areas of long-continued human urban settlement the accumulated debris of life has gradually raised the level of the land surface and occupation mounds (*tells*) are a fertile source of information to the archaeologist. Today, with the technical ability to build that man has, even estuaries may be converted from ecologically productive environments into suburban sprawl (figure 6.4) by the processes of dredging and filling. The ocean floors are also being affected because of the vast bulk of waste material that man is creating. Waste-solid disposal by coastal cities is now sufficient to modify shorelines and it covers adjacent ocean bottoms

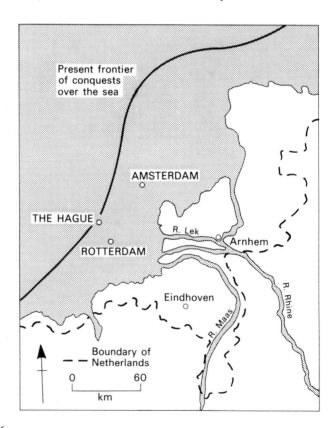

FIG. 6.2
The coastline of the Netherlands in the absence of coast protection works. The solid line indicates the approximate position of the protected coastline (after Graftdijk, in R. C. Ward, 1978, figure 4.2)

196

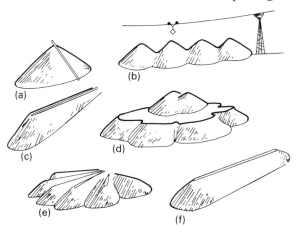

FIG. 6.3
*Some shapes produced by shale
tipping (after Haigh, 1978,
figure 2.1)*
*(a) Conical resulting from
    MacClane tipping*
*(b) Multiple cones tipped from
    aerial ropeways*
*(c) High 'fan-ridges' by tramway
    tipping over slopes*
*(d) High plateau mounds topped
    with cones*
*(e) Low multiple 'fan-ridges' by
    tramway tipping*
*(f) Lower ridge by tramway
    tipping*

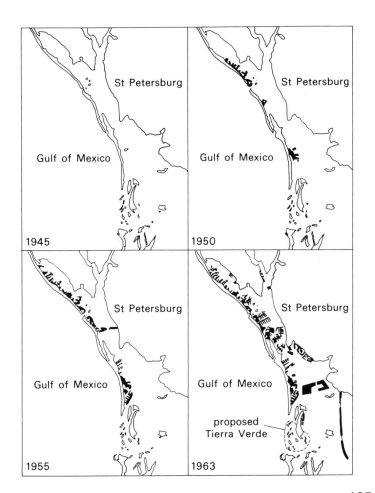

FIG. 6.4
*Boca Ciega Bay on the Gulf of
Mexico near St Petersburg is
rapidly being converted by
dredging and filling into a
typical suburban sprawl (after
Lauf, in Wagner, 1974,
figure 7.4)*

197

with characteristic deposits on a scale large enough to be geologically significant. This has been brought out dramatically by Gross (1972: 3174) who has undertaken a quantitative comparison of the quantity of solid wastes dumped into the Atlantic by man in The New York Metropolitan region with the amount of sediment brought into the ocean by rivers:

The discharge of waste solids exceeds the suspended sediment load of any single river along the U.S. Atlantic coast. Indeed, the discharge of wastes from the New York Metropolitan region is comparable to the estimated suspended-sediment yield (6.1 megatons per year) of all rivers along the Atlantic coast between Maine and Cape Hatteras, North Carolina.

Not only are the rates of sedimentation high, but the sediments also tend to contain abnormally high contents of such substances as carbon and heavy metals (Goldberg *et al.*, 1978) (table 6.4).

TABLE 6.4
Fluxes of heavy metals to coastal environments in the USA
(μg cm^{-2} year^{-1})

Chemical	Santa Barbara Basin California	Naragansett Bay Rhode Island	Chesapeake Bay Cove 1411	Cove 1314
Lead				
anthropogenic	2.1	124	7.6	1.9
natural	1.0	2.6	5.3	3.9
Zinc				
anthropogenic	2.2	230	34	4.1
natural	9.7	14	19	15
Copper				
anthropogenic	1.4	193	4.5	0.8
natural	2.6	3.1	4.0	3.6

Source: Goldberg *et al.*, 1978

Many of the features created by excavation in one generation are filled in by another, because phenomena like water-filled hollows produced by mineral extraction are often both wasteful of land and a suitable location for the receipt of waste. The same applies to natural hollows such as karstic or ground ice depressions. Watson (1976), for example, has mapped the distribution of hollows which were largely created by marl diggers in the lowlands of south-west Lancashire and north-west Cheshire as they were represented on mid-nineteenth-century topographic maps (figure 6.5a). When this distribution is compared with the present distribution (figure 6.5b) it is evident that a very substantial proportion of the holes have been infilled and obliterated by man, with only 2 114 out of 5 380 remaining. Hole densities have fallen from $121/km^2$ to $47/km^2$.

Accelerated sedimentation

An inevitable consequence of the accelerated erosion produced by man (see p. 126) has been accelerated sedimentation. This has been heightened by the deliberate addition of sediments to stream channels as a result of the need to get rid of mining and other wastes.

In a classic study, G. K. Gilbert (1917) demonstrated that hydraulic mining in the Sierra Nevada mountains of California led to the addition of great quantities of sediments into the river valleys draining the range. This in itself raised their bed levels, changed their channel configurations and thereby caused flooding of lands that had previously been immune. Of even greater significance was the fact that the rivers transported increased quantities of debris into the estuarine

32
Gold washing in a long sluice at Yale, British Columbia, in the 1890s. Such activities caused rivers to become choked with debris

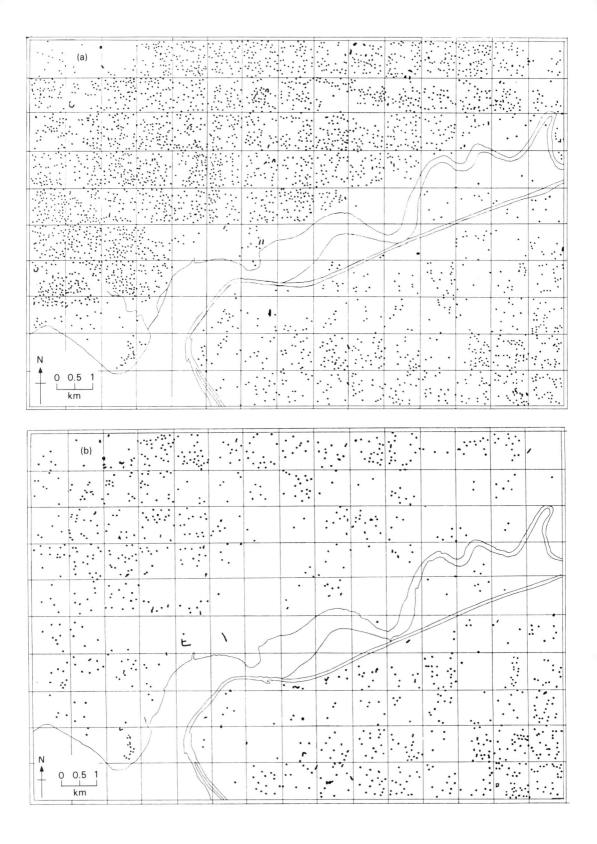

bays of the San Francisco system, and caused extensive shoaling which in turn diminished the tidal prism of the bay. The volume of shoaling, Gilbert calculated, produced by hydraulic mining since the discovery of gold, was 846 million cubic metres. Comparably serious sedimentation of bays and estuaries has also been brought about by man on the eastern coast of America. As Gottschalk (1945: 219) wrote:

Both historical and geological evidence indicates that the preagricultural rate of silting of eastern tidal estuaries was low. The history of sedimentation of ports in the Chesapeake Bay area is an epic of the effects of uncontrolled erosion since the beginning of the wholesale land clearing and cultivation more than three centuries ago.

He has calculated that at the head of the Chesapeake Bay, 65 million cubic metres of sediment were deposited between 1846 and 1938. The average depth of water over an area of 83 km^2 was reduced by 0.76m. New land comprising 318 ha was added to the State of Maryland and, as Gottschalk remarked, 'the Susquahanna River is repeating the history of the Tigris and Euphrates'. Much of the material entrained by erosive processes on upper slopes as a result of agriculture in Maryland, however, was not evacuated as far as the coast. Costa (1975) has suggested on the basis of the study of sedimentation that only about a third of the eroded material left the river valleys. The remainder accumulated on floodplains as alluvium and colluvium at rates of up to 1.6 cm/year. Similarly, Happ (1944), working in Wisconsin, did an intensive augering survey of floodplain soils and identified that since the development of agriculture flood plain aggradation had proceeded at a rate of about 0.85 cm/year. He noted that channel and floodplain aggradation had caused the flooding of low alluvial terraces to be more frequent, extensive and deeper. The rate of sedimentation has since declined (Trimble, 1976).

Ground subsidence

Not all ground subsidence is caused by man. For example, limestone solutional processes can in the absence of man create a situation where a cavern can collapse to produce a surface depression, and permafrost will sometimes melt to produce a thermokarst depression without the intervention of man. Nonetheless, ground subsidence can be caused or accelerated by man for a variety of reasons: by the transfer of subterranean fluids (such as oil, gas, and water); by the removal of solids by underground mining, or through dissolving solids and removing them in solutions (e.g., sulphur and

FIG. 6.5 (opposite)
The distribution of pits and ponds in a portion of north-western England:
(a) in the mid-nineteenth century
(b) in the mid twentieth century
(after Watson, 1976)

salt); by the disruption of permafrost; and by the compaction or reduction of sediments because of drainage and irrigation.

Some of the most dangerous and dramatic collapses have occurred in limestone areas because of the dewatering of limestone caused by mining activities. In the Far West Rand of South Africa, gold mining has required the abstraction of water to such a degree that the local water-table has been lowered by more than 300 m. The fall of the water-table caused miscellaneous clays and other materials filling the roofs of large caves to dry out and shrink so that they collapsed into the underlying void. One collapse created a depression 30 m deep and 55 m across, killing twenty-nine people. In Alabama, USA, water level decline consequent upon pumping has had equally serious consequences in a limestone terrain, and Newton (1976) has estimated that since 1900 about 4 000 induced sink-holes or related features have been formed, while fewer than fifty natural sink-holes have been reported over the same interval.

In some limestone areas, however, a reverse process can operate. The application of water to overburden above the limestone may render it more plastic so that the likelihood

33
A gaping chasm in the Transvaal, South Africa became the world's biggest grave in August, 1964. The sinkhole opened because ground-water conditions had been altered by mining activity and swallowed up a family of five, their servants and homes

of collapse is increased. This has occurred beneath reservoirs, such as the May Reservoir in central Turkey, and as a result of the application of waste water and sewerage to the land surface.

The process can be accelerated by the direct solution of susceptible rocks. For example, collapses have occurred in gypsum bedrock because of solution brought about by the construction of a reservoir. In 1893 the MacMillan Dam was built on the Pecos River in New Mexico but within 12 years the whole river flowed through caves which had developed since construction. Likewise both the San Fernando and Rattlesnake Dams in California suffer severe leakage due to this cause.

Subsidence produced by oil abstraction is an increasing problem in some parts of the world. The classic area is Los Angeles, where 9.3 m of subsidence occurred as a result of exploitation of the Wilmington oilfield between 1928 and 1971. The Inglewood oilfield displayed 2.9 m of subsidence between 1917 and 1963. Some coastal flooding problems occurred at Long Beach because of this process, while in Japan this has now emerged as a major problem (Nakano and Matsuda, 1976). In 1960 only 35.2 km^2 of the Tokyo lowland was below sea level, but continuing subsidence meant that by 1974 this had increased to 67.6 km^2, exposing a total of 1.5 million people to major flood hazard. Similar subsidence is known from the Lake Maracaibo field in Venezuela (Prokopovich, 1972) and from some Russian fields (Nikonov, 1977). A more widespread problem is posed by ground-water abstraction for industrial, domestic, and agricultural purposes. Table 6.5 presents some data for such subsidence from various parts of the world. This ratio of subsidence to water level decline are strongly dependent on the nature of the sediments composing the aquifer, and so ratios range from 1 : 7 for Mexico City, to 1 : 80 for the Pecos in Texas, and to less than 1 : 400 for London, England (Rosepiler and Reilinger, 1977).

Some subsidence is created by a process called hydro-compaction, which is explained thus. Moisture-deficient, unconsolidated, low-density sediments tend to have sufficient dry strength to support considerable effective stresses without compacting. However, when such sediments, which may include alluvial fans or loess, are thoroughly wetted for the first time, as they might be by percolating irrigation water, the intergranular strength of the deposits is diminished, rapid compaction takes place, and ground surface subsidence follows. Unequal subsidence can create problems for irrigation schemes.

203

TABLE 6.5
Ground subsidence

(a)   GROUND SUBSIDENCE PRODUCED BY OIL AND GAS ABSTRACTION

Location	Amount (m)		Rate (mm/year)
Azerbaydzhan, USSR	2.5	(1912–62)	50
Atravopol, USSR	1.5	(1956–62)	125
Wilmington, USA	9.3	(1928–71)	216
Inglewood, USA	2.9	(1917–63)	63

(b)   GROUND SUBSIDENCE PRODUCED BY GROUND-WATER
         ABSTRACTION

Location	Amount (m)		Rate (mm/year)
London, England	0.06–0.08	(1865–1931)	0.91–1.21
Savanna, Georgia	0.1	(1918–55)	2.7
Mexico City	7.5	–	250–300
Houston, Galveston, Texas	1.52	(1943–64)	60–76
Central Valley, California	8.53	–	–
Tokyo, Japan	4	(1892–1972)	500
Osaka, Japan	> 2.8	(1935–72)	76
Niigata	> 1.5	–	–
Pecos, Texas	0.2	(1935–66)	6.5
South central Arizona	2.9	(1934–77)	96

Source: data in Cooke and Doornkamp, 1974; Prokopovich, 1972;
          Rosepiler and Reilinger, 1977; Holzer, 1979

The subsidence produced by mining (which produced court cases in England as early as the fifteenth century) is perhaps the most familiar, though its importance varies according to such factors as the thickness of seam removed, its depth, the width of working, the degree of filling with solid waste after extraction, the geological structure, and the method of working adopted (Wallwork, 1974). In general terms, however, the vertical displacement by subsidence is less than the thickness of the seam being worked, and becomes slighter with an increase in the depth of mining. This is because the collapse of the overlying strata causes them to fragment and fracture and the mass of rock fills a greater space than it did when naturally compacted. Consequently the surface expression of deep-seated subsidence may be equal to no more than a third of the thickness of the mineral removed. Subsidence associated with coal-mining may cause the disruption of surface drainage and the resultant depressions then become permanently flooded. In England, the valleys of the Aire and Calder in the Castleford– Knottingley area, the Anker valley in east Warwickshire, and

204

the Wigan–Leigh area of Lancashire, provide examples of subsidence lakes formed on stream floodplains.

Coal-mining areas are not the only ones where subsidence problems are serious. In Cheshire, north-west England, salt is extracted from two major seams, each of about 30 m in thickness. Moreover, these seams occur at no great depth – the uppermost being at about 70 m below the surface. A further factor to be considered is that the rock salt is highly soluble in water so that the flooding of mines may cause additional collapse. These three conditions – thick seams, shallow depth and high solubility – have produced optimum conditions for subsidence and many subsidence lakes called 'flashes' have developed (Wallwark, 1956). Some of these are illustrated in figure 6.6. The main railway line between Crewe and Manchester at Elton subsided no less than 4.9 m between 1892 and 1956 (Wallwork, 1960). Likewise, salt extraction at Windsor, Canada, is known to have produced a water-filled depression 150 m in diameter and about 8 m deep (Martinez, 1971).

Land drainage can promote subsidence of a different type, notably in areas of organic soils (see p. 124). The lowering of the water-table makes peat susceptible to oxidation and deflation so that its volume decreases. One of the

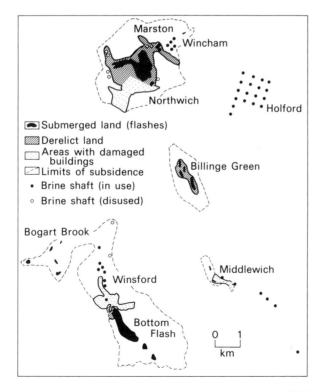

FIG. 6.6
Subsidence in mid-Cheshire's salt area in 1954 (after Wallwork, 1956, figure 3)

205

longest records of this process, and one of the clearest demonstrations of its efficacy, have been provided by the measurements at Holme Post in the English Fenlands. Approximately 3.8 m of subsidence occurred between 1848 and 1957 (Fillenham, 1963), with the fastest rate occurring soon after drainage had been initiated (figure 6.7). The present rate averages about 1.4 cm/year (Richardson and Smith, 1977).

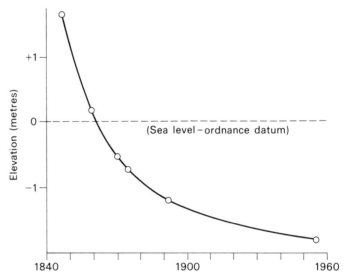

FIG. 6.7
The subsidence of the English fenlands peat at Holme Fen Post from 1842 to 1960 following drainage (from data in Fillenham, 1963)

A further type of subsidence, sometimes associated with earthquake activity, results from the effects on the earth's crust of large masses of water impounded behind reservoirs. Seismic effects can be generated in areas with susceptible fault systems and this may account for earthquakes recorded at Koyna (India) and elsewhere. The process whereby a mass of water causes coastal depression is called hydro-isostasy, and the degree of subsidence that has been monitored for various large man-made reservoirs is listed in table 6.6.

TABLE 6.6
Hydro-isostatic subsidence caused by the creation of man-made reservoirs

Reservoir	Maximum downwarping (cm)	Period
Lake Mead, USA	20.1	1950–63
Kariba, Central Africa	12.7	1959–68
Koyna, India	8–14	1962–8
Bratsk, Siberia	5.6	1961–6
Krasnoyarsk, Siberia	3	1967–71
Plyava, Baltic	0.5	1965–70

Source: from data in Nikonov, 1977

In permafrost areas ground subsidence is associated with thermokarst development, thermokarst being irregular, hummocky terrain produced by the melting of ground ice, permafrost. The development of thermokarst is due primarily to the disruption of the thermal equilibrium of the permafrost and an increase in the depth of the active layer. This can be illustrated by reference to figure 6.8. Following French (1976: 106) consider an undisturbed tundra soil with an active layer of 45 cm. Assume also that the soil beneath 45 cm is supersaturated permafrost and yields upon a volume basis upon thawing 50% excess water and 50% saturated soil. If the top 15 cm were removed, the equilibrium thickness of the active layer, under the bare ground conditions, might increase to 60 cm. As only 30 cm of the original active layer remained, 60 cm of the permafrost must thaw before the active layer can thicken to 60 cm, since 30 cm of supernatant water will be released. Thus, the surface subsides 30 cm because of the thermal melting associated with the degrading permafrost, to give an overall depression of 45 cm.

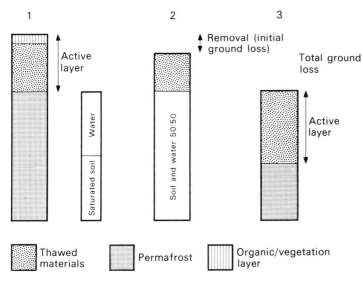

FIG. 6.8
Diagram illustrating how the disturbance of high ice content terrain can lead to permanent ground subsidence (after Mackay, in French, 1976, figure 6.1). 1–3 indicate stages before, immediately after, and subsequent to, disturbance

Thus the key process involved in thermokarst subsidence is the state of the active layer and its thermal relationships. When, for example, surface vegetation is cleared for agricultural or constructional purposes the depth of thaw will tend to increase. The movement of tracked vehicles has been particularly destructive of the surface vegetation and deep channels may soon result from permafrost degradation. Likewise, similar effects may be produced by the siting of heated buildings on permafrost, and by the laying of oil, sewer and water pipes in or on the active layer (Ferrians *et al.*, 1969).

Arroyo trenching

In the south-western United States many broad valleys and plains became deeply incised with valley bottom gullies (arroyos) over a short time-period between 1865 and 1915, with the 1880s being especially important (Cooke and Reeves, 1976). This cutting had a rapid and detrimental effect on the flat, fertile, and easily irrigated valley floors, the most desirable sites for settlement and economic activity in a harsh environment.

Many students of this phenomenon have believed that thoughtless human actions caused the entrenchment and the apparent coincidence of white settlement and arroyo development tended to give credence to this viewpoint. The range of actions that could have been culpable is large: timber-felling, over-grazing, cutting of grass for hay in valley bottoms, compaction along well-travelled routes, chanelling of runoff from trails and railways, disruption of valley-bottom sods by animals' feet, and the invasion of grasslands by miscellaneous types of scrub.

On the other hand the decipherment of the long-term history of the valley fills shows that there have been repeated phases of aggradation and incision and some of these took place before the influence of man could have been a significant factor. This has caused a debate as to whether it was the arrival of the white man which was responsible for this particular severe phase of environmental degradation. Huntington (1914), for example, argued that valley filling would be a consequence of a move to more arid climatic conditions. These, he believed, would cause a reduction in vegetation which in turn would promote rapid removal of soil from devegetated mountain slopes during storms, and overload streams with sediment. With a return to humid conditions vegetation would be re-established, sediment yields would be reduced and entrenchment of valley fills would take place. Bryan (1928) put forward a contradictory climatic explanation. He argued that a slight shift towards drier conditions, by causing a depletion of vegetation cover and reducing the soil infiltration capacity, would produce significant increases in storm runoff which would erode valleys. Another climatic interpretation was advanced by Leopold (1951), involving a change in rainfall intensity rather than quantity. He indicated that a reduced frequency of low-intensity rains would weaken the vegetation cover while an increased frequency

208

of heavy rains at the same time increased the incidence of erosion.

It is therefore clear that the possible mechanisms that can lead to alternations of cut-and-fill of valley sediments are extremely complex and that any attribution of all arroyos in all areas to human activities may be a serious oversimplification of the problem (figure 6.9). It is also possible that natural environmental changes, such as changes in rainfall characteristics, have operated at the same time and in the same direction as human actions.

In the Mediterranean lands there have also been controversies surrounding the age and causes of alternating phases of aggradation and erosion in valley-bottoms. Vita-Finzi (1969) has suggested that at some stage during historical times many of the streams in the Mediterranean area, which had hitherto been engaged primarily in downcutting, began to build up their beds. Renewed downcutting, still seemingly in operation today, has since incised the channels into the alluvial fill. He proposed that the reversal of the downcutting trend in the Middle Ages was both ubiquitous and confined in time, and that some universal and time-specific agency was required to explain it. He believed that devegetation by man was not a medieval innovation and that some other mechanism was required. A solution he gave to account for the phenomenon was precipitation change during the climatic fluctuation known as the Little Ice Age (AD 1550–1850). This was not an interpretation which found favour with Butzer (1974). He reported that his investigations showed plenty of post-Classical and pre-1500 alluviation (which could not therefore be ascribed to the Little Ice Age), and he doubted whether Vita-Finzi's dating was precise enough to warrant a 1550–1850 date. Instead he suggested that man was responsible for multiple phases of accelerated erosion from slopes and accelerated sedimentation in valley-bottoms from as early as the mid-first millennium BC.

Accelerated weathering

Although fewer data are available, and the effects are generally not so immediately obvious, there is some evidence that human activities have led to changes in the nature and rate of weathering (Winkler, 1970). The prime cause of this is probably brought about by air pollution (see p. 271). It is clear that as a result of increased emissions of sulphur dioxide because of the burning of fossil fuels, there are increased levels of sulphuric acid in rain over many industrial areas. This in itself may react with stones and cause their

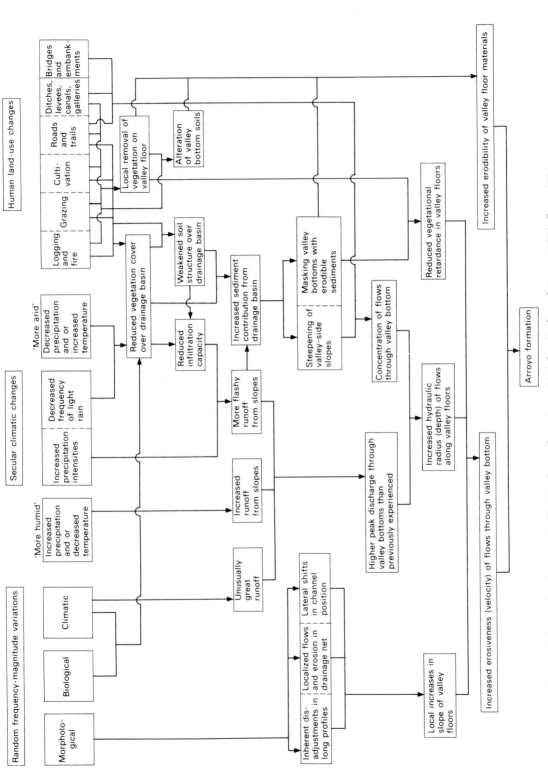

FIG. 6.9 *A model for the formation of arroyos (gullies) in the south-western USA (after Cooke and Reeves, 1976, figure 1.2)*

decay. Chemical reactions involving sulphur dioxide can also generate salts such as calcium sulphate and magnesium sulphate, which may be effective in causing the physical breakdown of rock through the mechanism of salt weathering.

Similarly, atmospheric carbon dioxide levels have been rising steadily because of the burning of fossil fuels, and deforestation. Carbon dioxide may combine with water, especially at lower temperatures, to produce weak carbonic acid which can dissolve limestone, marbles, and dolomites. Weathering can also be accelerated by changes in ground-water levels caused by irrigation. This can be illustrated by a consideration of the Indus Plain in Pakistan (Goudie, 1977b), where irrigation has caused the water-table to be raised by about 6 m since 1922. This has caused increased evaporation and salinization (see p. 113). The salts that are precipitated by evaporation above the capillary fringe include sodium sulphate, a very effective cause of stone decay, and buildings, such as the great archaeological site of Mohenjo-Daro, are decaying at a catastrophic rate.

34
The ancient city of Mohenjo-Daro in Pakistan was excavated in the 1920s. Irrigation has been introduced into the area causing ground-water levels to be raised. This has brought salt into the bricks of the ancient city causing severe disintegration

In other cases accelerated weathering has been achieved by moving stone from one environment to another. Cleopatra's Needle, an Egyptian obelisk in New York City, is an example of rapid weathering of stone in an inhospitable environment. Originally erected on the Nile opposite Cairo about 1500 BC, it was toppled in about 500 BC by Persian invaders, and lay partially buried in Nile sediments until, in 1880, it was moved to New York. It immediately began to scale and the inscriptions were largely obliterated within 10 years because of the penetration of moisture which enabled frost-wedging and hydration of salts to occur.

Accelerated mass movements

There are many examples of mass movements being triggered by man through his miscellaneous activities (Selby, 1979). For instance, landslides can be created either by undercutting or by unloading (figure 6.10). When a road is constructed, material derived from undercutting the upper hillside may be cast onto the lower hillslope as a relatively loose fill to widen the road bed. Storm-water is then often diverted from the road on to the loose fill.

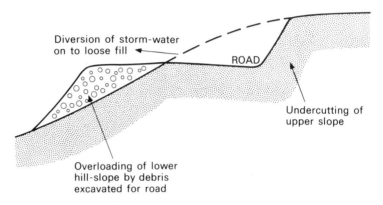

FIG. 6.10
Slope instability produced by road construction

Because of the hazards presented by both natural and accelerated mass movements man has developed a whole series of techniques to attempt to control them. Such methods, many of which are widely used by engineers, are listed in table 6.7. However, such techniques are increasingly necessary as man's power to change a hillside, and to make it more prone to slope failure, has been transformed by engineering developments. Excavations are going deeper, man-made structures are larger, and many sites which are at best marginally suitable for engineering activities are now being used because of increasing pressure on land. This applies especially to some of the expanding urban areas in the humid parts of low latitudes — Hong Kong, Kuala Lumpur, Rio de Janeiro, and many others. It is very seldom that man deliberately accelerates mass movements: most are accidentally caused, the exception possibly being the deliberate triggering of a threatening snow avalanche (Perla, 1978).

The forces producing slope instability and landsliding can usefully be divided into disturbing forces and resisting properties (Cooke and Doornkamp, 1974: 130–2). The factors leading to an increase in shear stress (disturbing forces) are listed in table 6.8a. Some of the factors are natural, while others (italicized) are affected by man. In table 6.8b the factors leading to a decrease in the shearing

Type of movement	Method for control
Falls	Flattening the slope
	Benching the slope
	Drainage
	Reinforcement of rock walls by grouting with cement, anchor bolts
	Covering of wall with steel mesh
Slides and flows	Grading or benching to flatten the slope
	Drainage of surface water with ditches
	Sealing surface cracks to prevent infiltration
	Subsurface drainage
	Rock or earth buttresses at foot
	Retaining walls at foot
	Pilings through the potential slide mass

TABLE 6.7
Examples of methods of controlling mass movements

Source: after Baker, R. F. and Marshall, H. E. in Dunne and Leopold, 1978, table 15.16

resistance of materials making up a slope are listed. Once again there are various situations when man can play a role.

Some mass movements are created by man because he piles up waste soil and rock into unstable accumulations that fail spontaneously. At Aberfan, in South Wales, a major disaster occurred when a 180 m high coal-waste tip began to move as an earthflow. The tip had been constructed not only as a steep slope but also upon a spring line. This made an unstable configuration which eventually destroyed a school and claimed over 150 lives. Man-induced mass movements are also a problem in Los Angeles, California. Some result from the denudation of slope vegetation cover by fires, many of which are set by man (see p. 29), while others are triggered by infiltration of water from cesspools and from irrigation water applied to lawns and gardens. In Hong Kong, where a large proportion of the population is forced to occupy steep slopes developed on deeply weathered granites and other rocks, mass movements are a severe problem and So (1971) has shown that many of the landslips and washouts (70% of those in the great storm of June 1966, for example) were associated with road sections and slopes artificially modified through construction and cultivation.

One of the most serious mass movements in which man played a role was that which created the Vaiont Dam disaster in Italy in 1963, in which 2 600 people were killed (Kiersch, 1965). Heavy antecedent rainfall conditions and the presence of young, highly folded sedimentary rocks provided the

TABLE 6.8
Factors involved in slope failure

(a)   FACTORS LEADING TO AN INCREASE IN SHEAR STRESS

1   Removal of lateral or underlying support
      undercutting by water (e.g., river, waves), or glacier ice
      weathering of weaker strata at the toe of the slope
      washing out of granular material by seepage erosion
      man-made cuts and excavations, draining of lakes or reservoirs

2   Increased disturbing forces
      natural accumulations of water, snow, talus
      *man-made pressures (e.g., stock-piles of ore, tip-heaps, rubbish
          dumps, or buildings)*

3   Transitory earth stresses
      earthquakes
      continual passing of heavy traffic

4   Increased internal pressure
      build-up of pore-water pressures (e.g., in joints and cracks,
          especially in the tension crack zone at the rear of the slide)

(b)   FACTORS LEADING TO A DECREASE IN SHEARING RESISTANCE

1   Materials
      beds which decrease in shear strength if water content
          increases (clays, shale, mica, schist, talc, serpentine) (e.g.,
          *when local water-table is artificially increased in height by
          reservoir construction*, or as a result of stress release
          (vertical and/or horizontal) following slope formation
      low internal cohesion (e.g., consolidated clays, sands, porous
          organic matter
      in bedrock: faults, bedding planes, joints, foliation in schists,
          cleavage, brecciated zones, and pre-existing shears

2   Weathering changes
      weathering reduces effective cohesion, and to a lesser extent
          the angle of shearing resistance
      absorption of water leading to changes in the fabric of clays
          (e.g., loss of bonds between particles or the formation of
          fissures)

35 (opposite)
*The village of Aberfan in South
Wales where in 1966 a massive
debris flow caused severe loss
of life when it destroyed a
school and houses as it ran
down from a coal-waste tip*

3   Pore-water pressure increase
      high ground-water table as a result of increased precipitation
          *or as a result of human interference (e.g., dam
          construction)* (see 1 above)

Source: modified after Cooke and Doornkamp, 1974: 131

214

necessary conditions for a slip to take place, but it was the construction of the Vaiont Dam itself which changed the local ground-water conditions sufficiently to affect the stability of a rock mass on the margins of the reservoir. 240 million cubic metres of ground slipped with great speed into the reservoir and this caused a great rise in water level which overtopped the dam and caused flooding and loss of life downstream. Comparable slope instability was caused when the Franklin D. Roosevelt lake was impounded by the Columbia River in the USA (Coates, 1977) but the effects were, happily, less serious.

It is evident from what has been said about the predisposing causes of the slope failure *triggered* by the Vaiont Dam that man was only able to have such an impact because the natural conditions were broadly favourable. Exactly the same lesson can be learnt from the accelerated landsliding in southern Italy. Nossin (1972) has demonstrated how in Calabria road construction has triggered off (and been hindered by) landsliding, but he has also stressed that the area is fundamentally susceptible to such mass movement activity because of geological conditions. It is an area where rapid recent uplift has caused downcutting by rivers and the undercutting of slopes by erosion. It is also an area of incoherent metamorphic rocks, with frequent faulting. Further, water is often trapped by Tertiary clay layers, providing further stimulus to movement.

Deliberate modification of channels

Both for purposes of navigation and flood control man has deliberately straightened many river channels. Indeed, the elimination of meanders contributes to flood control in two ways. First, it eliminates some over-bank floods on the outside of curves, against which the swiftest current is thrown and where the water surface rises highest. Secondly, and more importantly, the resultant shortened course increases both the gradient and the velocity, and the floodwaters erode and deepen the channel, thereby increasing its flood capacity (see p. 149).

It was for this reason that a programme of channel cutoffs was initiated along the Mississippi in the early 1930s. By 1940 it had lowered flood stages by as much as 4 m at Arkansas City, Arkansas. By 1950 the length of the river between Memphis, Tennessee, and Baton Rouge, Louisiana (600 km down-valley) had been reduced by no less than 270 km as a result of 16 cutoffs.

Some landscapes have become dominated by man-made

channels, normally once again because of the need for flood alleviation and drainage. This is especially evident in an area like the English Fenlands where the straight artificial channels contrast with the sinuous courses of the original rivers such as the Great Ouse (figure 6.11).

Non-deliberate river channel changes

There are thus many examples of the deliberate modification of river channel geometry by man, by the construction of embankments, by channelization, and by other such processes (see, for example, p. 148). However, major changes in the configuration of channels can be achieved accidentally (table 6.9), either because of man-made changes in stream discharge or in their sediment load: both parameters affect channel capacity (Park, 1977).

For example, it is now widely recognized (see p. 151) that the urbanization of a river basin results in an increase in the peak flood flows in a river. It is also recognized that the morphology of stream channels is related to their discharge characteristics and especially to the discharge at which bank full flow occurs. Consequently, as a result of urbanization the frequency of discharges which fill the channel will increase, with the result that the beds and banks of channels in erodible materials will be eroded so as to enlarge the channel. This in turn will lead to bank caving, possible undermining of structures, and increases in turbidity (Hollis and Luckett, 1976).

Comparable changes in channel morphology result from discharge diminution resulting from flood-control works and diversions for irrigation. This can be shown for the North Platte and the South Platte in America. The North Platte, 762–1 219 m wide in 1890 near the Wyoming–Nebraska border, has narrowed to about 60 m at present, while the South Platte river was about 792 m wide, 89 km above its junction with the North Platte in 1897, but had narrowed to about 60 m by 1959 (Schumm, 1977: 161). The tendency of both rivers has been to form one narrow, well-defined channel in place of the previously wide, braided channels, and, in addition, the new channel is generally somewhat more sinuous than the old (figure 6.12).

Likewise the building of dams can lead to channel aggradation upstream from the reservoir and channel deepening downstream (see p. 142) because of the changes brought about in sediment loads (figure 6.13). Some data on observed rates of degradation below dams are presented in table 6.10. They show that the average rate of degradation

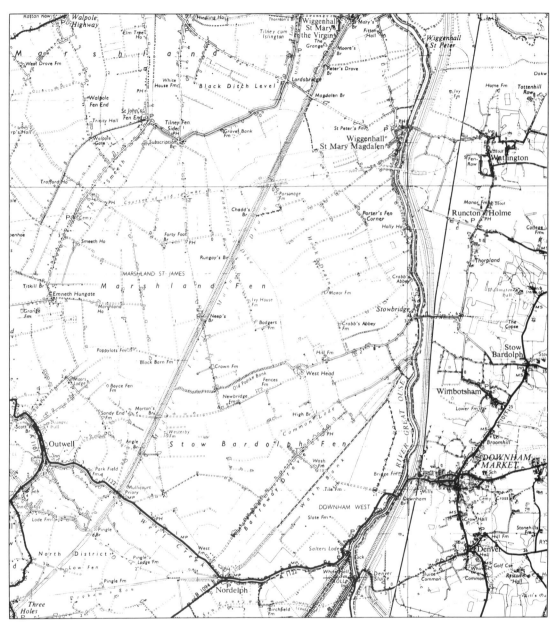

FIG. 6.11
*Natural and artificial waterways
of the English Fenland.
Reproduced from the Ordnance
Survey map with the permission
of the Controller of Her Majesty's
Stationery Office, crown
copyright reserved*

Phenomenon	*Cause*
Channel incision	'Clear-water erosion' below dams caused by sediment removal
Channel aggradation	Reduction in peak flows below dams Addition of sediment to streams by mining agriculture, etc.
Channel enlargement	Increase in discharge level produced by urbanization
Channel diminution	Discharge decrease following water abstraction or flood control
Channel diminution	Trapping and stabilizing of sediment by artificially introduced plants

TABLE 6.9
Accidental channel changes

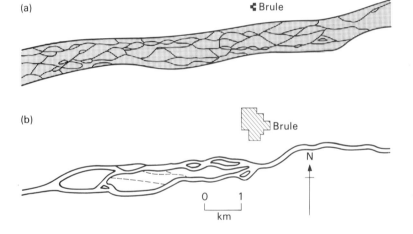

FIG. 6.12
The configuration of the channel of the South Platte River at Brule in Nebraska, USA: (a) in 1897 and (b) in 1959. Such changes in channel form result from discharge diminution from flood-control works and diversions for irrigation (after Schumm, 1977: figure 5.32)

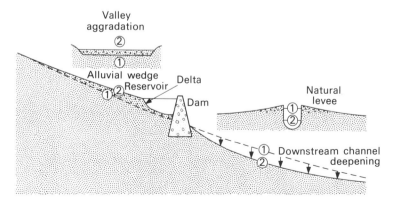

FIG. 6.13
Schematic profile and cross-section of a river showing upstream and downstream effects of a dam and reservoir (after Strahler and Strahler, 1973, figure 14.36)

219

TABLE 6.10
*Degradation below
selected dams*

	Period of record	Drainage area (km^2)	Average bed lowering (m)	Average degradation (m/year)
Missouri, Fort Peck	1936–50	149 508	0.308	0.0204
Missouri, Garrison	1949–57	469 826	0.198	0.0283
Arkansas, John Martin	1943–51	49 036	0.101	0.0125
North Platte, Guarnsey	1927–57	41 958	0.610	0.0202
Red, Dennison	1942–48	99 174	0.497	0.0311
North Canadian, Canton	1947–59	32 331	0.555	0.0457
South Canadian, Conchas	1935–42	19 037	0.808	0.1152
Salt Fork, Arkansas	1936–45	8 288	0.305	0.0381
Smoky Hill, Kanopolis	1946–61	20 357	0.232	0.0155
Rio Grande, Elephant Butte	1917–32	74 851	0.497	0.0311

Source: modified after Leopold *et al.*, 1964, table 11.2, p. 454

has been of the order of 30 mm/year over periods of about 10–15 years following closure of the dams. However, over a period of time the rate of degradation seems to become less or to cease altogether, and Leopold *et al.* (1964: 455) suggest that this can be brought about in several ways. First, because degradation results in a flattening of the channel slope in the vicinity of the dam, the slope may become so flat that the necessary force to transport the available materials is no longer provided by the flow. Secondly, the reduction of flood peaks by the dam reduces the competence of the transporting stream to carry some of the material on its bed. Thus if the bed contains a mixture of particle sizes the river may be able to transport the finer sizes but not the larger, and the gradual winnowing of the fines will leave an armour of coarser material that prevents further degradation.

The overall effect of the creation of a reservoir by the construction of a dam is to lead to a reduction in down-stream channel capacity (see Petts, 1979 for a review). This seems to amount to between about 30 and 70% (see Table 6.11).

Equally far-reaching changes in channel form are produced by land-use changes and the introduction of soil conservation measures. Figure 6.14 provides an idealized representation of how the river basins of Georgia, USA have been modified through human agency between 1700 (the time of European settlement) and the present. Clearing of the land for cultivation (b) caused massive slope erosion which caused the transference of large quantities of sediment into channels and floodplains. This phase of intense erosive land-use

220

TABLE 6.11
*Channel capacity reduction
below reservoirs*

River	Dam	Percentage channel capacity loss
Republican, USA	Harlan County	66
Arkansas, USA	John Martin	50
Rio Grande, USA	Elephant Butte	50
Tone, UK	Clatworthy	54
Meavy, UK	Burrator	73
Nidd, UK	Angram	60
Burn, UK	Burn	34
Derwent, UK	Ladybower	40

Source: modified after Petts, 1979, table 1

persisted particularly strongly during the nineteenth century and the first decades of the twentieth century, but thereafter (c) conservation measures, reservoir construction and a reduction in the intensity of agricultural land-use led to further channel changes (Trimble, 1974). Streams ceased to carry such a heavy sediment load, they became much less turbid, and incision took place into the floodplain sediments. By means of this active stream-bed erosion, streams incised themselves into the modern alluvium, lowering their beds as much as 3–4 m.

Reactivation and stabilization of sand dunes

To George Perkins Marsh the reactivation and stabilization of sand dunes, especially coastal dunes, was a theme of the greatest importance in his analysis of man's transformation of nature. He devoted fifty-four pages to it:

the preliminary steps, whereby wastes of loose, drifting, barren sands are transformed into wooded knolls and plains, and finally through the accumulation of vegetable mould, into arable ground, constitute a conquest over nature which precedes agriculture – a geographical revolution – and therefore, an account of the means by which the change has been effected belongs properly to the history of man's influence on the great features of physical geography (p. 393)

He was fascinated by 'the warfare man wages with the sand hills' and asked (p. 410) 'in what degree the naked condition of most dunes is to be ascribed to the improvidence and indiscretion of man'.

His analysis showed quite clearly that most of the coastal dunes of Europe and North America had been rendered mobile, and hence a threat to agriculture and settlement, because of man's actions, especially because of grazing and

221

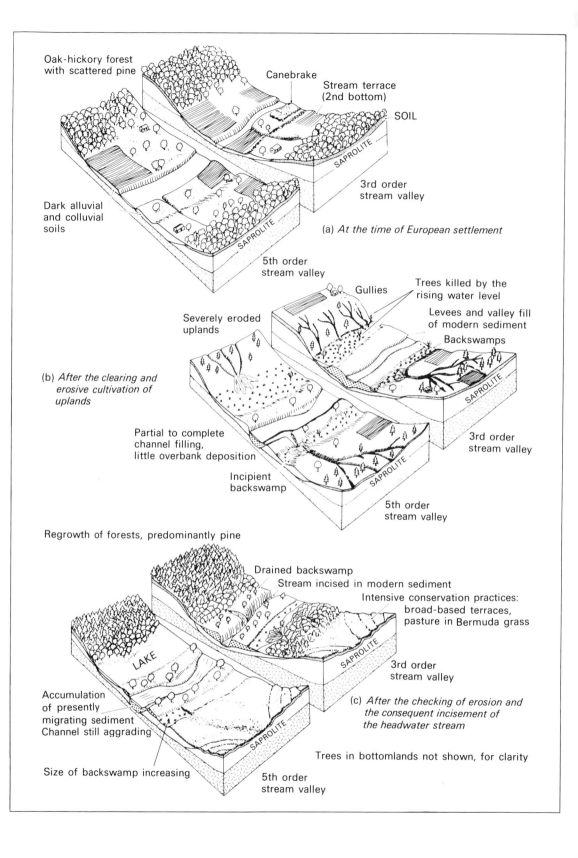

Oak-hickory forest
with scattered pine

Canebrake

Stream terrace
(2nd bottom)

SOIL

SAPROLITE

3rd order
stream valley

Dark alluvial
and colluvial
soils

SAPROLITE

(a) *At the time of European settlement*

5th order
stream valley

Gullies

Trees killed by the
rising water level

Levees and valley fill
of modern sediment

Backswamps

Severely eroded
uplands

(b) *After the clearing and
erosive cultivation of
uplands*

SAPROLITE

3rd order
stream valley

Partial to complete
channel filling,
little overbank deposition

Incipient
backswamp

SAPROLITE

5th order
stream valley

Regrowth of forests, predominantly pine

Drained backswamp
Stream incised in modern sediment
Intensive conservation practices:
broad-based terraces,
pasture in Bermuda grass

LAKE

SAPROLITE

3rd order
stream valley

Accumulation
of presently
migrating sediment
Channel still aggrading

(c) *After the checking of erosion and
the consequent incisement of
the headwater stream*

Trees in bottomlands not shown, for clarity

Size of backswamp increasing

SAPROLITE

5th order
stream valley

clearing. In Britain the cropping of dune warrens by rabbits was a severe problem and a most significant event in their long history was the myxomatosis outbreak (see p. 94) of the 1950s which severely reduced the rabbit population and led to dramatic changes in stability and vegetative cover.

Appreciation of the problem of dune reactivation on mid-latitude shorelines, and attempts to overcome it, go back a long way (Kittredge, 1948). For example, recognition of the menace of shifting sand following denudation is indicated by a decree of 1539 in Denmark which imposed a fine for destroying certain species of sand plants on the coast of Jutland. The fixation of coastal sand dunes by planting vegetation was initiated in Japan in the seventeenth century, while attempts at the reafforestation of the spectacular Landes dunes in south-west France began as early as 1717, and came to fruition in the nineteenth century through the plans of the great Brémontier. 81 000 ha of moving sand had been fixed in the Landes by 1865. In Britain possibly the most impressive example of sand control is provided by the reafforestation of the Culbin Sands in north-east Scotland with confier plantations (Edlin, 1976).

Man-induced dune instability is not, however, a problem that is restricted to mid-latitude coasts. In inland areas of Europe clearing, fire, and grazing has affected some of the late Pleistocene dune fields that were created on the arid steppe margins of the great ice sheets, and in eastern England the dunes of the Breckland created problems on many occasions. There are records of carriages being halted by sand-blocked roads, and of one village, Downham, being overwhelmed altogether. However, it is possibly on the margins of the great subtropical and tropical deserts that some of the greatest fears are being expressed about sand dune reactivation. This is one of the facets of the process of desertification and desertization (see p. 45). Increasing population levels of both man and his domestic animals, brought about by improvements in health and by the provision of boreholes, has led to an excessive pressure on the limited vegetation resources. As ground cover has been reduced so dune instability has increased. The problem is not so much that dunes in the desert cores are relentlessly marching onto moister areas, but that fossil dunes, laid down during the more arid phase peaking around 18 000 years ago, have been reactivated in place.

Most solutions to the problem of dune instability and sand blowing involve the establishment of a vegetation cover. This is not always easy. Species for the control of sand dunes are subject to undermining of the roots, to burying, to

FIG. 6.14 (opposite) *Changes in the evolution of the fluvial landscapes of The Piedment of Georgia, USA, in response to land-use change between 1700 and 1970 (after Trimble, 1974: 117)*

abrasion, and often to severe deficiencies of soil moisture. Thus the species that are selected need to have the ability to recover after partial burying, to have deep and spreading roots, to have rapid height growth in the seedling stages, to promote rapid litter development, and to add nitrogen to the soil through root nodules. During the early stages of growth they may need to be protected by the erection of fences, sand traps, and surface mulches. Growth can also be stimulated by the addition of synthetic fertilizers.

In the hearts of deserts sand dunes are naturally mobile because of the sparse vegetation cover. Even here, however, man sometimes attempts to stabilize sand surfaces to protect settlements, pipelines, industrial plant and agricultural land. The use of relatively porous barriers to stop or divert sand movement has proved to be relatively successful, and palm fronds or chicken wire have been found adequate. Elsewhere surfaces have been stabilized by the application of high-gravity oil or by salt-saturated water (which promotes the development of wind-resistant surface crusts).

On desert margins in many parts of the world successful dune stabilization has been achieved by the planting of the types of species listed in table 6.12.

In temperate areas coastal dunes have been successfully stabilized by the use of various trees and other plants. In Japan *Pinus thumbergii* has been successful, while in the great Culbin sands plantations of Scotland *P. nigra* and

TABLE 6.12
Species used for sand dune fixation in desert areas

Tamarix:
    Tamarix aphylla
    Tamarix stricta
Acacias
Gumtrees (Eucalyptus)
Egyptian cane: *Saccharum spontaneum*
Balsam euphorb: *Euphorbia balsamifera*
Castor bean: *Ricinus communis*
Saxaoul: *Halyxolon persicum* (less than 100 mm)
Calligonum: *C. azel, C. arich, C. arborescens, C. comosum,*
                  C. polygonoides
Perennial grasses such as:
    Panicum antidotale   *Aristida pennata*
    Panicum turgidum   *Aristida kareliana*
    Pennisetum dichtomum
Legumes shrubs such as:
    Retama raetam
Other sand-adapted shrubs could be tested, such as:
    Leptadenia pyrotechnica   *Salvadora persica*
    Ochradenus baccatus   *Genista saharae*

Source: after Le Houérou, 1976, table 9.4

P. laricio have been used initially, followed by *P. sylvestis.* Of the smaller shrubs, *Hippophaë* has proved highly efficient, sometimes too efficient, at spreading. Clearance of it from areas where it is not welcome is a problem because of some of the properties that make it such an efficient sand stabilizer: vigorous suckering growth and the rapid regrowth of cut stems (Boorman, 1977). There are also different types of grass that have been employed, especially in the early stages of stabilization. These include two grasses which are moderately tolerant of salt: *Agropyron junceiforme* (sand twitch) and *Elymus arenarius* (lyme grass). Another grass which is much used, not least because of its rapid and favourable response to burial by drifting sand, is *Ammophila arenaria* (marram). In certain areas a hybrid occurs between *A. arenaria* and *Calamagrostis epigeios*; *Ammocalamagrostis baltica* (baltic marram grass). Though more vigorous even than *Ammophila* it is completely sterile and has to be propagated vegetatively.

Further stabilization of coastal dunes has been achieved by the mechanism of sand fences. These generally consist of slats about 1.0—1.5 m high, and having a porosity of 25—50%. They have proved to be effective in building incipient dunes in most coastal areas. By installing new fences with regularity large dunes can be created with some rapidity (see figure 6.15). Alternative methods, such as using junk cars on the beaches at Galveston, Texas, have been attempted without much success.

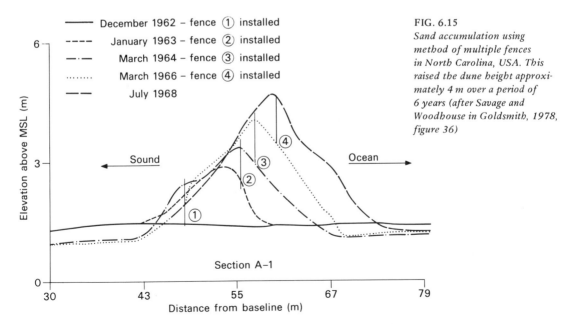

FIG. 6.15
Sand accumulation using method of multiple fences in North Carolina, USA. This raised the dune height approximately 4 m over a period of 6 years (after Savage and Woodhouse in Goldsmith, 1978, figure 36)

225

The Human Impact

Accelerated coastal erosion

Because of the concentration of so many settlements, industries, transport facilities, and recreational developments on coastlines, the pressures that are placed on coastal landforms are often acute and the consequences of excessive erosion will be serious. While most areas are subject to some degree of natural erosion and accretion, the balance can be upset by man in a whole range of different ways (table 6.13). However, man seldom attempts to accelerate coastal erosion deliberately. More normally, coast erosion is an unexpected or unwelcome result of various economic activities. Frequently coast erosion has been accelerated as a result of man's attempts to reduce it.

One of the best forms of coastal protection is a good beach. Thus, if material is removed from a beach accelerated cliff retreat may take place. Such removal may take place to provide minerals of economic worth, including heavy minerals, or to provide aggregates for construction purposes. The classic example of the latter was the mining of 660 000

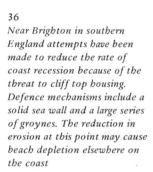

36
Near Brighton in southern England attempts have been made to reduce the rate of coast recession because of the threat to cliff top housing. Defence mechanisms include a solid sea wall and a large series of groynes. The reduction in erosion at this point may cause beach depletion elsewhere on the coast

tonnes of shingle from the beach at Hallsands in Devon in 1887 to provide material for the construction of dockyards at Plymouth. The shingle proved to be undergoing little or no natural replenishment and in consequence the shore level was reduced by about 4 m and the loss of the protective shingle soon resulted in cliff erosion to the extent of 6 m

TABLE 6.13

Mechanisms of man-induced erosion in coastal zones

Man-induced erosion zones		Effects	
1	Beach mining for placer deposits (heavy minerals) such as zircon, rutile, ilmenite and monazite	1	Loss of sand from frontal dunes and beach ridges
2	Construction of groynes, breakwaters, jetties and other structures	2	Downdrift erosion
3	Construction of offshore breakwaters	3	Reduction in littoral drift
4	Construction of retaining walls to maintain river entrances	4	Interruption of littoral drift resulting in downdrift erosion
5	Construction of sea-walls revetments, etc.	5	Wave reflection and accelerated sediment movement
6	Deforestation	6	Removal of sand by wind: sand drift
7	Fires	7	Migrating dunes and sand drift after destruction of vegetation
8	Grazing of sheep and cattle	8	Initiation of blow-outs and transgressive dunes: sand drift
9	Off-road recreational vehicles (dune buggies: trail bikes, etc.)	9	Triggering mechanism for sand drift attendant upon removal of vegetative cover
10	Reclamation schemes	10	Changes in coastal configuration: and interruption of natural processes, often causing new patterns in sediment transport
11	Increased recreational needs	11	Accelerated deterioration, and destruction, of vegetation on dunal areas, promoting erosion by wind and wave action

Source: Hails, 1977, table 9.II, p. 348

between 1907 and 1957. The village of Hallsands was cruelly attacked by waves and is now in ruins.

Another common cause of beach and cliff erosion at one point is coast protection at another. Because, as already stated, a broad beach serves to protect the cliffs behind, beach formation is often encouraged by the construction of groynes. However, the construction of such structures may merely displace the erosion (possibly in an even more marked form) further along the coast. This is illustrated in figure 6.16.

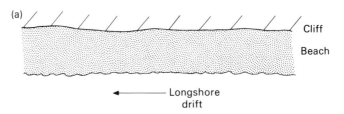

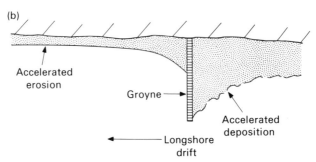

FIG. 6.16
Diagrammatic illustration of the effects of groyne construction on sedimentation on a beach

Piers or breakwaters can have similar effects to groynes. This has occurred at various places along the British coast: erosion at Seaford resulted from the Newhaven breakwater, while erosion at Lowestoft resulted from the pier at Gorleston. Figure 6.17 illustrates the changes in the location of beach erosion achieved by the building of jetties or breakwaters in various locations. At Madras in south-east India, for example, a 1 000 m long breakwater was constructed in 1875 to create a sheltered harbour on a notoriously inhospitable coast, dominated by sand transport from north to south. On the south side of the breakwater over 1 million square metres of new land formed by 1912, but erosion occurred for 5 km north of the breakwater. At Ceará in Brazil, also in 1875, a detached breakwater was erected over a length of 430 m more or less parallel to the shore. The idea in using a detached structure was that littoral drift material would be able to move along the coast uninterrupted by the presence of a

228

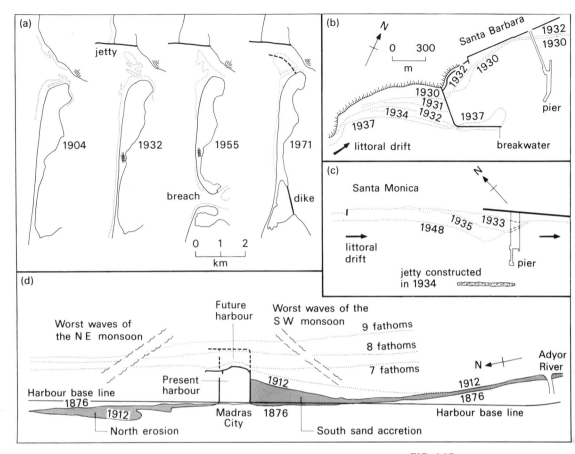

FIG. 6.17

Examples of the effects of man-made shoreline installations on beach and shoreline morphology

(a) Erosion of Bayocean Spit, Tillamook Bay, Oregon, after construction of a north jetty in 1914–17. The heavy dashed line shows the position of the new south jetty under construction

(b) The deposition–erosion pattern around the Santa Barbara breakwater in California

(c) Sand deposition in the protected lee of Santa Monica breakwater in California

(d) Madras Harbour, India, showing accretion on updrift side of the harbour and erosion on the downdrift side

(Komar, Beach processes and sedimentation, p. 334, © 1976. Reprinted by permission of Prentice-Hall, Inc.)

conventional structure built across the surf zone. This, however, proved to be a fallacy (Komar, 1976) since the removal of the wave action which provided the energy for transporting the littoral sands resulted in their deposition within the protected area.

Plate 37 shows the evolution of the coast at West Bay in Dorset, southern England following the construction of a jetty. As time goes on the beach in the foreground builds outwards while the cliff behind the jetty retreats and needs to be protected with a sea wall. Likewise, the construction of some sea walls, erected to reduce coastal erosion and flooding, has had the opposite effect to that which was intended (see figure 6.18).

Problems of this type are exacerbated because there is now abundant evidence to indicate that much of the reservoir of sand and shingle that creates beaches is in some respects a relict feature. Much of it was deposited on the continental shelf during the maximum of the last glaciation (around 18 000 years BP), when sea level was about 120–140 m below its present level. It was transported shoreward and

37

A jetty was built at West Bay to facilitate entry to the harbour:

Top: In 1860 it has had little effect on the coastline

Centre: By 1900 sediment accumulation had taken place in the foreground but there was less sediment in front of the cliff behind the town

Bottom: By 1976 the process had gone even further and the cliff had to be protected by a sea wall. Even this has since been severely damaged by a winter storm

incorporated in present-day beaches during the phase of rapidly rising post-Glacial sea levels that characterized the Flandrian transgression until about 6000 years BP. Since that time, with the exception of minor oscillations of the order of a few metres, world sea levels have been stable and much less material is as a consequence being added to beaches and shingle complexes. Therefore, according to Hails

230

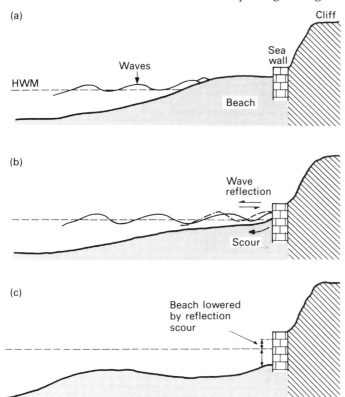

FIG. 6.18
Sea walls and erosion: a broad, high beach prevents storm waves breaking against a sea wall and will persist, or erode only slowly; but where waves are reflected by the wall (b), scour is accelerated, and the beach is quickly removed and lowered (c) (modified after Bird, 1979, figure 6.3)

(1977: 322): 'in many areas, there is virtually no offshore supply to be moved onshore, except for small quantities resulting from seasonal changes'. It is because of these problems that many erosion prevention schemes now involve beach replenishment (by the artificial addition of appropriate sediments to build up the beach) or employ miscellaneous sand bypassing techniques (including pumping and dredging) whereby sediments are transferred from the accumulation side of a man-made barrier to the erosional side (King, 1974).

In some areas, however, sediment-laden rivers bring material into the coastal zone which becomes incorporated into beaches through the mechanism of long shore drift. Thus any change in the sediment load of such rivers may result in a change in the sediment budget of neighbouring beaches. When accelerated soil erosion occurs in a river basin the increased sediment load may cause coastal accretion and siltation (see p. 119), but where the sediment load is reduced through such action as the construction of large reservoirs, behind which sediments accumulate, coastal erosion may result. This is believed to be one of the less desirable consequences of the construction of the Aswan

231

Dam on the Nile: parts of its delta have shown recently accelerated recession. Likewise in Texas, where over the last century four times as much coastal land has been lost as has been gained, one of the main reasons is believed to be the reduction in the suspended loads of some of the rivers discharging into the Gulf of Mexico (table 6.14). The four rivers listed carried, in 1961–70, only about one fifth of what they carried in 1931–40.

TABLE 6.14
Suspended loads of Texas rivers discharging into the Gulf of Mexico

River	*Suspended load* (million tonnes)		*Percentage* *
	1931–40	*1961–70*	
Brazos	350	120	30
San Bernard	1	1	100
Colorado	100	11	10
Rio Grande	180	6	3
TOTAL	631	138	20

* Of 1931–40 loads
Source: modified from Hails, 1977, table 9.1 (after data from Stout *et al.* and Curtis *et al.*)

Construction of great levees on the Mississippi River since 1717 have also affected the Gulf of Mexico coast. The channelization of the river (discussed also on p. 216) has increased its velocity, has reduced over-bank deposition of silt onto swamps, marshes and estuaries, and has changed the salinity conditions of marshland plants (Cronin, 1967). As a result the coastal marshes and islands have suffered from increased erosion or a reduced rate of development. This has been vividly described by Biglane and Lafleur (1967: 691):

Like a bullet through a rifle barrel, waters of the mighty Mississippi are thrust toward the Gulf between the confines of the flood control levees. Before the day of these man-made structures, these waters poured out over tremendous reaches of the coast....Freshwater marshes (salinities averaging 4–6%) were formed by deposited silts and vegetative covers of wire grass....As man erected his flood protection devices, these marshes ceased to form an extensively as before.

In some areas anthropogenic vegetation modification creates increased erosion potential. This has been illustrated for the hurricane-afflicted coast of Belize, Central America (Stoddart, 1971). He showed that natural dense vegetation thickets on low sandy islands (cays) acted as a baffle against waves and served as a massive sediment trap for coral blocks, shingle, and sand transported during extreme storms. However, on many islands the natural vegetation had been replaced by coconut plantations. These had an open structure easily penetrated by sea water, they tended to have little or no ground vegetation (thus exposing the cay surface to stripping and channelling), and they had a dense but shallow root net easily undermined by marginal sapping. Thus Stoddart found (p. 191) that 'where the natural vegetation had been replaced by coconuts before the storm [Hurricane Hattie], erosion and beach retreat led to net vertical decreases in height of 3—7 ft; whereas where natural vegetation remained, banking of storm sediments against the vegetation hedge led to net vertical increases in height of 1—5 ft'.

Other examples of markedly accelerated coastal erosion and flooding result from anthropogenic degradation of dune ridges (see p. 221). Frontal dunes are a natural defence against erosion, and coastal changes may be long-lasting once they are breached. Many of those areas in eastern England which best resisted the great storm and surge of 1952 were those where man had not weakened the coastal dune belt.

Not all dune stabilization and creation schemes have proved desirable (Dolan *et al.*, 1973). In North Carolina (see figure 6.19), the natural barrier island system along the coastline met the challenge of periodic extreme storms, such as hurricanes, by placing no permanent obstruction in the path of the powerful waves. Most of the initial stress of such storms is sustained by relatively broad beaches (figures 6.19a). Because no resistance is created by impenetrable landforms water can flow between the dunes (which do not form a continuous line) and across the islands, with the result that

FIG. 6.19
Cross-sections of two barrier islands in North Carolina, USA, the upper diagram (a) is typical of the natural systems, and the lower (b) illustrates the stabilized systems (after Dolan et al., *1973, figure 4)*

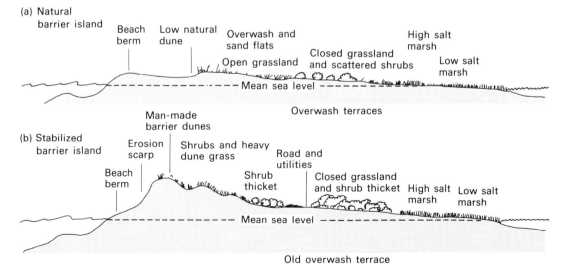

(a) Natural barrier island

Beach berm | Low natural dune | Overwash and sand flats | High salt marsh

Closed grassland and scattered shrubs | Low salt marsh

Open grassland

Mean sea level

Overwash terraces

(b) Stabilized barrier island

Man-made barrier dunes

Erosion scarp | Shrubs and heavy dune grass | Road and utilities

Beach berm

Shrub thicket | Closed grassland and shrub thicket | High salt marsh | Low salt marsh

Mean sea level

Old overwash terrace

wave energy is rapidly exhausted. However, between 1936 and 1940, 1000 km of sand fencing was erected to create an artificial barrier dune along part of the Outer Banks, and 2.5 million trees and various grasses (especially *Ammophila breviligulata*) were planted to create large artificial dunes. The altered barrier islands (see figure 6.19b) not only have the artificial barrier dune system; they also have beaches that are often only 30 m wide compared with 140 m for the unaltered islands. This beach-narrowing process, combined with the presence of a permanent dune structure, has created a situation in which high wave energy is concentrated in an increasingly restricted run-up area, resulting in a steeper beach profile, increased turbulence and greater erosion. Another problem associated with this artificial dune stabilization is the flooding that occurs when north-east storms pile the water of the lagoon, Pamlico Sound, up against the barrier islands. In the past, these surge waters simply flowed out between the low, discontinuous dunes and over the beach to the sea, but with the altered dune chain the water cannot drain off readily and vast areas of land are at times submerged.

Man's influence on seismicity and volcanoes

The seismic and tectonic forces which mould the relief of the earth and cause such hazards to man are one of the fields in which human attempts at control have had least success and where least has been attempted. Nonetheless, the fact that man has been able inadvertently to trigger off small earthquakes by nuclear blasts (as in Nevada) (Pakiser *et al.*, 1969), by injecting water into deep wells (as in Colorado), by mining, by building reservoirs, and by fluid extraction, suggests that in the course of time it may be possible to 'defuse' earthquakes by relieving tectonic strains gradually in a series of non-destructive low-intensity earthquakes. One problem, however, is that there is no assurance than an earthquake which is deliberately triggered by man will be a small one, or that it will be restricted to a small area. The legal implications are immense.

The demonstration that increasing water pressures could initiate small-scale faulting and seismic activity was inadvertently demonstrated near Denver (Evans, 1966) where nerve-gas waste was being disposed of at great depth in a well in the hope of avoiding contamination of useful ground-water supplies. The waste was pumped in at high pressures and triggered off a series of earthquakes (see figure 6.20) the timing of which corresponded very closely to the timing of

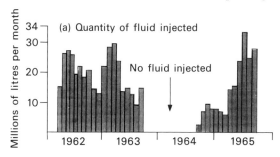

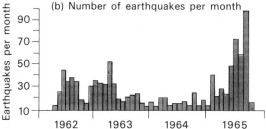

FIG. 6.20
*Correlation between quantity
of waste-water pumped into a
deep well and the number of
earthquakes near Denver,
Colorado (after Birkeland
and Larson, 1978: 573)*

waste disposal in the well. It is also now thought that the
pumping of fluids into the Inglewood Oil Field, Los Angeles,
to raise the hydrostatic pressure and increase oil recovery
may have been responsible for triggering the 1963 earthquake
which fractured a wall of the Baldwin Hills Reservoir. It
appears that increased fluid pressure reduces the frictional
force across the contact surface of a fault, allows slippage to
occur, and thereby creates an earthquake.

The significance of these 'accidents' has now been verified
experimentally at an oilfield at Rangely in Colorado, USA,
where variations in seismicity have been produced by deliberately controlled variations in the fluid pressure in a zone
that is seismically active (Raleigh *et al.*, 1976).

Perhaps the most important anthropogenically induced
seismicity results from the creation of large reservoirs. With
the ever-increasing number and size of reservoirs (see p.
142) the threat increases. There are at least six cases (Koyna,
Kremasta, Hsinfengkiang, Kariba, Hoover, and Marathon)
where earthquakes of a magnitude greater than 5, accompanied by a long series of foreshocks and aftershocks, have
been related to reservoir impounding. However, as table 6.15
shows, there are many more locations where the filling of
reservoirs behind dams has led to lesser levels of seismic
activity. Detailed monitoring has shown that earthquake
clusters occur in the vicinity of some dams after their reservoirs have been filled, whereas prior to construction activity
was less clustered and less frequent. Similarly, there is evidence from Vaiont (Italy), Lake Mead (USA), Kariba (Central

235

Dam	Year of completion	Year of largest earthquake
Marathon, Greece	1929/30	1938
Oued Fodda, Algeria	1932	—
Boulder, USA	1936	1939
Pieve di Cadore, Italy	1949	—
Clark Hill, USA	1952	1974
Kariba, Zimbabwe/Zambia	1959	1963
Grandval, France	1959	1963
Hsingfengkiang, China	1959	1962
Kurobe, Japan	1960	1961
Camarillas, Spain	1960	1961
Canelles, Spain	1960	1962
Vaiont, Italy	1961	1963
Monteynard, France	1962	1963
Koyna, India	1962	1967
Benmore, New Zealand	1965	1966
Kremasta, Greece	1965	1966
Piastra, Italy	1965	1966
Contra, Switzerland	1965	1965
Najina Bašta, Yugoslavia	1966	1967
Grančarevo, Yugoslavia	1967	—
Oroville, USA	1968	1975
Kastraki, Greece	1968	—
Nurek, USSR	1969	1972
Vouglans, France	1970	1971
Karnafusa, Japan	1970	—
Talbingo, Australia	1971	1972
Schlegeis, Austria	1971	—
H. Verwoerd, South Africa	1972	—
Jocasses, USA	1972	1975
Keban, Turkey	1973	1974
Manic 3, Canada	1975	1975

Source: from data in Judd, 1974 and Milne, 1976, processed by author

Africa), Koyna (India), and Kremasta (Greece) that there is a linear correlation between the storage level in the reservoir and the logarithm of the frequency of shocks. This is illustrated for Vaiont (figure 6.21a) and for Koyna (figure 6.21b), and Nurek (figure 6.21c). It is also apparent from Nurek that as the great reservoir has filled so the depth of the more shallow-seated earthquakes appears to have increased (figure 6.22).

The reasons why seismicity takes place when some dams are built include the hydro-isostatic pressure (see p. 206) exerted by the mass of the water impounded in the reservoir, together with changing water pressures across the contact surfaces of faults. Given that the deepest reservoirs provide

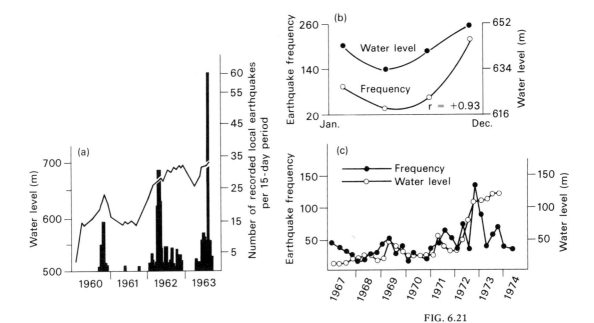

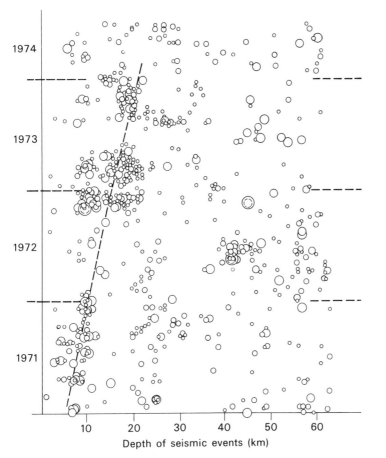

FIG. 6.21
Relationships between reservoir
levels and earthquake
frequencies for:
(a) Vaiont Dam, Italy
(b) Koyna, India (these curves
show the 3-monthly average
of water level and the
total number of earthquakes
for the same months from
1964 to 1968)
(c) The Nurek Dam, Tajik, SSR
(after Judd, 1974 and
Tajikistan Academy of Sciences,
1975)

FIG. 6.22
As the dashed line indicates,
there has been a progressive
increase in the depth of the
shallower seismic events in the
vicinity of the Nurek
Reservoir, Tajik SSR since the
dam was first used to pond up
the lake that now lies behind it
(after Tajikistan Academy of
Sciences, 1975)

237

surface loads of only 20 bars or so, direct activation by the mass of the impounded water seems an unlikely cause (Bell and Nur, 1978) and the role of changing pore pressure assumes greater importance. Paradoxically, there are some possible examples of reduced seismic activity induced by reservoirs (Milne, 1976). One possible explanation of this phenomenon is the increased incidence of stable sliding (fault creep) brought about by higher pore water pressure in the vicinity of the reservoir.

Miscellaneous other human activities appear to affect seismic levels. In Johannesburg, South Africa, for example, gold mining and associated blasting activity have produced tens of thousands of small tremors, and there is a notable reduction in the number that occur on Sundays, a day of rest. In Staffordshire, England, coal mining has caused increased seismic activity. There are also cases where seismicity and faulting can be attributed to fluid extraction as in the oilfields of Texas and California, and the gas-fields of the Po Valley in Italy.

When it comes to the question of human influence on volcanic activity the impotence of man becomes apparent, though some success has been achieved in the control of lava flows. Thus in 1937 and 1947 the US Army attempted to divert lava from the city of Hilo, Hawaii, by bombing threatening flows, while elsewhere, where lava rises in a crater, breaching of the crater wall to direct lava toward uninhabited ground may be possible. In 1973 an attempt was made to halt advance of lava with cold water during the Icelandic eruption of Kirkjufell. Using up to 4 million litres of pumped water per hour, the lava was cooled sufficiently to decrease its velocity at the flow front so that the chilled front acted as a dam to divert the still fluid lava behind (Williams and Moore, 1973).

CHAPTER 7

The Impact of Man on Climate and the Atmosphere

World climates

The climate of the world is now known to have fluctuated frequently and extensively in the three or so million years during which man has been an inhabitant of the earth (Goudie, 1977a). The bulk of these changes have nothing to do with the intervention of man. Climate has changed, and is currently changing, because of a wide range of different natural factors which operate over a variety of time scales (figure 7.1).

Nonetheless with the increasing human population and the rising level of technology it is now apparent that over the last century man has probably become a significant factor in the variations in world climate which are taking place, but it remains extremely difficult to ascertain whether it is human influence rather than natural forces which are responsible for observed trends. If man can be considered a factor then this is particularly because of his inadvertent effects on atmospheric quality and on the albedo of land masses (table 7.1).

The CO_2 problem

Since the beginning of the Industrial Revolution man has been taking stored carbon out of the earth in the form of coal, petroleum and natural gas, and burning it to make carbon dioxide (CO_2), heat, water vapour and smaller

239

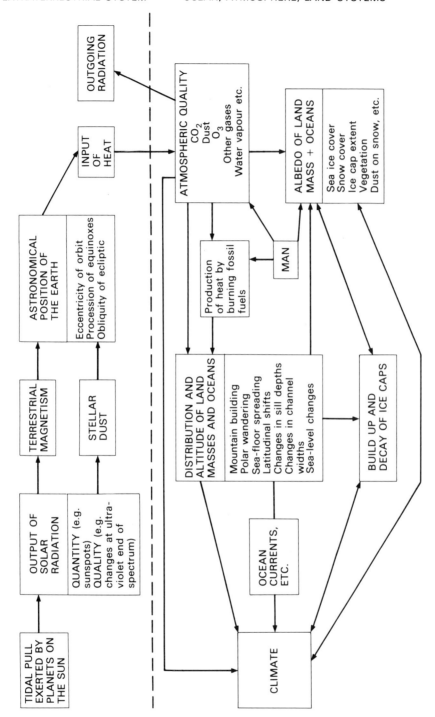

FIG. 7.1 *A schematic representation of some of the possible influences causing climatic change (after Goudie, 1977a, figure 7.1)*

TABLE 7.1
Man's impact on global climate

Possible Mechanisms	
CO_2 emission	— industrial
	— agricultural
Chlorofluoromethane	
Water vapour	
Ozone	
Krypton 85	
Nitrous oxide	
Aerosols	— industrial
	— agricultural
Thermal pollution	
Albedo change	
dust addition to ice caps	
deforestation	
overgrazing	
Alteration of ocean currents by constriction of straits, etc.	
Diversion of fresh waters into oceans, changing the salinity and, therefore, the freezing point of the sea water	

amounts of SO_2 and other gases. The CO_2 in the atmosphere has risen from an estimated 280–290 ppm by volume to a present level of over 320 ppmv, and the upward trend is evident in records from various parts of the world (figure 7.2). Forecasts suggest that it will reach some 380–390 ppmv by the turn of the century and may double by the middle of the next century (Kellogg, 1978: 211).

At one time it was believed that global warming of about 0.6°C between the 1880s and the 1940s was caused by the CO_2 build-up associated with industrialization, but a subsequent fall of 0.3°C between 1940 and 1970 has caused this relationship to be doubted. The temperature fluctuation probably reflects a change in the planetary heat budget.

Industrialization, however, is not the only cause of change in CO_2 levels. Changes in land-use, especially deforestation and agricultural expansion, have reduced the overall quantity of plant biomass, thereby releasing large amounts of CO_2 into the atmosphere. Recent calculations indicate that this process may have been especially important since the expansion of European communities and technology into the

241

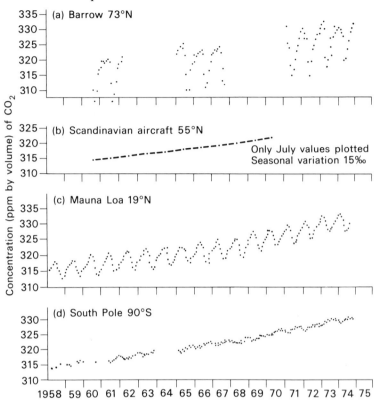

FIG. 7.2

Changes in the atmospheric concentration of carbon dioxide (after Rotty and Weinberg in Lockwood, 1979, figure 6.19)

Americas and elsewhere (Wilson, 1978). It has been calculated that whereas the CO_2 released by the worldwide combustion of fossil fuels amounts to about 5×10^{15} g of carbon per year at the present time, the amount being released by deforestation is of the order of 6×10^{15}, and that from the decay of soil humus 2×10^{15} g/year (Woodwell, 1978). Thus the release of CO_2 by agricultural expansion plus deforestation may be equal to, or rather larger than, that produced by the burning of fossil fuels, though the data presented by different workers are not always consistent (see table 7.2) and there are still uncertainties surrounding the world carbon budget (Bach, 1979). Indeed Broecker *et al.* (1979) suggest that forest cutting in the last couple of decades has not dramatically changed world CO_2 levels because the regrowth of previously cut forests and the enhancement of forest growth resulting from the excess CO_2 in the atmosphere have probably roughly balanced the recent rate of forest destruction.

The CO_2 levels in the atmosphere have an effect on the heat balance, since CO_2 is virtually transparent to incoming solar radiation but absorbs outgoing terrestrial infra-red

A

TABLE 7.2
Inputs of CO_2 into the atmosphere from various sources (especially non-fossil wood burning)

Plant community	Net release of carbon (10^{15} g/year)
Tropical forests	3.5
Temperate zone forests	1.4
Boreal forests	0.8
Other vegetation	0.2
Total land vegetation	5.8
Detritus and humus	2.0
LAND TOTAL	7.8

Source: Woodwell *et al.*, 1978

B

Source	Gross input of carbon (10^{15} g/year)	Net input of carbon (10^{15} g/year)
Fires in boreal forests and non-wooded areas	0.07	0.0
Fires in temperate forests and non-wooded areas	0.4	0.0
Tropical shifting cultivation on land already in use	3.0	0.0
New tropical forest clearings	1.5 (0.7–2.2)	1.5 (0.7–2.2)
Fuel wood burning	0.2	0.006 (0.004–0.008)
Paper waste burning	0.08	0.0008
Soil carbon loss in agriculture	0.3	0.3
Soil carbon loss on burning	0.4	0.02
Desertification	0.5	0.05
Urbanization of farmland	0.01	0.01
Fossil fuel burning	5.0	5.0
Respiration of land biota	63.0	0.0
Decomposition of land detritus	37.0	0.0
Respiration of ocean biota	25.0	0.0
Decomposition of ocean detritus	35.0	0.0
TOTAL	~ 171.0	~ 6.9

Source: Wong, 1978

radiation; radiation that would otherwise escape to space and result in loss of heat from the lower atmosphere (figure 7.3).

Consequently one would expect increased CO_2 levels to lead to an increase in surface temperatures. The degree of resultant change is the subject of debate, but it is thought that by AD 2050 when CO_2 levels have increased by 100%

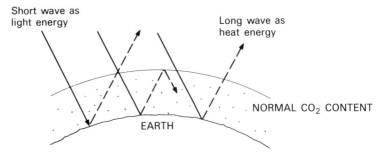

Short wave as
light energy

Long wave as
heat energy

NORMAL CO₂ CONTENT

EARTH

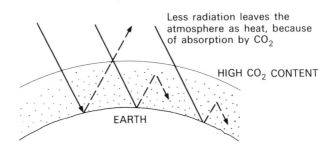

Less radiation leaves the
atmosphere as heat, because
of absorption by CO₂

HIGH CO₂ CONTENT

EARTH

FIG. 7.3
The greenhouse effect:
short-wave radiation strikes
the earth's surface and is
transformed into long-wave
radiation (heat). Since CO_2
absorbs long-wave radiation,
the greater the atmospheric CO_2
content the more heat is
retained and the warmer the
atmosphere becomes

over natural levels, mean surface temperatures might increase by between 1.5 and 3°C, with rather larger values being attained in high latitudes.

It is difficult to assess the consequences of such a temperature increase should it occur. On the bonus side growing seasons in the world's cereal-growing lands would be increased, but on the debit side is the possibility that the extent of deserts might expand and that sea levels might rise a few metres to flood coastal areas as a result of the partial melting of ice caps and glaciers (Mercer, 1978). As Woodwell (1978: 43) has stated: 'Carbon dioxide, until now an apparently innocuous trace gas in the atmosphere, may be moving rapidly toward a central role as a major threat to the present world order'. If temperatures do indeed rise by 1.5–3°C then we shall have conditions similar to those that existed during the warmest phases of the Holocene (the hypsithermal) and to those of the warmest portions of earlier Pleistocene inter-Glacials.

Other gases

In addition to CO_2, other gases influence climate, and their rate of emission by man is increasing, as illustrated for SO_2 in figure 7.4.

A recent contaminant of the atmosphere is a group of gases called chlorofluoromethanes, which are used both as

244

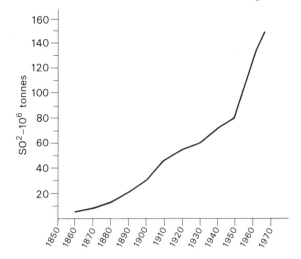

FIG. 7.4
*Estimated historical global
SO$_2$ emissions. (After Robinson
and Robbins in Matthews et al.,
1971, figure 24.1, reprinted
from* Man's impact on the
climate, *ed. Matthews* et al. *by
permission of The MIT Press,
Cambridge, Massachusetts
© 1971 by The Massachusetts
Institute of Technology)*

refrigerants and as household aerosol propellants. These gases are extremely stable and can persist in the troposphere for relatively long periods (a residence time of 40 years has been calculated). The present mean tropospheric concentration amounts to only about 0.2 ppb by volume, but this could treble by the turn of the century (Kellogg, 1978: 212), unless appropriate legislation is introduced.

The effect of these gases is probably twofold. On the one hand it is thought that photodissociation of these gases in the stratosphere produces significant amounts of chlorine atoms and leads to the partial destruction of an important control on radiation — ozone. On the other, the chloro-fluoromethanes, like CO_2, prevent some of the infra-red terrestrial radiation from the surface, that would otherwise escape to space, from passing through the lower atmosphere, thereby leading to an increase in the surface temperature.

Other gases which are being introduced into the atmosphere, with possible effects on temperatures, are nitrous oxide and water vapour (Panofsky, 1976). Thus, for example, supersonic aircraft, both civil and military, discharge some water vapour into the stratosphere as contrails. At the present the water content of the stratosphere is low, as is the exchange of air between the lower stratosphere and other regions. Consequently, comparatively modest amounts of water vapour discharged by aircraft could have a significant effect on the natural balance. It has been calculated that 400 supersonic aircraft, making four flights per day, would place 150×10^6 kg of water into the lower stratosphere. This could, over a period of years, double the existing water content of the atmosphere, thereby leading to a small rise in temperature, perhaps 0.6°C (Sawyer, 1971).

Statistics, however, on the increase of cirrus levels as a result of stratospheric aircraft movements are still meagre (SCEP Report, in Matthews *et al.*, 1971: 39) and their statistical significance is not always proven, though studies at Salt Lake City and Denver between 1949 and 1969 do show an upward trend in cirrus cloudiness which paralleled the increase in jet aircraft activity (figure 7.5). The expected rapid development of civil aviation in future decades may make this an important element of anthropogenic atmospheric modification.

Nitrous oxide (which may, for example, be derived from supersonic aircraft and from the breakdown of nitrate fertilizers – Hutchinson and Mosier, 1979), methane, ammonia and a number of other trace constituents which man is adding to the earth's atmosphere, have infrared absorption bands in the spectral region $7-14$ μm and contribute to the atmospheric greenhouse effect (Wang *et al.*, 1976).

Warnings have been circulated (Boeck *et al.*, 1975) about the possible role of a substance which is emitted from nuclear reactors, called Krypton 85. It is believed that its increasing presence will decrease the electrical resistance of the atmosphere between the oceans and the ionosphere. This in turn would affect the electrification of thunderclouds and, through that, precipitation levels.

Aerosols

One consequence of the Industrial Revolution, which is probably of no lesser significance than CO_2 emission, is the increased quantity of dust or smoke particles that are emitted into the lower atmosphere. A striking illustration of this is provided by the analysis of dust levels in glacier ice of known age in the southern USSR. Layers of ice dated AD $1800-1920$ show a dust content of 10 mg/l, whereas by the 1950s the figure had increased twenty-fold to 200 mg/l (Davitaya, 1969).

Figure 7.6 shows that the average turbidity factor for the atmosphere (Linke turbidity) has increased by 30% in a decade (the dot-and-dash line). It also shows the effect of a natural source of turbidity, the Mount Agung (Bali) eruption of 1963. In the figure the dotted line represents the linear trend for the same period if the effects of the eruption are excluded from the computations.

An increase in atmospheric aerosols would have an effect on temperatures through its effect on the scattering and absorption of solar radiation. The exact effects, however, are still not clear, for whether added aerosols cause heating

246

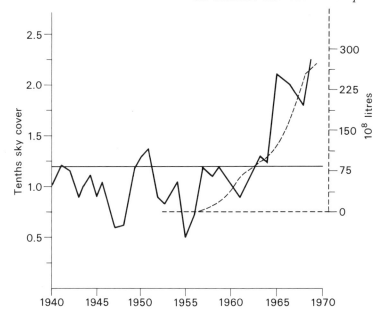

FIG. 7.5
The history of the annual high cloudiness at Denver, Colorado. The dashed line shows the growth in jet-fuel consumption by domestic commercial jet aircraft. (After Matthews et al., 1971, figure 33.1, reprinted from Man's impact on the climate, *ed. Matthews et al. by permission of The MIT Press, Cambridge, Massachusetts © 1971 by The Massachusetts Institute of Technology)*

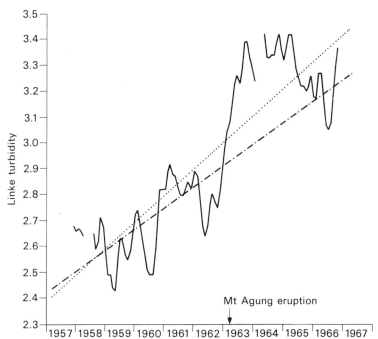

FIG. 7.6
Increasing turbidity at Mauna Loa Observatory (after Peterson in Bryson and Kutzbach, 1968, figure 1); symbols are explained in the text (p. 246)

or cooling of the earth–atmosphere system is a function not only of their intrinsic absorption–backscatter characteristics, but also of their location in the atmosphere with respect to such variables as cloud-cover, cloud reflectivity, and underlying surface reflectivity (Weare *et al.*, 1974). So, for example,

247

over ice caps 'grey' aerosol particles would cause warming of the atmosphere because they would be less reflective than the white snow surfaces beneath, whereas over a dark reflected surface they would reflect a greater amount of radiation, leading to a cooling (Peck, 1975). Thus precise quantitative assessment of the effects of an increased atmospheric aerosol content is hazardous, but Rasool and Schneider (1971) have suggested that an increase by a factor of four or five in global aerosol concentrations could be sufficient to lower temperatures by as much as 3.5°C.

Similarly Idso and Brazel (1978) and Brazel and Idso (1979) point to the two contrasting tendencies of dust — the backscattering effect producing cooling and the thermal blanketing effect causing warming. The latter mechanism would absorb some of the earth's thermal radiation that would otherwise escape to space, and then reradiate a portion of this radiation back to the land surface, causing a rise in surface temperatures. They believe that natural dust provided by volcanic emissions would tend to go into the stratosphere (where backscattering and cooling would be the prime consequences) whereas anthropogenic dust would tend to occur in the lower levels of the atmosphere causing thermal blanketing and warming.

Industrialization is not, however, the sole source of atmospheric particulate matter, nor is a change in temperature the only possible consequence. Bryson and Barreis (1967), for example, argue that intensive agricultural exploitation of desert margins such as in Rajasthan, India, would create a dust pall in the atmosphere by exposing greater areas of surface materials to deflation in dust storms. This dust pall, they believe, would change atmospheric temperature to the extent that convective activity, and thus rainfall, would be reduced. Observations on dust levels over the Atlantic during the drought years of the late 1960s and early 1970s in the Sahel suggest that the degraded surfaces of that time led to a great (× 3) increase of atmospheric dust (Prospero and Nees, 1977). There is thus the possibility that man-induced desertization creates dust which could in turn increase the degree of desertization by its effect on rainfall levels.

When assessing the likely consequences of human production of aerosols it needs to be borne in mind that the natural production of aerosol materials is of a very much higher order. This is brought out in table 7.3 which shows the estimated mass of global emissions of atmospheric particulate material for 1968. Nonetheless the data suggest that on a global scale man is now emitting 280 million tonnes/year of small particulate matter into the atmosphere compared to a natural rate of 1250 million tonnes/year, or a ratio of about 4.5 : 1.

Thermal pollution

One consequence of the burning of fossil fuels is the production of heat. This is probably most important on the local scale where it can be identified as the 'urban heat island' (see p. 254). On a broader scale the amount of energy used by man has been negligible compared both to the resources of solar energy and to the energy of photosynthesis by plants. On a global basis the total amount of heat released by all of mankind's activities is roughly 0.01% of the solar energy absorbed at the surface (Kellogg, 1978: 215) and such a small fraction would have a negligible effect on the total heat balance of the earth.

Vegetation and albedo

Incoming radiation of all wavelengths is partly absorbed and partly reflected. Albedo is the term used to describe the proportion of energy reflected and hence is a measure of the ability of the surface to reflect radiation.

Land-use changes create differences in albedo which have important effects on the energy balance, and hence on the water balance of an area. Tall rain forest may have an albedo as low as 9%, while the albedo of a desert is as high as 37% (table 7.4).

There has been increased interest recently in the possible

Source	Diameter < 5 µm	All sizes
Sea salt	500	1000
Converted natural sulphate	335	420
Natural windblown dust	250	500
Converted man-made sulphate	200	220
Converted natural hydrocarbons	75	75
Converted natural nitrates	60	75
Converted man-made nitrates	35	40
Man-made particles	30	135
Volcanoes	25	?
Converted man-made hydrocarbons	15	15
Forest fires	5	35
Meteoric debris	0	10
TOTAL	1530	2525 +

TABLE 7.3
Estimated mass of global emissions of atmospheric particulate material, 1968 (million tonnes)

Source: Matthews *et al.*, 1971, table 24.1

consequences of deforestation on climate through the effect of albedo change. Ground deprived of a vegetation cover as a result of deforestation and over-grazing (as in parts of the Sahel) has a very much higher albedo than ground covered in plants. This could affect temperature levels. Satellite imagery of the Sinai–Negev region of the Middle East shows a very great difference in image between the relatively dark Negev and the very bright Sinai–Gaza Strip area. This line coincides with the 1948–9 armistice line between Israel and Egypt and results from different land-use and population pressures. Otterman (1974) has suggested that this land-use-changed albedo has produced temperature changes of the order of 5°C.

TABLE 7.4
Albedo values for different land-use types

Surface type	Location	Albedo (%)
Tall rain forest	Kenya	9
Lake	Israel	11.3
Peat and moss	England and Wales	12
Pine forest	Israel	12.3
Heather moorland	England and Wales	15
Evergreen scrub (maquis)	Israel	15.9
Bamboo forest	Kenya	16
Conifer plantation	England and Wales	16
Citrus orchard	Israel	16.8
Towns	England and Wales	17
Open oak forest	Israel	17.6
Deciduous woodland	England and Wales	18
Tea bushes	Kenya	20
Rough grass hillside	Israel	20.3
Agricultural grassland	England and Wales	24
Desert	Israel	37.3

Source: from miscellaneous data in Pereira, 1973, collated by author

Charney and others (1975) have argued that the increase in surface albedo, resulting from a decrease in plant cover, would lead to a decrease in the net incoming radiation, and an increase in the radiative cooling of the air. As a consequence of this, they maintain, the air would sink to maintain thermal equilibrium by adiabatic compression, and cumulus convection and its associated rainfall would be suppressed. A positive feedback mechanism would appear at this stage, for the lower rainfall would in turn have an adverse effect on plants and lead to a further decrease in plant cover. However, this view is disputed by Ripley (1976) who suggests that Charney and his co-workers, while considering the effect of vegetative changes on albedo, completely ignored the effect of vegetation on evapotranspiration. He points out that vegetated surfaces are usually cooler than bare ground because much of the absorbed solar energy is used to evaporate water, and concludes from this that protection from overgrazing and deforestation might, in contrast to Charney's views, be expected to lower surface temperatures and thereby reduce rather than increase convection and precipitation.

The removal of the humid tropical rain forests, which is proceeding at a fast rate (see p. 38), has also been seen as a possible mechanism of anthropogenic climatic change through its effect on albedo. A model for such change as proposed by Potter *et al.* (1975) is shown in table 7.5.

Budyko (1974) believes that the present extension of irrigation to about 0.4% of the earth's surface (1.3% of the land surface) would decrease their albedo, possibly on average by 10%. The corresponding change of the albedo of the entire earth—atmosphere system would amount to about 0.03%; enough, according to Budyko, to maintain the global mean temperature at a level nearly 0.1°C higher than it would otherwise be.

Deforestation

↓

Increased surface albedo

↓

Reduced surface absorption of solar energy

↓

Surface cooling

↓

Reduced evaporation and sensible heat flux
from the surface

↓

Reduced convective activity and rainfall

↓

Reduced release of latent heat, weakened Hadley circulation
and cooling in the mid and upper troposphere

↓

Increased tropical lapse rates

↓

Increased precipitation in the latitude bands
5—25°N and 5—25°S, and a decrease in the
equator—pole temperature gradient

↓

Reduced meridional transport of heat and
moisture out of equatorial regions

↓

Global cooling and a decrease in precipitation
between 45—85°N and 40—60°S

TABLE 7.5
A simulation of the possible worldwide climatic impact of tropical deforestation through albedo change

Source: modified by author after Potter *et al.*, 1975

251

Forests and rain

The belief that forests can increase precipitation levels has a long history (Thornthwaite, 1956), and it has been the basis of action programmes in many lands. For example, the American Timber Culture Act of 1873 was passed in the belief that if settlers were induced to plant trees in the Great Plains and prairies, precipitation would be increased sufficiently to eliminate the climatic hazards to agriculture. On the other hand, at much the same time, the view was expressed that 'rain follows the plough'. Aughey, working in Nebraska, for example, believed that after the soil is 'broken' rain as it falls is absorbed by the soil 'like a huge sponge', and that the soil gives this absorbed moisture slowly back to the atmosphere by evaporation (cited by Thornthwaite, 1956: 569), and so increases the rainfall.

These two early and contradictory views illustrate the confusion that still surrounds this question today. Forests undoubtedly influence rates of evapotranspiration, the flow of streams, the level of ground-water, and microclimates, but there is little reliable evidence to suggest that regional rainfall is either significantly increased by afforestation or decreased by deforestation. Certainly schemes to augment the rainfall levels on desert margins by widespread planting of forest belts are likely to achieve relatively little, for the aridity of deserts and their margins is controlled dominantly by the gross features of the general circulation, especially the subsiding air associated with the big high-pressure cells of the sub-tropics.

Although forests may not necessarily have a proven effect on regional or continental rainfall levels they are far more effective than other vegetation types at trapping other types of precipitation, especially cloud, fog and mist. Hence deforestation or afforestation can affect water budgets through their effect on the degree to which non-rainfall precipitation is intercepted. For example, in Hawaii, Norfolk Island Pines (*Araucaria heterophylla*) in an area where the annual rainfall is 2600 mm, condensed an additional 760 mm from heavy cloud. In the San Francisco area, Parsons (1960) recorded about 250 mm of drip from a pine tree on the Berkeley Hills during each of four rainless summers. In Japan this phenomenon has been used to good effect: trees are planted along the coast to intercept the inland drift of sea fogs.

There is one other land-use change that may result in measurable changes in precipitation; namely large-scale crop irrigation in semi-arid regions. In the High Plain of the USA the region is normally one of sparse grasses and it has dry soils throughout the summer; evapotranspiration is then very low. In the last three decades irrigation has been developed through large parts of the area, greatly increasing summer evapotranspiration levels. Strahler and Strahler (1973: 147) report that increases in July rainfall amounting to 20—50% have been recorded over the main irrigated areas, compared with the average for the previous 60—70-year period. If irrigation is indeed responsible for the precipitation increase the mechanism remains uncertain. One possibility is that the added water vapour resulting from the increased evapotranspiration increases instability of the lower air layer and acts as a triggering mechanism to set off more frequent and more intense convection in the air mass above.

The possible effects of water diversion schemes

The levels of the Aral and Caspian Seas in Soviet Central Asia are falling, as are water-tables all over the wide continental region. There are proposals to divert some major rivers to help overcome these problems. However, this raises difficult questions 'because it appears to touch a peculiarly sensitive spot in the existing climatic regime of the northern hemisphere' (Lamb, 1977: 671). The low-salinity water which forms a 100—200 m upper layer to the Arctic Ocean is in part caused by the input of fresh water from the large Russian and Siberian rivers. This low-salinity water is the medium in which the pack ice at present covering the polar ocean is formed. Tapping of any large proportion of this river flow might augment the area of salt water in the Arctic Ocean and thereby reduce the area of pack ice correspondingly. Temperatures over large areas might rise, and this in turn might tend to change the position and alignment of the main thermal gradients in the northern hemisphere and, with them, the jet-stream and the development and steering of cyclonic activity.

Lakes

It has often been implied that the presence of a large body of inland water must modify the climate around its shores, and therefore that man-made lakes might have a significant effect on local or regional climates. Climatic changes produced by the construction of a reservoir are produced by a variety of factors (Vendrov, 1965): the creation of a body of water with a large heat capacity that reduces the continentality of the climate; the substitution of a water surface for a land surface and the rise of the ground-water level in the littoral zone supplying moisture to the evaporating surface (leading to a rise in relative humidity and a drop in temperature); and the substitution of a smooth water surface for a rough land surface (leading to a rise in wind velocity above the lake and in the littoral zone). Schemes have been put forward for augmenting desert rainfall by flooding desert basins in the Sahara, Kalahari, and Middle East (see, for example, Schwarz, 1923). However, whether evaporation from lake surfaces can raise local precipitation levels is open to question, for precipitation depends more on atmospheric instability than upon the humidity content of the air. Moreover, most lakes are too small to affect the atmosphere materially in depth so that their influence falls heavily under the sway of the regional circulation. In addition, one needs to remember that some of the world's driest deserts occur along coastlines. Thus a relatively small man-made lake would be even more impotent in creating rainfall (see Crowe, 1971: 443–50).

However, the climatic effect of man-made lakes is evident in other ways, notably in terms of a local reduction in frost hazard. In the case of the Rybinsk reservoir (c. 4500 km^2) in the USSR, it has been calcualted that the climatic influence extends 10 km from the lake and that the frost-free season has been extended by 5–15 days on average (D'Yakanov and Reteyum, 1965).

Urban climates

It has been said that 'the city is the quintessence of man's capacity to inaugurate and control changes in his habitat' (Detwyler and Marcus, 1972). One way in which such control becomes evident is in a study of urban climates. Individual urban areas can at times, with respect to their weather, 'have similar impacts as a volcano, a desert, and as an irregular forest' (Changnon, 1973: 146). Some of the changes that can be produced are listed in table 7.6.

In comparison with rural surfaces, city surfaces absorb significantly more solar radiation, because a higher proportion of the reflected radiation is retained by high walls and dark-coloured roofs of the city streets. The concreted city surfaces have both great thermal capacity and conductivity so that heat is stored during the day and released by night. By contrast the plant cover of rural areas acts like an insulating blanket, so that rural areas tend to experience relatively lower temperatures by day and night, an effect that is enhanced by the evaporation and transpiration taking place.

A second thermal change in cities which contributes to the development of the 'urban heat island' is the large amount of artificial heat produced in the city by industrial, commercial, and domestic users.

In general the highest temperature anomalies are associated with the densely built-up area near the city centre, and decrease markedly at the city perimeter. Observations in Hamilton, Ontario, and Montreal, Quebec, suggested temperature changes of 3.8 and 4.0°C respectively per kilometre (Oke, 1978). Temperature differences also tend to be highest during the night. The form of the urban temperature effect has often been likened to an 'island' protruding distinctly out of the cool 'sea' of the surrounding landscape. The rural–urban boundary exhibits a steep temperature gradient or 'cliff' to the urban heat island. Much of the rest of the urban

TABLE 7.6
Average changes in climatic elements caused by cities

Element	Parameter	Urban compared with rural (−, *less*; +, *more*)
Radiation	On horizontal surface	−15%
	Ultraviolet	−30% (winter); −5% (summer)
Temperature	Annual mean	+0.7°C
	Winter maximum	+1.5°C
	Length of freeze-free season	+2 to 3 weeks (possible)
Wind speed	Annual mean	−20 to −30%
	Extreme gusts	−10 to −20%
	Frequency of calms	+5 to 20%
Relative humidity	Annual mean	−6%
	Seasonal mean	−2% (winter); −8% (summer)
Cloudiness	Cloud frequency + amount	+5 to 10%
	Fogs	+100% (winter; +30% (summer)
Precipitation	Amounts	+5 to 10%
	Days	+10%
	Snow days	−14%

Phenomenon	Consequence
Heat production (the heat island)	Rainfall + Temperature +
Retention of reflected radiation by high walls and dark coloured roofs	Temperature +
Surface roughness increase	Wind − Eddying +
Dust increase (the dust dome)	Fog + Rainfall +(?)

Source: after H. Landsberg in Griffiths, 1976: 108

area appears as a 'plateau' of warm air with a steady but weaker horizontal gradient of increasing temperature towards the city centre. The urban core may be a 'peak' where the urban maximum temperature is found. The difference between this value and the background rural temperature defines the *urban heat island intensity* (ΔT_{u-r}) (Oke, 1978: 255).

Table 7.7 lists the average annual urban–rural temperature differences for several large cities. Values range from 0.6 to 1.3°C. The relationship between city size and urban–rural difference, however, is not necessarily linear; sizeable nocturnal temperature contrasts have been measured even in relatively small cities. Factors such as building density are at least as important as city size, and high wind velocities will tend to eliminate the heat island effect.

TABLE 7.7
Annual mean urban–rural temperature differences of cities

City	Temperature difference (°C)
Chicago, USA	0.6
Washington DC, USA	0.6
Los Angeles, USA	0.7
Paris, France	0.7
Moscow, USSR	0.7
Philadelphia, USA	0.8
Berlin, Germany	1.0
New York, USA	1.1
London, UK	1.3

Source: from data in Peterson, J. T., table 11.2, p. 136 and other sources, in Detwyler, 1971

Nonetheless, Oke (1978: 257) has found that the heat island intensity is related to city size. Using population as a surrogate of city size, ΔT_{u-r} is found to be proportional to the log of the population. Other interesting results of this study include the tendency for quite small centres to have a heat island, the observation that the maximum thermal modification is about 12°C, and the recognition of a difference in slope between the North American and the European relationships (figure 7.7). The explanation for this last result is not clear, but it may be related to the fact that population is a surrogate index of the central building density.

The existence of the urban heat island has a number of implications; city plants bud and bloom earlier, some birds are attracted to the thermally more favourable urban habitat, humans find the added warmth stressful if the city is already

256

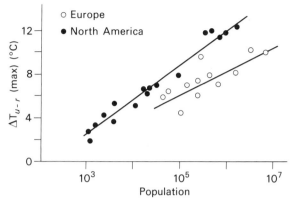

FIG. 7.7
Relationship between maximum observed heat island intensity (ΔT_{u-r}(max)) and population for North American and European settlements (after Oke, 1978, figure 8.16)

situated in a warm area, less winter space-heating is required, but, conversely, more summer air-conditioning is necessary.

The urban-industrial effects on clouds, rain, snowfall, and associated weather hazards such as hail and thunder are harder to measure and explain than the temperature changes (Darungo *et al.*, 1978). The changes can be related to various influences (Changnon, 1973: 143):

thermal induced upward movement of air,
increased vertical motions from mechanically induced turbulence,
increased cloud and raindrop nuclei,
industrial increases in water vapour.

Table 7.8 illustrates the differences in summer rainfall, thunderstorms, and hailstorms between various rural and urban areas in the USA. These data indicate that rainfall increases ranged from 9 to 27%, the incidence of the thunderstorms increased by 10 to 42%, and hailstorms increased by 67 to 430%.

TABLE 7.8
Areas of maximum increases (urban–rural difference) in summer rainfall and severe-weather events for eight American cities

City	Rainfall Percentage	Location*	Thunderstorms Percentage	Location*	Hailstorms Percentage	Location*
St Louis	+15	B	+25	B	+276	C
Chicago	+17	C	+38	A,B,C	+246	C
Cleveland	+27	C	+42	A,B	+ 90	C
Indianopolis	0	—	0	—	0	—
Washington DC	+ 9	C	+36	A	+ 67	B
Houston	+ 9	A	+10	A,B	+430	B
New Orleans	+10	A	+27	A	+350	A,B
Tulsa	0	—	0	—	0	—

* A = within city perimeter
  B = 8–24 km downwind
  C = 24–64 km downwind
Source: after Changnon, 1973, figure 1.5, p. 144

257

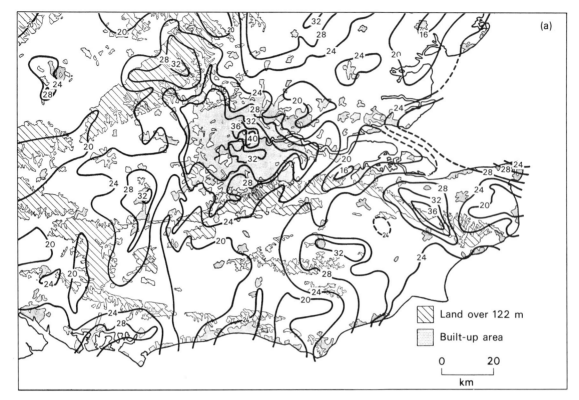

(a)

Land over 122 m

Built-up area

0   20

km

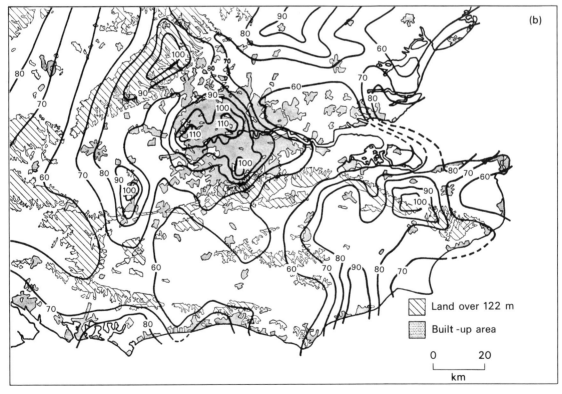

(b)

Land over 122 m

Built -up area

0   20

km

One of the most celebrated examples of the effect of a city on local precipitation is provided from the Chicago area. At La Porte, Indiana, some 48 km downwind of a large industrial complex between Chicago and Gary, Indiana, the amount of precipitation and the number of days with thunderstorms and hail have increased markedly since 1925. There has been a 30–40% increase in precipitation, and this seems to parallel the curve of increase in atmospheric pollution associated with the production curve of the Chicago iron and steel industrial complex. Moreover, peaks in steel production are seen to be associated with highs in the La Porte precipitation curve. Thunderstorms have also increased in frequency and since 1949 there have been 38% more thunderstorm days at La Porte than expected on the data from surrounding areas. Similarly the incidence of hail days is 59% greater over the total period, but reached 246% higher in the period 1951–65.

The industrial complex west of La Porte increases the number of condensation and freezing nuclei, the amount of water vapour and the air temperature (Changnon, 1968).

Another interesting example of the effects of major conurbations on precipitation levels is provided by the London area. In this case it seems that the mechanical effect of the city was dominant in creating localized maxima of precipitation both by being a mechanical obstacle to airflow on the one hand, and by causing frictional convergence of flow on the other (Atkinson, 1975). A long-term analysis of thunderstorm records in south-east England is highly suggestive — indicating the higher frequencies of thunderstorms over the conurbation compared to elsewhere (Atkinson, 1968). The similarity in the morphology of the thunderstorm isopleth and the urban area is striking (figures 7.8a and b). Moreover, Brimblecombe (1977) shows a steadily increasing thunderstorm frequency as the city has grown (figure 7.8c).

Similarly the detailed Metromex investigation of St Louis in the USA (Changnon, 1978) shows that in the summer the city affects precipitation and other variables within a distance of 40 km. Increases were found in various thunderstorm characteristics (about + 10 to + 115%), hailstorm conditions (+ 3 to 330%), various heavy rainfall characteristics (+ 35 to + 100%) and strong gusts (+ 90 to + 100%).

Two main factors are involved in the effect that cities have on winds: the rougher surface they present in comparison with rural areas; and the frequently higher temperatures of the city fabric.

Buildings, especially those in cities with a highly differentiated skyline, exert a powerful frictional drag on air moving

FIG. 7.8 (opposite)
Thunder in south-east England:
(a) total thunder rain in south-east England, 1951–60 expressed in inches (after Atkinson, 1968, figure 6)
(b) number of days with thunder overhead in south-east England, 1951–60 (after Atkinson, 1968, figure 5)

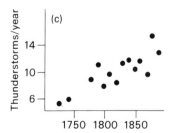

(c) thunderstorms per year in London (decadal means for whole year) (after Brimblecombe, 1977, figure 2)

over and around them (Chandler, 1976). This creates turbulence, with characteristically rapid spatial and temporal changes in both direction and speed. The average speed of the winds is lower in built-up areas than over rural areas, but Chandler found that in London when winds are light, speeds are greater in the inner city than outside, whereas the reverse relationship exists when winds are strong. The overall annual reduction of wind speed in Central London is about 6%, but for the higher velocity winds (more than 1.5 m/s) the reduction is more than doubled.

Studies in both Leicester and London, England, have shown that on calm, clear nights when the urban heat island effect is at its maximum there is a surface inflow of cool air towards the zones of highest temperatures. These so-called 'country breezes' have low velocities and become quickly decelerated by intense surface friction in the suburban areas.

Smoke haze and photochemical smog

The emission of miscellaneous pollutants, especially into the atmospheres of industrial cities, produces an increase in the number of days with smoke-haze conditions as in eighteenth and nineteenth century London (figure 7.9a). This is also illustrated by the data for some Illinois cities (figure 7.9b). Chicago, the only major city in the group, was the first to show a sizeable increase, though the moderately industrialized cities of Moline, Springfield, and Peoria also show sizeable increases beginning in the 1930s. Cairo, a non-industrial city with minimal twentieth-century growth, has had no great temporal increase in smoke-haze day frequencies (Changnon, 1973). In general, Landsberg (1970) estimates that on average the number of particles present over urban areas is 10 times greater than that over rural environs. The degree of pollution increases with city size (table 7.9). Many of these atmospheric particulates are hygroscopic and so tend to promote fog formation as water vapour readily condenses on them. However, although fog generally occurs more frequently in metropolitan areas, this is not true for very dense fog, for the heat island effect of greater warmth often prevents the thickest night fogs from reaching the densities reported in outlying districts (see table 7.10).

Local dust plumes can create changes in precipitation. A notable example of this comes from a coal-fired power station near Boulder, Colorado where fly-ash aerosols inadvertently seeded supercooled fog and induced local snowfall. The shape of the plume and the area of snowfall were the same (Darungo *et al.*, 1978).

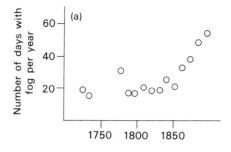

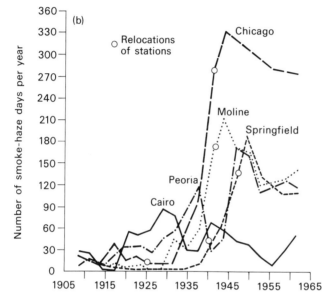

FIG. 7.9
(a) *Number of fogs per year in London as based on decadal means (after Brimblecombe, 1977, figure 1)*
(b) *Annual number of days with smoke-haze conditions in Illinois cities as based on a 3-year moving average (after Changnon, 1973, figure 1.5)*

Measures can be taken to control smoke haze. Edward I ordered a man put to torture for burning coal and fouling the air in the fourteenth century, while more recently the clear-air acts in Britain have led to a reduction in smog in major cities. In London, emissions of smoke had, by 1970, been reduced to one-tenth of what they were in 1956 (see figure 7.10) and in Manchester fog and sulphur dioxide levels decreased, while sunshine levels went up.

Smog produced by the burning of coal is often sulphurous. Sulphur dioxide (SO_2) is generated which in air may oxidize to sulphur trioxide (SO_3) which reacts with water vapour (H_2O) in the presence of catalysts to form sulphuric acid mist (H_2SO_4). The precipitation of such acid droplets with sulphate particles creates the so-called 'acid rain' which is liable to contaminate rivers and lakes. The acidification of fresh waters in Scandinavia may be caused by emissions from the industrial heartland of western Europe and Britain (see p. 271).

261

TABLE 7.9
Air pollution mechanisms

(a) URBAN–RURAL AIR POLLUTION GRADIENTS
(concentrations in $\mu g/m^3$)

	Urban	Non-urban		
		Proximate	Intermediate	Remote
Suspended particulates	102.0	45.0	40.0	21.0
Benzene soluble organics	6.7	2.5	2.2	1.1
Ammonium	0.9	1.22	0.28	0.15
Nitrate	2.4	1.40	0.85	0.46
Sulphate	10.1	10.0	5.29	2.51
Copper	0.16	0.16	0.08	0.06
Iron	1.41	0.56	0.27	0.15
Manganese	0.07	0.02	0.01	0.01
Nickel	0.02	0.01	0.00	0.00
Lead	1.11	0.21	0.10	0.00

(b) AIR POLLUTION RELATED TO CITY SIZE

Population class	Concentration ($\mu g/m^3$)		
	Total suspended particulates	SO_2	NO_2
Non-urban	25	10	33
c. 10 000	57	35	116
10 000	81	18	64
25 000	87	14	63
50 000	118	29	127
100 000	95	26	114
400 000	100	28	127
700 000	101	29	146
1 000 000	134	69	163
3 000 000	120	85	153

Source: Berry, 1974, tables 2.3 and 2.4, modified by author

TABLE 7.10
Fog frequencies in London

Location	Hours per year (based on four observations per day) with visibility less than			
	40 m	200 m	400 m	1000 m
Kingsway (Central London)	19	126	230	940
Kew (inner suburbs)	79	213	365	633
London Airport (outer suburbs)	46	209	304	562
South-east England (mean of 7 stations)	20	177	261	494

Source: after Chandler, 1965

38
In December 1952 the city of London was affected by severe smog. Visibility was reduced and smog masks had to be worn out-of-doors. Many people with weak chests died. Since then, because of legislation, the incidence of smog has declined markedly

While smog produced by the burning of coal is common, there is a second widespread type: the photochemical smog. The name originates from the fact that most of the less desirable properties of such fog result from the products of chemical reactions induced by sunlight (Cadle, in Matthews, *et al.*, 1971: 340 *et seq.*).

Photochemical smog appears 'cleaner' than other types of fog in the sense that it does not contain the very large particles of soot that are so characteristic of smog derived from coal-burning. However, the eye irritation and damage to

263

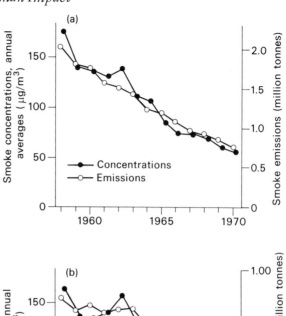

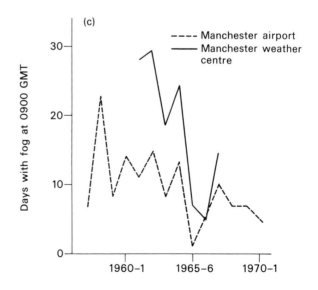

FIG. 7.10
*Trends in atmospheric quality
in the United Kingdom and in
the Manchester area:
(a) trends in regional smoke
concentrations and
emissions in the United
Kingdom
(b) trends in sulphur dioxide
concentrations and
emissions in the United
Kingdom
(c) changing number of days
with fog (visibility less than
1000 m in Manchester
(d) comparative urban annual
mean sulphur dioxide
concentrations;
(e) number of hours of sunshine
November to January in
Manchester
(after Chandler, 1976, figure
14.2 and Wood et al., 1974,
figures 14, 17, and 18)*

264

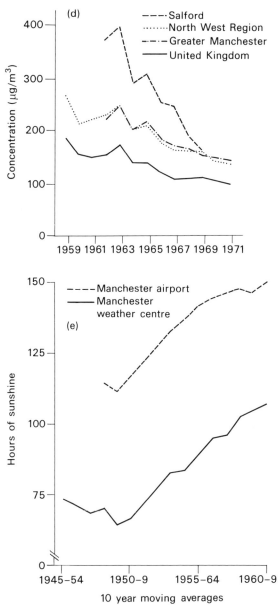

plant leaves which it produces make it unpleasant. Photochemical smog occurs particularly where there is large-
scale combustion of petroleum products, as in automobile-
dominated cities like Los Angeles. Its unpleasant properties
include a high lead content; also a series of chemical reactions
are triggered by sunlight (figure 7.11). For example, a photochemical decomposition of nitrogen dioxide into nitric oxide
and atomic oxygen occurs, and the atomic oxygen can react

265

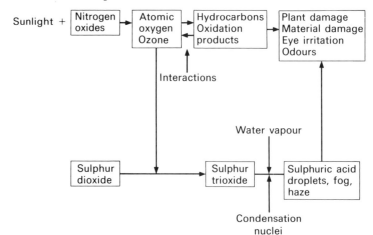

FIG. 7.11
Possible reactions involving primary and secondary pollutants. (After Haagen-Smit, in Reid E. Bryson and John E. Kutzbach, Air Pollution (Association of American Geographers, 1968), figure 4. Reprinted by permission.)

with molecular oxygen to form ozone. Further ozone may be produced by the reaction of atomic oxygen with various hydrocarbons.

Photochemical smogs are not universal. Because sunlight is a crucial factor in their development they are most common in the tropics or during seasons of strong sunshine. Their especial notoriety in Los Angeles is due to a meteorological setting dominated at times by sub-tropical anticyclones with weak winds, clear skies, and a subsidence inversion, combined with the general topographic situation and the high vehicle density (> 1500 vehicles/km^2).

Because of the presence of particulate matter, the duration of bright sunshine shows significant reductions over urban areas, and in large cities a progressive decline can be traced towards the city centre. Over the period 1921–50, for example, the mean daily sunshine duration outside London was 4.33 h, whereas in the Central Area it was 3.60 h (Chandler, 1965). Since that time, on account of clean air legislation, the situation has improved.

Rainmaking and other methods of deliberate climate modification

The most fruitful attempts by man to augment natural precipitation have been through cloud seeding. Rainmaking experiments of this type are based on three main assumptions (Chorley and More, 1967: 159).

1　Either the presence of ice crystals in a super-cooled cloud is necessary to release snow and rain; or the presence of comparatively large water droplets is necessary to initiate the coalescence process.

2   Some clouds precipitate inefficiently or not at all, because these components are naturally deficient.

3   The deficiency can be remedied by seeding the clouds artificially, either with solid carbon dioxide (dry ice) or silver iodide to produce crystals, or by introducing water droplets or large hygroscopic nuclei.

These methods of seeding are not universally productive. Under conditions of orographic lift and in thunderstorm cells, when nuclei are insufficient to generate rain by natural means, some augmentation may be attained, especially if cloud temperatures are of the order of −10 to −15°C. The increase of precipitation gained under favourable conditions may be of the order of 10–20% in any one storm. In lower latitudes, where cloud-top temperatures frequently remain above 0°C, silver iodide or dry ice seeding is not applicable. Methods have been introduced therefore whereby small water droplets of 50 μm diameter are sprayed into the lower layers of deep clouds so the growth of cloud particles will be stimulated by coalescence.

Other techniques of warm cloud seeding include the feeding of hygroscopic particles into the lower air layers near the updraught of a growing cumulus cloud (Breuer, 1980).

The results of the many experiments now carried out on cloud seeding are still controversial, very largely because we have an imperfect understanding of the physical processes involved. This means that the evidence has to be evaluated on a statistical rather than a scientific basis, so that although precipitation may occur after many seeding trials, it is difficult to decide to what extent artificial stimulation and augmentation is responsible as opposed to natural mechanisms. It also needs to be remembered that this form of planned weather modification applies to small areas for short periods of time. As yet, no means exist to change precipitation appreciably over large areas on a sustained basis.

Other types of deliberate climatic modification have also been attempted (Hess, 1974). For example, it has been thought that the production of many more hailstone embryos by silver iodide seeding will yield smaller hailstones which would both be less damaging and more likely to melt before reaching the ground. Some results in Russia have been encouraging but one cannot exclude the possibility that seeding may sometimes even increase hail damage (Atlas, 1977). Similar experiments have been conducted in lightning-suppression. The concept here is to produce in a thundercloud, again by silver iodide seeding, an abnormal abundance of ice crystals that would act as added corona points and thus relieve the electrical potential gradient by corona discharge before a lightning strike could develop (Panel on Weather and Climate Modification, 1966: 4–8).

Hurricane modification is perhaps the most desirable aim of those seeking to suppress severe storms, because of the extremely favourable benefit-to-cost ratio of the work. The principal once again is that by introducing freezing nuclei into the ring of clouds around the hurricane centre one would trigger the release of the latent heat of fusion in the eye-wall cloud system which, in turn, would diminish the maximum horizontal temperature gradients in the storm and cause a hydrostatic lowering of the surface temperature. This, eventually, should lead to a weakening of the damaging winds (K. Smith, 1975: 212). A 15% reduction in maximum winds is theoretically possible.

Much research has been devoted in the Soviet Union to the possibility of removing the Arctic Sea ice and to ascertain effects of such action on the climate of northern areas (see Lamb, 1977: 660). One proposal was to dam the Bering Strait, thereby blocking off water flow from the Pacific. The assumption was that more, and warmer, Atlantic water would be drawn into the Central Arctic, improving temperature conditions in that area. Critics have pointed to the possibility of adverse changes in temperatures elsewhere, together with undesirable change in precipitation character and amount.

Fog dispersal, vital for airport operation, is another aim of weather modification. Seeding experiments have shown that fog consisting of supercooled droplets can be cleared by using liquid propane or dry ice. In very cold fogs this seeding method causes rapid transformation of water droplets into ice particles.

In regions of high temperature dark soils often become overheated, and the resultant high evapotranspiration rates lead to moisture deficiencies. Applications of white powders (India and Israel) or of aluminium foils (Hungary) increase the reflection from the soil surface and reduce the rate at which insulation is absorbed. Temperatures of the soil surface and subsurface are lowered (by as much as 10°C) and soil moisture is conserved (by as much as 50%).

The planting of windbreaks is an even more important attempt by man to modify local climate deliberately. Shelter-belts have been in use for centuries in many windswept areas of the globe, both to protect soils from blowing and to protect the plants from the direct effects of high-velocity winds. The size and effectiveness of the protection depends on their height, density, shape, and frequency. However, the belts may have consequences for microclimate beyond those for which they were planted. Evaporation rates are curtailed; snow is arrested on, and its melting waters are available for the fields; but temperatures may become more excessive in the stagnant space in the lee of the belt, creating an increase in frost danger.

Traditional farmers in many societies have been aware of the virtues of microclimate management (Wilken, 1972). They manage shade by employing layered cropping systems or by covering the plants and soil with mulches; they may deliberately try to modify albedo conditions — Tibetan farmers, for example, reportedly throw dark rocks onto snow-covered fields to promote late spring melting; and in the Paris area of France some very dense stone walls were constructed to absorb and radiate heat.

Conclusion: the climatic impact

We can attempt to make certain general conclusions about the human impact on climate. The first is that man is undoubtedly effective, sometimes deliberately, at the microclimatic level by changing the nature of the land surface. He is also causing highly important changes, mainly inadvertently, in his environment at the scale of the individual city. When it comes to a consideration of larger scales (regional plus global) there is a great deal more controversy about the extent and direction of his impact, which is at such scales almost wholly inadvertent.

The fact remains that it is difficult to separate the effect of natural changes from those that may have been brought about by man. Moreover, we still know insufficient to be able to make deliberate climatic modifications of fully proven effectiveness even at a local scale. Finally, as some of the examples that have been discussed show, the possible feedback effects of some schemes for climatic or hydrological modification (such as the diversion of Siberian rivers into the Arctic) could be hazardous, given our present state of limited knowledge.

Air pollution: some further effects

This chapter has already made much reference to the way in which man has changed the turbidity of the atmosphere and the gases within it. However, the consequences of air pollution go further than either their direct impact on human health or their impact on local, regional, and global climates.

269

The Human Impact

FIG. 7.12
Trends in atmospheric quality:
(a) The chart shows the lead
content of the Greenland ice
cap due to atmospheric
fallout of the mineral
on the snow surface. A
dramatic upturn in
worldwide atmospheric
levels of lead occurred at the
beginning of the Industrial
Revolution of the
nineteenth century and again
after the more recent spread
of the automobile (after
Murozumi et al., 1969:
1247)
(b) The sulphate concentration
on a sea-salt free basis in
north-west Greenland glacier
ice samples as a function of
year. The curve represents
the world production of
thermal energy from coal,
lignite, and crude oil
(modified after Koide and
Goldberg, 1971, figure 1)

First of all, the atmosphere acts as a major channel for the transfer of pollutants from one place to another. Thus some harmful substances have been transferred long distances from their source of emission. DDT is one example; lead is another. Thus, since the start of the Industrial Revolution the lead content of the Greenland ice cap, although far removed from the source of the pollutant (which is largely derived from either industrial or automobile emissions) has gone up very substantially (figure 7.12a). The same applies to its sulphate content (figure 7.12b). The analysis of pond sediments from a remote part of North America (Yosemite) indicates that lead levels there are also elevated as a result of human activities, being more than twenty times the natural levels. The lead, which came in from atmospheric sources, shows a five-fold elevation in the plants of the area and a fifty-fold elevation in the animals compared with natural levels (Shirahata *et al.*, 1980). Some estimates have also been made of the total quantities of heavy metals that man is emitting into the atmosphere compared with emissions from natural sources (Nriagu, 1979). The increase is eighteen-fold for lead, nine-fold for cadmium, seven-fold for zinc, and three-fold for copper.

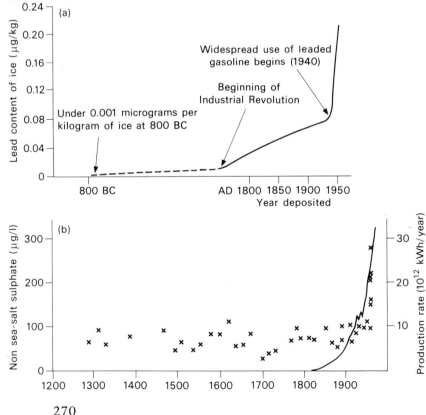

A second example of the possible widespread nature and ramifying ecological consequences of atmospheric pollution is provided by 'acid rain' (see p. 76 and Likens and Bormann, 1974). Normally, water in the atmosphere which is in equilibrium with CO_2 will have a pH of about 5.7. However, recently much stronger acids have been observed in snow and rain in the north-east USA, with pH values as low as 2.1, while in Scotland in one storm the rain was the acidic equivalent to vinegar (pH 2.4). In the same areas the annual acidity values average around pH 4 (see figure 5.25). The degree of acidulation of precipitation appears to be increasing (figure 7.13), though data are sparse, and Likens and Bormann propose that paradoxically this increase may be caused by two factors: the replacement of coal by oil and natural gas; and the implementation of air pollution control measures (particularly increasing the height of smoke stacks and installing particle precipitators). These appear to have transformed a local 'soot problem' into a regional 'acid rain problem'. Coal burning put out a great deal of sulphate but was neutralized by high calcium contents in the relatively unfiltered coal smoke emissions. Natural-gas burning creates less sulphate but that which is produced is not neutralized. The new higher chimneys pump the smoke high so that it is dispersed over wide areas.

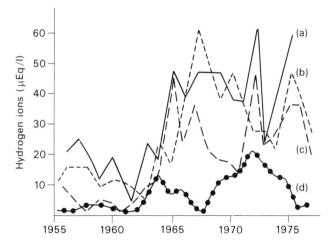

FIG. 7.13
Acidity of rain and snow for four Scandinavian localities. The acidity is expressed in terms of the annual volume-weighted concentration of hydrogen ions in microequivalents per litre:
(a) = Lista, Norway
(b) = Ås, Norway
(c) = Kise, Norway
(d) = Kiruna, Sweden
(modified after Likens et al., 1979: 45)

The ecological consequences of this acid rain are still largely the subject of conjecture but possible effects include a reduction in plant growth, changes in the rate at which soil nutrients are leached, the acidification of lakes and rivers (with consequent effects on flora and fauna), and the corrosion of engineering structures (Likens *et al.*, 1979).

It is perhaps worth concluding this chapter by reiterating

the fact that the variability of air pollution in both space and time, while undoubtedly owing much to man, is also highly dependent on natural conditions, and in particular on meteorological conditions (R. Thompson, 1978). This is brought out in figure 7.14. Climatic factors control the efficiency with which effluents are diluted and dispersed away from primary sources, while local relief and micro-climatic circumstances modify the interaction between the emission of pollutants and the atmosphere. Moreover, as we have already stated, not all pollutants are man-made: the vast majority of nitrogen oxides are emitted by bacteria rather than by car exhausts, most chlorides in rainwater come from the oceans, and a considerable proportion of atmospheric dust is injected into the air by such mechanisms as volcanic eruptions and by dust storms removing fine silt from glacial outwash fans or desert basins.

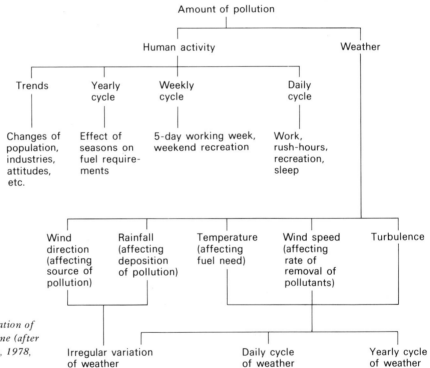

FIG. 7.14
Some causes of the variation of air pollution through time (after Meetham, in Thompson, 1978, figure 1)

CHAPTER 8

Conclusion

The power of non-industrial and pre-industrial man

Thus far in this book we have looked at the impact that human societies have had on the different components of man's physical environment: vegetation, animals, soil, water, landforms, and climate. It has become apparent that Marsh was correct over a century ago to express his cogently argued views on the importance of man as an agent of environmental change. Since his time the impact that man has had on his environment has increased, as has our awareness of this impact. However, it is worth making the point here that although much of the concern that is expressed about the undesirable effects that man is having on his own environment tends to focus on the role played by sophisticated industrial societies, this should not blind us to the fact that many highly important changes in environment were and are being achieved by non-industrial societies. In recent years it has become apparent that in particular fire was available to early man to achieve substantial alteration to vegetation so that plant assemblages that were once thought to be natural climatic climaxes may in reality be in part anthropogenic fire climaxes. This applies to many areas of both savanna and mid-latitude grassland (see p. 41). Such alteration of natural vegetation has been shown to pre-date the arrival of European settlers in the Americas, New Zealand, and elsewhere and the effects of fire may have been compounded by the use of the stone axe and by the grazing effects of domestic animals. In turn the removal and modification of vegetation would have led to adjustments in fauna. It is also apparent that soil erosion resulting from vegetation removal has a long history and that it was regarded as a threat by the classical authors. Recent studies (see p. 53) tend to suggest that some of the major environmental changes in Highland Britain and similar parts of western Europe that were once explained by climatic changes can be more effectively explained by the activities of Mesolithic and Neolithic peoples. This applies, for example, to the decline in the numbers of certain plants in the pollen record and to the development of peat bogs and podzolization (see p. 117). Even soil salinization was brought about at an early date because of the adaptation of irrigation practices in arid areas, and its effects on crop yields were noted in Iraq more than 4000 years ago (see p. 112). Similarly (see p. 98) there is an increasing body of evidence that early man in his capacity as an hunter may have caused great changes in the world's mega-fauna as early as 11 000 years ago.

In spite of the increasing pace of world industrialization and urbanization, it is ploughing and pastoralism which are responsible for many of our most serious environmental problems and which are still causing some of the most widespread changes in the landscape. Thus soil erosion brought about by agriculture is, it can be argued, a more serious pollutant of the world's waters than is industry; many of the habitat changes which so affect wild animals are brought about through agricultural expansion (see p. 80); and soil salinization and desertification can be regarded as two of the most serious problems facing the human race. Land-use changes, such as the conversion of forests to fields, may be at least as effective in causing anthropogenic changes in climate as the more celebrated burning of fossil fuels and emission of industrial aerosols into the atmosphere. The liberation of CO_2 into the atmosphere by means of agricultural expansion, changes in surface albedo values, and the production of dust, are all major ways in which agriculture may modify world climates (see p. 242).

The proliferation of impacts

A further point we can make is that with changes in technology the number of ways in which man is affecting his environment is proliferating. It is these recent changes, because of the uncertainty which surrounds them and the limited amount of experience we have of their potential effects, which have caused greatest concern. Thus it is only since the Second World War, for example, that man has had nuclear reactors for electricity generation, that he has used powerful pesticides such as DDT, and that he has sent supersonic aircraft into the stratosphere. Likewise, it is only since around the turn of the century that the world's oil resources have been extensively exploited, that chemical fertilizers have become widely used, and that the internal combustion engine has revolutionized the scale and speed of transport and communications.

Above all, however, the complexity, frequency, and magnitude of impacts is increasing, partly because of greatly increasing human populations and partly because of a general increase in *per capita* consumption. Thus some traditional methods of land-use such as shifting agriculture (see p. 39) and nomadism which have been regarded as involving some sort of equilibrium with the environment, seem to break down and to cause environmental deterioration when population pressures exceed a particular threshold.

This is illustrated for shifting agriculture systems by figure 8.1 which shows the relationship of soil fertility levels to cycles of slash-and-burn agriculture. Fertility can be maintained (figure 8.1a) under the long cycles characteristic of low-density populations. However, as population levels increase, the cycles of necessity become shorter, and soil fertility levels are not maintained, thereby imposing greater stresses on the land (figure 8.1b).

(a) Long cycle

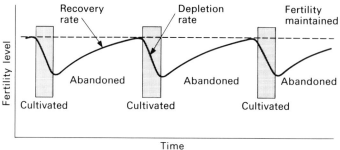

(b) Short cycle

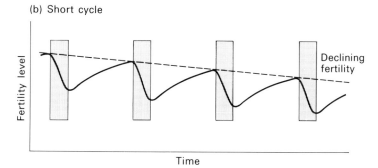

FIG. 8.1
Land rotation and population density. The graphs show the relationship of soil fertility to cycles of slash-and-burn agriculture. In (a) fertility levels are maintained under the long cycles characteristic of low-density populations. In (b) fertility levels are declining under the shorter cycles characteristic of increasing population density. Notice that in both diagrams the curves of both depletion and recovery have the same slope (after Haggett, 1979, figure 8.4)

At the other end of the spectrum increasing incomes, leisure, and ease of communication, have generated a greater demand for recreation and tourism in the developed nations and these have created additional environmental problems (see p. 79), especially in coastal and mountain areas (see, for example, Bayfield, 1973). Examples are given in table 8.1. Likewise, it is apparent when one considers the range of possible impacts of one major type of industrial development they are very considerable. As table 8.2 indicates, the exploitation of an oilfield and all the activities that involves (e.g., pipelines, new roads, refineries, drilling, etc.) have a wide range of likely effects on land, air, water, and organisms.

TABLE 8.1
*Some environmental
consequences of recreation*

Desecration of cave formations by speleologists
Trampling by human feet leading to soil compaction
Nutrient additions at camp sites by man and his pets
Decrease in soil temperatures because of snow compaction by
   snowmobiles
Footpath erosion and off-road vehicle erosion
Dune reactivation by trampling
Vegetation change due to trampling and collecting
Creation of new habitats by cutting trails and clearing camp sites
Pollution of lakes and inland waterways by gasoline discharge from
   outboard motors and by human waste
Creation of game reserves and protection of ancient domestic breeds
Disturbance of wildlife by proximity of persons and by hunting,
   fishing, and shooting
Conservation of woodland for pheasant shooting

Changes are reversible

It is evident that while man has achieved many undesirable and often unexpected changes in his environment he often has the capacity to modify the rate of such changes, or to reverse them. There are cases where this is not possible: once soil has been eroded from an area it cannot be restored, once a plant or animal has become extinct it cannot be brought back, and once a laterite iron pan has become established it is difficult to destroy.

However, through the work of George Perkins Marsh and other workers, man became aware that many of the changes that had been set in train needed to be reversed or reduced in degree. Sometimes this has simply involved giving up a practice (such as the cavalier use of DDT) which proved to be undesirable, or replacing it with another which had been less detrimental in effect. Often, however, specific measures have been taken (table 8.3) which have involved deliberate decisions of management and conservation. Many of these measures have been successful (see p. 261) while others have themselves created as many problems as they were intended to solve. This applies, for example, to certain schemes for the reduction of coast erosion (see p. 233).

(see p. 233)

TABLE 8.2

Qualitative environmental impacts of mineral industries with particular reference to an oil field

Facility	Direction of the impact and reaction of the environment			
	Land	Air	Water	Biocenosis
Well	Alienation of land land surface Extraction of oil, associated gas, ground-water Pollution by crude oil, refined products, drilling mud, Disturbance of of internal structure of soil and subsoil Destruction of soil	Pollution by associated gas and volatile hydrocarbons, products of combustion	Withdrawal of surface water and ground-water Pollution by crude oil and refined products; salination of fresh water Disturbance of water balance of both subsurface and and surface waters	Pollution by crude oil and refined products Disturbance and destruction over a limited surface area
Pipeline	Alienation of land Accidental oil spills Disturbance of land-forms and internal structure of soil and subsoil	Pollution by volatile hydrocarbons		Disturbance and destruction over a limited surface area
Motor roads	Alienation of land Pollution by oil products Disturbance of landforms and internal structure of soil and subsoil	Pollution by combustion products. volatile hydrocarbons, sulfur dioxide, nitrogen oxides		Pollution by combustion products Disturbance and destruction over limited surface area
Collection point	Alienation of land Pollution by crude oil and refined products (spills) Disturbance of internal structure of soil and subsoil	Pollution by volatile hydrocarbons		Disturbance and destruction over limited surface area

Source: Denisova, 1977, table 2, p. 650

The concern with preservation and conservation has been a long one, with many important landmarks; the interest has increased dramatically in recent years. In many countries major developments in land-use, construction, and industrialization have to be preceded by the production of an Environmental Impact Assessment.

In some countries and in connection with particular species conservation and protection has had a long and sometimes successful impact. In Britain, for example, the Wild Birds Protection Act dates back to 1880, and the Sea Birds Protection Act even further — to 1869. The various acts have been modified and augmented over the years to outlaw egg collecting, pole trapping, plumage importation, and the capture or possession of various species. The effectiveness of the various bird protection Acts can be measured in real terms. Over the last 50 years no species have been lost as British breeding birds due to lack of protection — the only major loss has been the Kentish plover which was in any case on the edge of its range. Perhaps more importantly several species have successfully recolonized Britain, the most celebrated being the avocet and the osprey. Today both are firmly established, together with other species lost in the nineteenth century: the black-tailed godwit, the goshawk and the bittern. Also as a result of protection the red kites of Wales have not only survived but increased in numbers, and the peregrine falcon maintains its largest numbers in Europe outside Spain.

One further ground which gives some basis for hope that man may be reconciled with his environment is that there are some signs of a widespread tendency for public attitudes

TABLE 8.3 *A six-stage model for wildlife conservation*	1 Immediate physical protection from man and from changes in the environment
	2 Educational efforts to awaken the public to the need of protection and so to gain acceptance of protective measures
	3 Life history studies of the species so as to determine their habitat requirements and the causes of their population decline
	4 Dispersion of the stock so as to prevent loss of the species by disease or by a chance event such as fire
	5 Captive breeding of the species so as to assure higher survival of young, to aid research, and to reduce the chances of catastrophic loss
	6 Habitat restoration or rehabilitation when this is necessary before re-introducing the species

Source: after Denson (1970)

39
*The impact of recreation
pressures is well displayed at a
prehistoric hill-fort, Bradbury
Rings, Dorset. Pedestrians and
motorcyclists have caused
severe erosion of the ramparts*

to nature and the environment to be changing. These changing social values, combined with scientific facts, influence
political action. This point of view, which acts as an antidote
for some of the more pessimistic views of the world's future,
has recently been elegantly argued by Ashby (1978). He
contends that the rudiments of a healthy environmental
ethic are developing, and explains (pp. 84—5):

Its premise is that respect for nature is more moral than lack of respect
for nature. Its logic is to put the Teesdale Sandwort...into the same
category of value as a piece of Ming porcelain; the Yosemite Valley in
the same category as Chartres cathedral; a Suffolk landscape in the
same category as a painting of the landscape by Constable. Its justifica-
tion for preserving these and similar things is that they are unique, or
irreplaceable, or simply part of the fabric of nature, just as Chartres
and the painting by Constable are part of the fabric of civilization; also
that we do not understand how they have acquired their durability and
what all the consequences would be if we destroyed them.

279

The susceptibility to change

Ecosystems respond in different ways to the human impact, and some are more vulnerable to man-made perturbation than others.

It has often been thought, for example, that complex ecosystems are more stable than simple ones. Thus in Clements' theory of Succession the tendency toward community stabilization was ascribed in part to an increasing level of integration of community functions. As Goodman (1975: 238) has expressed it:

In general the predisposition to expect greater stability of complex systems was probably a combined legacy of eighteenth century theories of political economics, esthetically and perhaps religiously motivated attraction to the belief that the wondrous variety of nature must have some purpose in an orderly world, and ageless folkwisdom regarding eggs and baskets.

Indeed as Murdoch (1975) has pointed out, it makes good intuitive sense that a system with many links, or 'multiple fail-safes' is more stable than one with few links or feedback loops. As an example, if a type of herbivore is attacked by several predatory species, the loss of any one of these species will be less likely to allow the herbivore to erupt or explode in numbers than if only one predator species were present and that single predator type disappeared.

Various other arguments have been marshalled to support the idea that great diversity and complexity causes greater ability to minimize the magnitude, duration, and irreversibility of changes brought about by some external perturbation such as man (Noy-Meir, 1974). It has been stated that natural systems, which are generally more diverse than artificial (man-made) systems such as crops or laboratory populations, are also more stable. Likewise, the tropical rain forest has been thought of as more diverse and more stable than simpler temperate communities, while simple Arctic ecosystems, exemplified by unstable lemming populations, are in turn held to be less stable than the more diverse temperate communities. In the same way the simple ecosystems of oceanic islands have always appeared highly vulnerable to disturbance brought about by anthropogenic plant and animal introductions (see p. 87).

However, considerable doubt has been expressed recently as to whether this classic concept of the causal linkage between diversity/complexity and stability is entirely valid (see, for example, Hurd *et al.*, 1971). Murdoch (1975) indicates that there is no convincing field evidence that diverse natural communities are in general more stable than simple ones. He cites various papers which show that fluctuations of microtine rodents (lemmings, field voles, etc.) are as violent in relatively complex temperate zone ecosystems as they are in the less complex Arctic zone ecosystems. This is supported by Goodman (1975, p. 239) who writes:

As for the apparent stability of tropical biota, that could well be an illusion attributable to insufficient study of bewilderingly complex assemblages in which many species are so poorly represented in samples of feasible size that even considerable fluctuations might go undetected. Indeed, there are countervailing anecdotes regarding ecological instability in the tropics, such as recent reports of an insect virtually defoliating the wild Brazil-nut trees in Bolivia and of monkeys succumbing in large numbers to epidemics.

He goes on to add: 'There is growing awareness of the surprising susceptibility of the rain forest ecosystem to man-made perturbation'. This is a point of view supported by May (1979), and discussed by Hill (1975). He points out that a very high species-diversity is frequently associated with areas which have relatively constant physical environmental conditions over the course of a year and a series of years. The rain forest may be construed to be such an environment, and one where this constancy has allowed the presence of many specialized species, each pursuing a narrow range of activities. It has been argued that because of the high degree of specialization of the indigenous species they have a low ability to recover from major stresses caused by the intervention of man.

Goodman (1975) has also queried the sufficiency of the argument based on the apparent instability of island ecosystems, suggesting that islands, being evolutionary backwaters and dead-ends, may accumulate species that are especially susceptible to competitive or exploitative displacement. Lack of diversity may not in this case therefore necessarily be the sole or prime cause of instability.

The apparent instability of agricultural compared to natural communities is also often put down to lack of diversity (see p. 21), and indeed modern agriculture does involve great ecosystem simplification. However, such instability as there is may not, once again, necessarily result from the simplification. Other factors could promote instability: agricultural communities are disrupted, even destroyed, more frequently and more massively as part of the cultivation process than those natural systems we tend to think of as stable; and the component species of natural systems are co-evolved (co-adapted), and this is not usually true of agricultural communities. As Murdoch (1975: 799) suggests it may be that:

natural systems are more stable than crop systems because their inter-acting species have had a long shared evolutionary history....In contrast with these natural communities the dominant plant species of a crop system is thrust into an often alien landscape...the crops have undergone radical selection in breeding programmes, often losing their genetic defence mechanisms.

Thus the ideas that complex natural ecosystems will be less susceptible to man-made perturbation and that simple artificial ecosystems will inevitably be unstable are not necessarily tenable. Nonetheless, it is apparent that there are differences in susceptibility between different ecosystem types, and these differences may result from factors other than the degree of diversity and complexity (Cairns and Dickson, 1977).

Some systems tend to be *vulnerable*. Lakes, for example, are natural traps and sumps and are thus more vulnerable to the effects of disadvantageous inputs than are rivers (which are continually receiving new inputs) or oceans (which are so much larger). Other systems display the property of *elasticity* – the ability to recover from damage. This may be because nearby epicentres exist to provide organisms to re-invade a damaged system. Small, isolated systems will often tend to possess low elasticity (see p. 103). Two of the most important properties, however, are termed *resilience* (being a measure of the number of times a system can recover after stress) and *inertia* (the ability to resist displacement of structural and functional characteristics).

Two systems which display resilience and inertia are deserts and estuaries. In both cases their indigenous organisms are highly accustomed to variable environmental conditions. Thus most desert fauna and flora evolved in an environment where the normal pattern is one of more or less random alternations of short favourable periods and long stress periods. They have pre-adapted resilience (Noy-Meir, 1974) so that they can tolerate extreme conditions, have the ability for rapid recovery, have various delay and trigger mechanisms (in the case of plants) and have flexible and opportunistic eating habits (in the case of beasts). Estuaries, on the other hand, though the subject of increasing human pressures, also display some resilience. The vigour of their water circulation continuously and endogenously renews the supply of water, food, larvae, etc.; this aids recovery. Also, many species have biological characteristics which provide special advantages in estuarine survival (Cronin, 1967). These characteristics usually protect the species against the natural violence of estuaries and they are often helpful in resisting external forces like man.

Man or nature?

From many of the examples given in this book it is apparent that in many cases of environmental change it is not possible to state without risk of contradiction that it is man rather than nature which is responsible. Most systems are complex and man is but one component of them, so that many of his actions can lead to end-products which are intrinsically similar to those that may be produced by natural forces. It is a case of equifinality, whereby different processes can lead to basically similar results. Man is not always responsible for some of the changes with which he is credited. This book has given many examples of this problem and a selection is presented in table 8.4. The decipherment of cause is often a ticklish problem given the intricate interdependence of different components of ecosystems, the frequency and complexity of environmental changes, and the varying relaxation times that different ecosystem components may have when subject to a new impulse. This problem plainly does not apply to the same extent to changes which have been brought about deliberately and knowingly by man, but it does apply to the many cases where man may have initiated change inadvertently and non-deliberately.

This fundamental problem means that environmental impact statements of any kind are extremely difficult to make. As we have seen, man has been living on the earth and modifying it in different degrees for several millions of years, so that it is problematical to reconstruct the environment before the intervention of man. We seldom have any clear baseline against which to measure man-made changes. Moreover, even without man's intervention, the environment would be in a perpetual state of flux at a great many different time-scales (Goudie, 1977). In addition, as Wall and Wright (1977: 3) have demonstrated, there are spatial and temporal discontinuities between cause and effect. For example, erosion in one locality may lead to deposition in another, while destruction of key elements of an animal's habitat may lead to population declines throughout its range. Likewise in a time context, a considerable interval may elapse before the full implications of an

	Causes		Page reference
Change	Natural	Anthropogenic	
Late Pleistocene animal extinction	Climatic	Hunting	97
Death of savanna trees	Soil salinization through climatically induced ground-water rise	Over-grazing	—
Desertification in semi-arid areas	Climatic change	Over-grazing, etc.	45
Holocene peat bog development in Highland Britain	Climatic change and progressive soil deterioration	Deforestation and ploughing	117
Holocene elm and linden decline	Climatic change	Feeding and stalling of animals	54
Tree encroachment into alpine pastures in USA	Temperature amelioration	Cessation of burning	—
Gully development	Climatic change	Land-use change	208
Early twentieth century climatic warming	Changes in solar emission and volcanic activity	CO_2-generated greenhouse effect	241
Increasing coast recession	Rising sea level	Disruption of sediment supply	231
Increasing coastal flood risk	Rising sea level, natural subsidence	Pumping of aquifers creating subsidence	203
Increasing river flood intensity	Higher intensity rainfall	Creation of drainage ditches	124
Ground collapse	Karstic process	Dewatering by over-pumping	201

TABLE 8.4
Man or nature?
Some examples

activity are apparent. Also, because of the complex interactions between different components of different environmental systems and subsystems it is almost impossible to measure total environmental impact. As an instance, changes in soil may lead to changes in vegetation, which in turn may trigger changes in water quality and in animal populations. Primary impacts give rise to a myriad of successive repercussions throughout ecosystems which may be impracticable to trace and monitor. Quantitative cause-and-effect relationships can seldom be established.

References

Abler, R., Adams, J. S. and Gould, P. 1971: *Spatial organization: the geographer's view of the world.* Englewood Cliffs: Prentice Hall.

Abul-Atta, A. A. 1978: *Egypt and the Nile after the construction of the High Aswan Dam.* Cairo: Ministry of Irrigation and Land Reclamation.

Ackerman, W. C., Harmeston, R. H. and Sinclair, R. A. 1970: Some long-term trends in water quality of rivers and lakes. *Eos* 51, 516–22.

Ahlgren, I. F. 1974: The effect of fire on soil organisms. In Kozlowski, T. T. and Ahlgren, C. C. (editor), *Fire and ecosystems.* New York: Academic Press, 47–72.

Alabaster, J. S. 1972: Suspended solids and fisheries. *Proceedings of the Royal Society* 180B, 395–406.

Allchin, B., Goudie, A. S. and Hegde, K. T. M. 1977: *The prehistory and palaeogeography of the Great Indian Desert.* London: Academic Press.

Almer, B., Dickson, W., Ekstrom, C., Hornstrom, E. and Miller, U. 1974: Effects of acidification on Finnish lakes. *Ambio* 3, 30–6.

Amin, M. A. 1977: Problems and effects of schistosomiasis in irrigation schemes in the Sudan. Worthington, E. B., editor, *Arid land irrigation in developing countries: environmental problems and effects.* Oxford: Pergamon, 407–11.

Arber, M. A. 1946: Dust-storms in the Fenland around Ely. *Geography* 31, 23–6.

Aron, W. I. and Smith, S. H. 1971: Ship canals and aquatic ecosystems. *Science* 174, 13–20.

Ashby, E. 1978: *Reconciling man with the environment.* London: Oxford University Press.

Atkinson, B. W. 1968: A preliminary examination of the possible effect of London's urban area on the distribution of thunder rainfall, 1951–60. *Transactions of the Institute of British Geographers* 44, 97–118.

Atkinson, B. W. 1975: The mechanical effect of an urban area on convective precipitation. *Occasional Paper No. 3*, Dept. of Geography, Queen Mary College, University of London.

Atlas, P. 1977: The paradox of hail suppression. *Science* 195, 139–45.

Aubertin, G. M. and Patric, J. H. 1974: Water quality after clearcutting a small watershed in West Virginia. *Journal of Environmental Quality* 3, 243–9.

Bach, W. 1979: Short-term climatic alterations caused by human activities: status and outlook. *Progress in Physical Geography* 3, 55–83.

Ball, D. F. 1975: discussion in Evans, J. G., Limbrey, S. and Cleere H., editor, *The effect of man on the landscape: the Highland zone*, Council for British Archaeology Research Report 11, 26.

Banks, H. O. and Richter, R. C. 1953: Sea-water intrusion into groundwater basins bordering the California coast and inland bays. *Transactions of the American Geophysical Union*, 34, 575–82.

Barrass, R. 1974: *Biology, food and people*. London: Hodder and Stoughton.

Bartlett, H. H. 1956: Fire, primitive agriculture, and grazing in the tropics. In Thomas, W. L., editor, *Man's role in changing the face of the earth*. Chicago: University of Chicago Press, 692–720.

Barton, B. A. 1977: Short term effect of highway construction on the limnology of a small stream in southern Ontario. *Freshwater Biology* 7, 99–108.

Bates, M. 1956: Man as an agent in the spread of organisms. In Thomas, W. L., editor, *Man's role in changing the face of the earth*. Chicago: University of Chicago Press, 788–804.

Batterbee, R. W. 1977: Observations in the recent history of Lough Neagh and its drainage basin. *Philosophical Transactions of the Royal Society of London* 281B, 303–45.

Baver, L. D., Gardner, W. H. and Gardner, W. R. 1972: *Soil physics* (4th edition). New York: Wiley.

Baxter, R. M. 1977: Environmental effects of dams and impoundments. *Annual Review of Ecology and Systematics*, 8, 255–83.

Bayfield, N. G. 1973: Human pressures on soils in mountain areas. *Welsh soils discussion group report* 14, 36–49.

1979: Recovery of four heath communities on Cairngorm, Scotland, from disturbance by trampling. *Biological Conservation* 15, 165–79.

Beamish, R. J., Lockhart, W. L., Van Loon, J. C. and Harvey, H. H. 1975: Long-term acidification of a lake and resulting effects on fishes. *Ambio* 4, 98–102.

Beaumont, P. 1978: Man's impact on river systems: a world-wide view. *Area* 10, 38–41.

Beckinsale, R. P. 1969: Human responses to river regimes. In Chorley, R. J., editor, *Water, Earth and Man*. London: Methuen, 487–509.

1972: The effect upon river channels of sudden changes in sediment load. *Acta Geographica Debrecina* 10, 181–6.

286

Bell, J. N. B. and Cox, R. A. 1975: Atmospheric ozone and plant damage in the United Kingdom. *Environmental Pollution* 8, 163–70.

Bell, M. L. and Nur, A. 1978: Strength changes due to reservoir-induced pore pressure and stresses and application to Lake Oroville. *Journal of Geophysical Research* 83, 4469–83.

Bendell, J. F. 1974: Effects of fire on birds and mammals. In Kozlowski, T. T. and Ahlgren, C. E., editors, *Fire and ecosystems.* New York: Academic Press, 73–138.

Bender, B. 1975: *Farming in prehistory from hunter-gatherer to food-producer.* London: Baker.

Bennett, C. F. 1968: Human influences in the zoogeography of Panama. *Ibero-Americana* 51.

Bennett, H. H. 1938: *Soil conservation.* New York: McGraw Hill.

Bernabo, J. C. and Webb, T. III. 1977: Changing patterns in the Holocene pollen record of northeastern North America: mapped summary. *Quaternary Research* 8, 64–96.

Berry, B. J. L. 1974: *Land use, urban form and environmental quality.* Chicago: Department of Geography Research Series.

Bidwell, O. W. and Hole, F. D. 1965: Man as a factor of soil formation. *Soil Science* 99, 65–72.

Biglane, K. E. and Lafleur, R. A. 1967: Notes on estuarine pollution with emphasis on the Louisiana Gulf Coast. *Publication 83, American Association for the Advancement of Science* 690–2.

Bird, E. C. F. 1979: Coastal processes. In Gregory, K. J. and Walling, D. E., editors, *Man and environmental processes.* Folkestone: Dawson, 82–101.

Birkeland, P. W. and Larson, E. E. 1978: *Putnam's geology.* New York: Oxford University Press.

Blackburn, W. H. and Tueller, P. T. 1970: Pinjon and juniper invasion in Black sagebrush communities in east-central Nevada. *Ecology* 51, 841–8.

Blumer, M. 1972: Submarine seeps: are they a major source of open ocean oil pollution? *Science* 176, 1257–8.

Böckh, A. 1973: Consequences of uncontrolled human activities in the Valencia lake basin. In M. T. Farvar and J. P. Milton, editors, *The careless technology*, London: Stacey, 301–17.

Boeck, W. L., Shaw, D. T. and Vonnegut, B. 1975: Possible consequences of global dispersion of Krypton 85. *Bulletin of the American Meteorological Society* 56, 527.

Boorman, L. A. 1977: Sand-dunes. In Barnes, R. S. K., editor, *The coastline.* London: Wiley, 161–97.

Bormann, F. H., Likens, G. E., Fisher, D. W. and Pierce, R. S. 1968: Nutrient loss accelerated by clear cutting of a forest ecosystem. *Science* 159, 882–4.

Bourne, W. R. P. 1970: Oil pollution and bird conservation. *Biological Conservation* 2, 300–2.

Boussingault, J. B. 1845: *Rural economy* (2nd edition). London: Baillière.

Brazel, A. J. and Idso, S. B. 1979: Thermal effects of dust on climate. *Annals of the Association of American Geographers* 69, 432–7.

287

Breuer, G. 1980: *Weather modification: prospects and problems.* Cambridge: Cambridge University Press.

Bridges, E. M. 1978: Interaction of soil and mankind in Britain. *Journal of Soil Science* 29, 125–39.

Brimblecombe, P. 1977: London air pollution 1500–1900. *Atmospheric Environment* 11, 1157–62.

Broecker, W. S., Takahashi, T., Simpson, H. J. and Peng, T. H. 1979: Fate of fossil fuel carbon dioxide and the global carbon budget. *Science* 206, 409–18.

Brown, A. A. and Davis, K. P. 1973: *Forest fire control and its use* (2nd edition). New York: McGraw Hill.

Brown, E. H. 1970: Man shapes the earth. *Geographical Journal* 136, 74–85.

Brunhes, J. 1920: *Human geography.* London: Harrap.

Bryan, G. W. 1979: Bioaccumulation of marine pollutants. *Philosophical Transactions of the Royal Society* 286B, 483–505.

Bryan, K. 1928: Historic evidence of changes in the channel of Rio Puerco, a tributary of the Rio Grande in New Mexico. *Journal of Geology* 36, 265–82.

Bryson, R. A. and Barreis, D. A. 1967: Possibility of major climatic modifications and their implications: northwest India, a case for study. *Bulletin of the American Meteorological Society* 48, 136–42.

Bryson, R. A. and Kutzbach, J. E. 1968: *Air pollution.* Commission on College Geography Resource Paper No. 2. Washington, DC: Association of American Geographers.

Budyko, M. I. 1974: *Climate and life.* New York: Academic Press.

Burcham, L. T. 1970: Ecological significance of alien plants in California grasslands. *Proceedings of the Association of American Geographers* 2, 36–9.

Burke, R. 1972: Stormwater runoff. In Oglesby, R. T., Carlson, C. A. and McCann, J. A., editors, *River ecology and man.* New York: Academic Press, 727–33.

Busack, S. D. and Bury, R. B. 1974: Some effects of off-road vehicles and sheep grazing on lizard population in the Mojave Desert. *Biological Conservation* 6, 179–83.

Bussing, C. 1972: The impact of feedlots. In MacPhail, D. D., editor, *The High Plains: problem of semiarid environments.* Fort William: Colorado State University, 78–86.

Butzer, K. W. 1972: *Environment and archaeology – an ecological approach to prehistory.* London: Methuen.

— 1974: Accelerated soil erosion: a problem of man–land relationships. In Manners, I. R. and Mikesell, M. W., editors, *Perspectives on environments.* Washington, DC: Association of American Geographers.

— 1976: *Early hydraulic civilization in Egypt.* Chicago: University of Chicago Press.

— 1977: Environment, culture and human evolution. *American Scientist* 65, 572–84.

Cadle, R. D. 1971: The chemistry of smog. In Matthews, W. H., Kellogg,

W. W. and Robinson, G. D., editors, *Man's impact on the climate*. Cambridge, Mass.: MIT Press, 339—59.

Cairns, J. and Dickson, K. L. 1977: Recovery of streams from spills of hazardous materials. In Cairns, J., Dickson, K. L. and Herricks, E. E., editors, *Recovery and restoration of damaged ecosystems*. Charlottesville: University Press of Virginia, 24—42.

Carlson, C. W. 1978: Research in A.R.S. related to soil structure. In Emerson, W. W., Bond, R. D. and Dexter, A. R., editors, *Modification of soil structure*. Chichester: Wiley, 279—84.

Carrara, P. E. and Carroll, T. R. 1979: The determination of erosion rates from exposed tree roots in the Piceance Basin, Colorado, *Earth Surface Processes* 4, 407—17.

Carter, D. L. 1975: Problems of salinity in agriculture. *Ecological Studies* 15, 26—35.

Carter, L. J. 1977: Soil erosion: the problem persists despite the billions spent on it. *Science* 196, 409—11.

Casey, H. and Clarke, R. T. 1979: Statistical analysis of nitrate concentrations from the River Frome (Dorset) for the period 1965—76. *Freshwater Biology* 9, 91—7.

Challinor, D. 1968: Alteration of surface soil characteristics by four tree species. *Ecology* 49, 286—90.

Chancellor, W. J. 1977: Compaction of soil by agricultural equipment. *Division of Agricultural Sciences, University of California Bulletin* 1881.

Chandler, T. J. 1965: *The climate of London*. London: Hutchinson.

—— 1976: The climate of towns. In Chandler, T. J. and Gregory, S., editors, *The climate of the British Isles*. London: Longman, 307—29.

Changnon, S. A. 1968: The La Porte weather anomaly — fact or fiction? *Bulletin of the American Meteorological Society* 49, 4—11.

—— 1973: Atmospheric alterations from man-made biospheric changes. In Sewell, W. R. D., editor, *Modifying the weather: a social assessment*. Adelaide: University of Victoria, 135—184.

—— 1978: Urban effects on severe local storms at St. Louis. *Journal of Applied Meteorology* 17, 578—86.

Charney, J., Stone, P. H. and Quirk, W. J. 1975: Drought in the Sahara: a biogeophysical feedback mechanism. *Science* 187, 434—5.

Chesters, G. and Konrad, J. F. 1971: Effects of pesticide usage on water quality. *Bio Science* 21, 565—9.

Childe, V. G. 1936: *Man makes himself*. London: Watts.

Chorley, R. J. and More, R. J. 1967: The interaction of precipitation and man. In Chorley, R. J., editor, *Water, earth and man*. London: Methuen, 157—66.

Clark, G. 1962: *World prehistory*. Cambridge: Cambridge University Press.

—— 1977a: Domestication and social evolution. In Hutchinson, J., Clark, J. G. G., Jope, E. M. and Riley, R., editors, *The early history of agriculture*. Oxford: Oxford University Press, 5—11.

—— 1977b: *World prehistory in new perspective*. Cambridge: Cambridge University Press.

Clark, J. R. 1977: *Coastal ecosystem management*. New York: Wiley.

Clark, R. R. 1963: *Grimes Graves.* London: HMSO.

Clarke, R. T. and McCulloch, J. S. G. 1979: The effect of land use on the hydrology of small upland catchments. In Hollis, G. E., editor, *Man's impact on the hydrological cycle in the United Kingdom.* Norwich: Geo Abstracts, 71–8.

Coates, D. R., editor, 1976: *Geomorphology and engineering,* Stroudsburg: Dowden, Hutchinson and Ross.
   1977: Landslide perspectives. *Reviews in Engineering Geology* 3, 3–28.

Coffey, M. 1978: The dust storms. *Natural History* (New York) 87, 72–83.

Cole, M. M. 1963: Vegetation and geomorphology in northern Rhodesia: an aspect of the distribution of the Savanna of Central Africa. *Geographical Journal* 129, 290–310.

Cole, S. 1970: *The Neolithic revolution* (5th edition). London: British Museum (Natural History).

Collier, C. R. 1964: Influences of strip mining on the hydrologic environment of parts of Beaver Creek Basin, Kentucky, 1955–59. *United States Geological Survey Professional Paper* 472–B.

Conacher, A. J. 1979: Water quality and forests in Southwestern Australia: review and evaluation. *Australian Geographer* 14, 150–9.

Cooke, G. W. 1977: Waste of fertilizers. *Philosophical Transactions of the Royal Society of London* 281B, 231–41.

Cooke, R. U. and Doornkamp, J. C. 1974: *Geomorphology in environmental management.* Oxford: Clarendon Press.

Cooke, R. U. and Reeves, R. W. 1976: *Arroyos and environmental change in the American south-west.* Oxford: Clarendon Press.

Cooper, C. F. 1961: The ecology of fire. *Scientific American* 204 (4), 150–60.

Costa, J. E. 1975: Effects of agriculture on erosion and sedimentation in the Piedmont Province, Maryland. *Bulletin of the Geological Society of America* 86, 1281–6.

Cott, H. B. 1969: Tourists and crocodiles in Uganda. *Oryx* 10, 153–60.

Coupland, R. T., editor, 1979: *Grassland ecosystems of the world: analysis of grasslands and their uses.* Cambridge: Cambridge University Press.

Cowell, E. B. 1976: Oil pollution of the sea. In Johnson, R., editor, *Marine pollution.* London: Academic Press, 353–401.

Crisp, D. T. 1977: Some physical and chemical effects of the Cow Green (Upper Teesdale) impoundment. *Freshwater Biology* 7, 109–20.

Cronin, L. E. 1967: The role of man in estuarine processes. *Publication 83, American Association for the Advancement of Science* 667–89.

Crowe, P. R. 1971: *Concepts in climatology.* London: Longman.

Crozier, M. J., Marx, S. L. and Grant, I. J. 1978: Impact of off-road recreational vehicles on soil and vegetation. *Proceedings of the 9th New Zealand Geography Conference, Dunedin,* 76–9.

Cumberland, K. B. 1961: Man in nature in New Zealand. *New Zealand Geographer* 17, 137–54.

Currey, D. T. 1977: The role of applied geomorphology in irrigation and groundwater studies. In Hails, J. R., editor, *Applied geomorphology*. Amsterdam: Elsevier, 51–83.

Cwynar, L. C. 1978: Recent history of fire and vegetation from laminated sediment of Greenleaf Lake, Algonquin Park, Ontario. *Canadian Journal of Botany* 56, 10–21.

Daniel, T. C., McGuire, P. E., Stoffel, D. and Millfe, B. 1979: Sediment and nutrient yield from residential construction sites. *Journal of Environmental Quality* 8, 304–8.

Darby, H. C. 1956: The clearing of the woodland in Europe. In Thomas, W. L., editor, *Man's role in changing the face of the Earth*. Chicago: University of Chicago Press, 183–216.

Darling, F. F. 1956: Man's ecological dominance through domesticated animals on wild lands. In Thomas, W. L., editor, *Man's role in changing the face of the Earth*. Chicago: University of Chicago Press, 778–87.

Darungo, F. P., Allee, P. H. and Weickmann, H. K. 1978: Snowfall induced by a power plant plume *Geophysical Research Letters* 5, 515–17.

Daubenmire, R. 1968: Ecology of fire in grassland. *Advances in Ecological Research* 5, 209–66.

Davis, B. N. K. 1976: Wildlife, urbanisation and industry. *Biological Conservation* 10, 249–91.

Davis, D. H. 1942: *The Earth and Man: a human geography*. New York: Macmillan.

Davitaya, F. F. 1969: Atmospheric dust content as a factor affecting glaciation and climatic change. *Annals of the Association of American Geographers* 59, 552–60.

Denisova, T. B. 1977: The environmental impact of mineral industries. *Soviet Geography* 18, 646–59.

Denson, E. P. 1970: The trumpeter swan, *Olor Buccinator*: a conservation success and its lessons. *Biological Conservation* 2, 253–6.

Detwyler, T. R., editor, 1971: *Man's impact on environment*. New York: McGraw Hill.

Detwyler, T. R. and Marcus, M. G. 1972: *Urbanisation and environment: the physical geography of the city*. Belmont: Duxbury Press.

Dicks, B. 1977: Changes in the vegetation of an oiled Southampton water salt marsh. In Cairns, J., Dickson, K. L. and Herricks, E. E., editors, *Recovery and restoration of damaged ecosystems*. Charlottesville: University Press of Virginia, 72–101.

Dimbleby, G. W. 1974: The legacy of prehistoric man. In Warren, A. and Goldsmith, F. B., editor, *Conservation in practice*. London: Wiley, 279–89.

Dodd, A. P. 1959: The biological control of the prickly pear in Australia. In Keast, A., Crocker, R. L. and Christian, C. S., editors, *Biogeography and Ecology in Australia*. The Hague: Junk, 565–77.

Doerr, A. and Guernsely, L. 1956: Man as a geomorphological agent: the example of coal mining. *Annals of the Association of American Geographers* 46, 197–210.

Dolan, R., Godfrey, P. J. and Odum, W. E. 1973: Man's impact on the barrier islands of North Carolina. *American Scientist* 61, 152–62.

Doughty, R. W. 1974: The human predator: a survey. In Manners, I. R. and Mikesell, M. W., editors, *Perspectives on environment.* Washington, DC: Association of American Geographers, 152–80.

— 1978: The English sparrow in the American landscape: a paradox in nineteenth century wildlife conservation. *Research Paper 19, School of Geography, University of Oxford.*

Douglas, I. 1969: The efficiency of humid tropical denudation systems. *Transactions of the Institute of British Geographers* 46, 1–16.

Down, G. C. and Stocks, J. 1977: *Environmental impact of mining.* London: Applied Science Publishers.

Drennan, D. S. H. 1979: Agricultural consequences of groundwater development in England. In Hollis, G. E., editor, *Man's impact on the hydrological cycle in the United Kingdom.* Norwich: Geo Abstracts, 31–8.

Dunne, T. and Leopold, L. B. 1978: *Water in environmental planning.* San Francisco: Freeman.

D'Yakanov, K. N. and Reteyum, A. Y. 1965: The local climate of the Rybinsk reservoir. *Soviet Geography* 6, 40–53.

Eden, M. J. 1974: Palaeoclimatic influences and the development of savanna in southern Venezuela. *Journal of Biogeography* 1, 95–109.

Edington, J. M. and Edington, M. A. 1977: *Ecology and environmental planning.* London: Chapman and Hall.

Edlin, H. L. 1976: The Culbin sands. In Leniham, J. and Fletcher, W. W., editors, *Reclamation.* Glasgow: Blackie, 1–31.

Edmonson, W. T. 1975: Fresh water pollution. In Murdoch, W. W., editor, *Environment.* Sunderland: Sinauer Associates, 251–71.

Edwards, A. M. C. 1975: Long term changes in the water quality for agricultural catchments. In Hey, R. D. and Daniels, T. D., editors, *Science, technology and environmental management.* Farnborough: Saxon House, 111–22.

Ehrenfield, D. W. 1972: *Conserving life on Earth.* New York: Oxford University Press.

Ehrlich, P. R. and Ehrlich, A. H. 1970: *Population, resources, environment: issues in human ecology.* San Francisco: Freeman.

Ehrlich P. R., Ehrlich, A. H. and Holdren J. P. 1977: *Ecoscience: population, resources, environment.* San Francisco: Freeman.

Ellenberg, H. 1979: Man's influence on tropical mountain ecosystems in South America. *Journal of Ecology* 67, 401–16.

Ellis, J. B. 1975: Urban stormwater pollution. *Middlesex Polytechnic Research Report* 1.

Elton, C. S. 1958: *The ecology of invasions by plants and animals.* London: Methuen.

Evans, D. M. 1966: Man-made earthquakes in Denver. *Geotimes* 10, 11–18.

Evans, J. G., Limbrey, S. and Cleere, H., editors (1975) *The effect of man on the landscape: the Highland Zone.* Council for British Archaeology Research Report 11.

Evans, R. and Nortcliff, S. 1978: Soil erosion in North Norfolk. *Journal of Agricultural Science* 90, 185—92.

Evenari, M., Shanan, L. and Tadmor, N. H. 1971: Runoff agriculture in the Negev Desert of Israel. In McGinnies, W. G., Goldman, R. J. and Paylore, P., editors, *Food, Fiber and the Arid Lands*. Tucson: University of Arizona Press, 312—22.

Eyre, S. R. 1978: Nuclear power and nuclear waste. *Progress in Physical Geography* 2 (1), 151—6.

Feare, C. J. 1978: The decline of booby (Sulidae) population in the Western Indian Ocean. *Biological Conservation* 14, 295—305.

Ferrians, O. J., Kachadoorian, R. and Greene, G. W. 1969: Permafrost and related engineering problems in Alaska. *United States Geological Survey Professional Paper* 678.

Fillenham, L. F. 1963: Holme Fen Post. *Geographical Journal* 129, 502—3.

Fisher, J., Simon, N. and Vincent, J. 1969: *The Red Book — wildlife in danger*. London: Collins.

Flenley, J. R. 1979: *The equatorial rain forest: a geological history*. London: Butterworth.

Foster, T. 1976: *Bushfire*. Sydney: Reed.

Fox, H. L. 1976: The urbanizing river: a case study in the Maryland Piedmont. In Coates, D. R., editor, *Geomorphology and engineering*. Stroudsburg: Dowden, Hutchinson and Ross, 245—71.

French, H. M. 1976: *The periglacial environment*. London: Longman.

Frenkel, R. E. 1970: Ruderal vegetation along some California roadsides. *University of California Publications in Geography* 20.

Gade, D. W. 1976: Naturalization of plant aliens: the volunteer orange in Paraguay. *Journal of Biogeography* 3, 269—79.

Gameson, A. L. H. and Wheeler, A. 1977: Restoration and recovery of the Thames Estuary. In Cairns, J., Dickson, K. L. and Herricks, E. E., editors, *Recovery and restoration of damaged ecosystems*. Charlottesville: University Press of Virginia, 92—101.

Geertz, C. 1963: *Agricultural involution: the process of ecological change in Indonesia*. Berkeley: University of California Press.

Gerasimov, I. P. 1976: Problems of natural environment transformation in Soviet constructive geography. *Progress in Geography* 9, 75—99.

Gerasimov, I. P., Armand, D. L. and Yefron, K. M. 1971: *Natural resources of the Soviet Union: their use and renewal*. San Francisco: Freeman.

Gifford, G. F. and Hawkins, R. H. 1978: Hydrologic impact of grazing on infiltration: a critical review. *Water Resources Research* 14, 305—13.

Gilbert, G. K. 1917: Hydraulic mining debris in the Sierra Nevada. *United States Geological Survey Professional Paper* 105.

Gilbert, O. L. 1970: Further studies on the effect of sulphur dioxide on lichens and bryophytes. *New Phytologist* 69, 605—27.

293

Gilbert, O. L. 1975: Effects of air pollution on landscape and land-use around Norwegian aluminium smelters. *Environmental Pollution* 8, 113–21.

Gillespie, R., Horton, D. R., Ladd, P., Macumber, P. G., Rich, T. H., Thorne, R. and Wright, R. V. S. 1978: Lancefield Swamp and the extinction of the Australian megafauna. *Science* 200, 1044–8.

Glacken, C. J. 1956: Changing ideas of the habitable world. In Thomas, W. L., editor, *Man's role in changing the face of the Earth.* Chicago: University of Chicago Press, 70–92.

— 1963: The growing second world within the world of nature. In Fosberg, F. R., editor, *Man's place in the island ecosystem.* Honolulu: Bishop Museum Press, 75–100.

— 1967: *Traces on the Rhodian Shore: nature and culture in western thought from ancient times to the end of the eighteenth century.* Berkeley: University of California Press.

Godbole, N. N. 1972: Theories on the origin of salt lakes in Rajasthan India. *Proceedings of the 24th International Geological Congress,* Section 10, 354–7.

Goldberg, E. D. *et al.,* 1978: A pollution history of Chesapeake Bay. *Geochimica et Cosmochimica Acta* 42, 1413–25.

Goldsmith, V. 1978: Coastal dunes. In Davis, R. A., editor, *Coastal sedimentary environments.* New York: Springer-Verlag.

Goodman, D. 1975: The theory of diversity–stability relationships in ecology. *Quarterly Review of Biology* 50, 237–66.

Gorman, M. 1979: *Island ecology.* London: Chapman and Hall.

Gottschalk, L. C. 1945: Effects of soil erosion on navigation in Upper Chesapeake Bay. *Geographical Review* 35, 219–38.

Goudie, A. S. 1972: The concept of post-glacial progressive desiccation. *School of Geography, University of Oxford, Research Paper* 4.

— 1973: *Duricrusts of tropical and subtropical landscapes.* Oxford: Clarendon Press.

— 1977a: *Environmental change.* Oxford: Clarendon Press.

— 1977b: Sodium sulphate weathering and the disintegration of Mohenjo-Daro, Pakistan. *Earth Surface Processes* 2, 75–86.

Goudie, A. S. and Wilkinson, J. C. 1977: *The warm desert environment.* Cambridge: Cambridge University Press.

Gourou, P. 1961: *The tropical world* (3rd edition). London: Longman.

Graf, W. K. 1977: Network characteristics in suburbanizing streams, *Water Resources Research* 13, 459–63.

Grayson, D. K. 1977: Pleistocene avifaunas and the overkill hypothesis. *Science* 195, 691–3.

Green, F. H. W. 1976: Recent changes in land use and treatment. *Geographical Journal* 142, 12–26.

— 1978: Field drainage in Europe. *Geographical Journal,* 144, 171–4.

Greenland, D. J. 1977: Soil drainage by intensive arable cultivation: temporary or permanent. *Philosophical Transactions of the Royal Society of London,* 281B, 193–208.

Greenland, D. J. and Lal, R. 1977: *Soil conservation and management in the humid tropics.* Chichester: Wiley.

Gregory, K. J. and Walling, K. E. 1973: *Drainage basin form and process: a geomorphological approach.* London: Arnold.

Gregory, K. J. and Walling, D. 1979: *Man and environmental processes.* Folkestone: Dawson.

Griffiths, J. F. 1976. *Applied climatology, an introduction,* 2nd edition. Oxford: Oxford University Press.

Grigg, D. 1970: *The harsh lands.* London: Macmillan.

Gross, M. G. 1972: Geological aspects of waste solids and marine waste deposits, New York Metropolitan region. *Bulletin of the Geological Society of America,* 83, 3163–76.

Guilday, J. E. 1967: Differential extinction during late Pleistocene and Recent times. In Martin, P. S. and Wright, H. E., editors, *Pleistocene extinctions.* New Haven: Yale University Press, 121–40.

Haggett, P. 1979: *Geography: a modern synthesis* (3rd edition). London: Prentice Hall.

Haigh, M. J. 1978: Evolution of slopes on artificial landforms – Blaenavon, U. K. *University of Chicago, Department of Geography Research Paper,* 183.

Hails, J. R., editor, 1977: *Applied geomorphology.* Amsterdam: Elsevier.

Hanes, T. L. 1971: Succession after fire in the Chaparral of Southern California. *Ecological Monographs* 41, 27–52.

Happ, S. C. 1944: Effect of sedimentation on floods in the Kickapoo Valley, Wisconsin. *Journal of Geology* 52, 53–68.

Harlan, J. R. 1975a: Our vanishing genetic resources. *Science* 188, 617–22.

1975b: *Crops and man.* Madison: American Society of Agronomy.

1976: The plants and animals that nourish man. *Scientific American* 235 (3), 88–97.

Harris, D. R. 1966: Recent plant invasions in the arid and semi-arid southwest of the United States. *Annals of the Association of American Geographers* 56, 408–22.

Hay, J. 1973: Salt cedar and salinity on the Upper Rio Grande. In Farvar, M. T. and Milton, J. P., editors, *The careless technology.* London: Tom Stacey, 288–300.

Heinselman, M. L. and Wright, H. E. 1973: The ecological role of fire in natural conifer forests of western and northern North America. *Quaternary Research* 3, 317–482.

Helliwell, D. R. 1974: The value of vegetation for conservation. II: M1 Motorway area. *Journal of Environmental Management* 2, 75–8.

Hess, W. N., editor, 1974: *Weather and climate modification.* New York: Wiley.

Hickey, J. J. and Anderson, O. W. 1968: Chlorinated hydrocarbons and eggshell changes in reptorial and fish-eating birds. *Science* 162, 271–2.

Hill, A. R. 1975: Ecosystems stability in relation to stresses caused by human activities. *Canadian Geographer* 19, 206–20.

Hill, M. N., Chandler, J. A. and Highton, R. B. 1977: A comparison of mosquito populations in irrigated and non-irrigated areas of the Kano Plains, Byanza Province, Kenya. In Worthington, E. B., editor (1977). *Arid land irrigation in developing countries: environmental problems and effects.* Oxford: Pergamon, 307–15.

Hillel, D. 1971: Artificial inducement of runoff on a potential source of water in arid lands. In McGinnies, W. G., Goldman, B. J. and Paylore, P., editors, *Food, fiber and the arid lands.* Tucson: University of Arizona Press, 324—30.

Hills, T. L. 1965: Savannas: a review of a major research problem in tropical geography. *Canadian Geographer* 9, 216—28.

Holdgate, M. W. 1979: *A perspective of environmental pollution.* Cambridge: Cambridge University Press.

Holdgate, M. W. and Wace, N. M. 1961: The influence of man on the floras and faunas of southern Islands. *Polar Record* 10, 473—93.

Hollis, G. E. 1975: The effects of urbanization on floods of difference recurrence interval. *Water Resources Research* 11, 431—5.

Hollis, G. E. and Luckett, J. K. 1976: The response of natural river channels to urbanization: two case studies from Southeast England. *Journal of Hydrology* 30, 351—63.

Holzer, T. L. 1979: Faulting caused by groundwater extraction in Southcentral Arizona. *Journal of Geophysical Research* 84, 603—12.

Hopkins, B. 1965: Observations on Savanna burning in the Olokemeji forest reserve, Nigeria. *Journal of Applied Ecology* 2, 367--81.

Hotes, F. L. and Pearson, E. A. 1977: Effects of irrigation on water quality. In Worthington, E. B., editor, *Arid land irrigation in developing countries: environmental problems and effects.* Oxford: Pergamon, 127—58.

Howe, G. M., Slaymaker, H. O. and Harding, D. M. 1966: Flood hazard in Mid-Wales. *Nature* 212, 584—5.

Hudson, N. 1971: *Soil conservation.* London: Batsford.

Hughes, M. K., Lepp, N. W. and Phipps, D. A. 1980: Aerial heavy metal pollution and terrestrial ecosystems. *Advances in ecological research* 11, 217—327.

Huntington, E. 1914: The climatic factor as illustrated in arid America. *Carnegie Institution of Washington Publication* 192.

Hurd, L. E., Mellinger, M. V., Wold, L. L. and McNaughton, S. J. 1971: Stability and diversity at three trophic levels in terrestrial successional ecosystems. *Science* 173, 1134—6.

Hutchinson, G. E. 1973: Eutrophication. *American Scientist* 61, 269—79.

Hutchinson, G. L. and Mosier, A. R. 1979: Nitrous oxide emissions from an irrigated cornfield. *Science* 205, 1125—7.

Idso, S. B. and Brazel, A. J. 1978: Climatological effects of atmospheric particulate pollution. *Nature* 274, 781—2.

Illies, J. 1974: *Introduction to zoogeography.* London: Macmillan.

Imeson, A. C. 1971: Heather burning and soil erosion on the North Yorkshire Moors. *Journal of Applied Ecology* 8, 537—41.

Isaac, E. 1970: *Geography of domestication.* Englewood Cliffs: Prentice Hall.

Isachenko, A. G. 1974: On the so-called anthropogenic landscapes. *Soviet Geography* 15, 467—75.

1975: Landscape as a subject of human impact. *Soviet Geography* 16, 631—43.

296

Jacks, G. V. and White, R. O. 1939: *The rape of the Earth: a world survey of soil erosion.* London: Faber and Faber.

Jacobs, J. 1969: *The economy of cities.*

1975: Diversity, stability and maturity in ecosystems influenced by human activities. In Van Dobben, W. H. and Lowe-McConnell, R. H., editors, *Unifying concepts in ecology.* The Hague: Junk, 187—207.

Jacobsen, T. and Adams, R. M. 1958: Salt and silt in ancient Mesopotamian agriculture. *Science* 128, 1251—8.

Jarman, M. R. 1977: Early animal husbandry. In Hutchinson, J., Clark, J. G. G., Jope, E. M. and Riley, R., editors, *The early history of agriculture.* Oxford: Oxford University Press, 85—97.

Jarvis, P. J. 1979: The ecology of plant and animal introductions. *Progress in Physical Geography* 3, 187—214.

Jennings, J. N. 1952: The origin of the Broads. *R. G. S. Research Series* No. 2.

1966: Man as a geological agent. *Australian Journal of Science* 28, 150—6.

Jenny, H. 1941: *Factors of soil formation,* New York: McGraw Hill.

Johannessen, C. L. 1963: Savannas of interior Honduras. *Ibero-Americana* 46.

Johnson, N. M. 1979: Acid rain: neutralization within the Hubbard Brook ecosystem and regional implications. *Science* 204, 497—9.

Johnston, D. W. 1974: Decline of DDT residues in migratory songbirds. *Science* 186, 841—2.

Jones, E. L. 1972: The bird pests of British agriculture in recent centuries. *Agricultural History Review* 20, 107—25.

Judd, W. R. 1974: Seismic effects of reservoir impounding. *Engineering Geology,* 8, 1—212.

Karnes, L. B. 1971: Reclamation of wet and overflow lands. In Smith, G-H., editor, *Conservation of Natural Resources.* New York: Wiley, 241—55.

Keller, E. A. 1976: Channelisation: environmental, geomorphic and engineering aspects. In Coates, D. R., editor, *Geomorphology and engineering.* Stroudsburg: Dowden, Hutchinson and Ross, 115—40.

Kellman, M. 1975: Evidence for late glacial age fire in a tropical montane Savanna. *Journal of Biogeography* 2, 57—63.

Kellogg, W. W. 1978: Global influences of mankind on the climate. In Gribbin, J., editor, *Climatic change.* London: Cambridge University Press, 205—27.

Kiersch, G. A. 1965: The Vaiont reservoir disaster. *Mineral Information Service* 18, 129—38.

Kilgore, B. M. and Taylor, D. 1979: Fire history of a sequoia—mixed conifer forest. *Ecology* 60, 129—42.

King, C. A. M. 1974: Coasts. In Cooke, R. U. and Doornkamp, J. C., editors, *Geomorphology in environmental management.* Oxford: Clarendon Press, 188—222.

1975: *Introduction to physical and biological oceanography.* London: Edward Arnold.

Kittredge, J. 1948: *Forest influences.* New York: McGraw Hill.

Koide, M. and Goldberg, E. D. 1971: Atmospheric sulfur and fossil fuel combustion. *Journal of Geophysical Research* 76, 6589—96.

Komar, P. D. 1976: *Beach processes and sedimentation.* Englewood Cliffs: Prentice Hall.

Komarov, B. 1978: *The destruction of nature in the Soviet Union.* London: Pluto Press.

Krantz, G. S. 1970: Human activities and megafaunal extinctions. *American Scientist* 58, 164—70.

Lamb, H. H. 1977: *Climate: present, past and future. 2: Climatic history and the future.* London: Methuen.

Lambert, J. H., Jennings, J. N., Smith, C. T., Green, C. and Hutchinson, J. N. 1970: The making of the Broads: a reconsideration of their origin in the light of new evidence. *R. G. S. Research Series* No. 3.

Lamprey, H. 1978: The integrated project on arid lands. *Nature and Resources* 14, 2—11.

Landes, K. K. 1973: Mother nature as an oil polluter. *Bulletin of the American Association of Petroleum Geologists* 57, 637—41.

Landsberg, H. E. 1970: Man-made climatic changes. *Science* 170, 1265—8.

Langford, T. E. 1972: A comparative assessment of thermal effects in some British and North American rivers. In Oglesby, R. T., Carlson, C. A. and McCann, J. A., editors, *River ecology and man.* New York: Academic Press, 318—51.

Laporte, L. F. 1975: *Encounter with the Earth.* San Francisco: Canfield Press.

La Roe, E. T. 1977: Dredging — ecological impacts. In Clarke, J. R., editor, *Coastal ecosystem management.* New York: Wiley, 610—14.

Larson, F. 1940: The role of bison in maintaining the short grass plains. *Ecology* 21, 113—21.

Le Houérou, H. N. 1976: Rehabilitation of degraded arid lands. *Ecological Bulletin* 24, 189—205.

  1977: Biological recovery versus desertization. *Economic Geography* 63, 413—20.

Lemon, P. C. 1968: Effects of fire on an African plateau grassland. *Ecology* 49, 316—22.

Leopold, L. B. 1951: Rainfall frequency: an aspect of climatic variation. *Transactions of the American Geophysics Union* 32, 347—57.

Leopold, L. B., Wolman, M. G. and Miller J. P. 1964: *Fluvial processes in geomorphology.* San Francisco: Freeman.

Likens, G. E. and Bormann, F. H. 1974: Acid rain: a serious regional environmental problem. *Science* 184, 1176—9.

Likens, G. E., Wright, R. F., Galloway, J. N. and Butler, T. J. 1979: Acid rain. *Scientific American* 241 (4), 39—47.

Lockwood, J. G. 1979: *Causes of climate,* London: Arnold.

Lowe-McConnell, R. H. 1975: Freshwater life on the move. *Geographical Magazine* 47, 768—75.

Luke, R. H. 1962: *Bush fire control in Australia.* Melbourne: H & S.

Lund, J. W. G. 1972: Eutrophication. *Proceedings of the Royal Society of London*, 180B, 371–82.

Lyell, C. 1836: *Principles of geology* (4th edition), vol. III. London: Murray.

Macfarlane, M. J. 1976: *Laterite and landscape.* London: Academic Press.

Maignien, R. 1966: A review of research on laterite. *UNESCO, Natural Resources Research* 4.

McKnight, T. L. 1959: The feral horse in Anglo-America. *Geographical Review* 49, 506–25.

1971: Australia's buffalo dilemma. *Annals of the Association of American Geographers* 61, 759–73.

Makkaveyev, N. I. 1972: The impact of large water engineering projects on geomorphic processes in stream valleys. *Soviet Geography* 13, 387–93.

Mandel, S. 1977: The overexploitation of groundwater resources in dry regions. In Mundlak, Y. and Singer S. F., editors, *Arid zone development: potentialities and problems.* Cambridge, Mass.: Ballinger, 31–52.

Manners, I. R. 1978: Agricultural activities and environmental stress. In Hammond, K. A., editor, *Sourcebook of the environment.* Chicago: University of Chicago Press, 263–94.

Manners, I. R. and Mikesell, M. W., editors, 1974: *Perspectives on environment.* Washington, DC: Association of American Geographers.

Manshard, W. 1974: *Tropical agriculture.* London: Longman.

Marks, P. L. and Bormann, F. H. 1972: Revegetation following forest cutting: mechanisms for return to steady-state nutrient cycling. *Science* 176, 914–15.

Marquiss, M., Newton, I. and Ratcliffe, D. A. 1978: The decline of the raven, *Corvus corax*, relation to afforestation in southern Scotland and northern England. *Journal of Applied Ecology* 15, 129–44.

Marsh, G. P. 1864: *Man and Nature.* New York: Scribner.

1965: *Man and Nature*, edited by D. Lowenthal. Cambridge, Mass.: Belknap Press.

Martens, L. A. 1968: Flood inundation and effects of urbanization in Metropolitan Charlotte, North Carolina. *United States Geological Survey Water Supply Paper* 1591–C.

Martin, P. S. 1967: Prehistoric overkill. In Martin, P. S. and Wright, H. E., editors, *Pleistocene extinctions.* New Haven: Yale University Press, 75–120.

1974: Palaeolithic players on the American stage: man's impact on the late Pleistocene megafauna. In Ives, J. D. and Barry, R. G., editors, *Arctic and alpine environments.* London: Methuen.

Martin, P. S. and Wright, H. E., editors, 1967: *Pleistocene extinctions.* New Haven: Yale University Press, 75–120.

Martinez J. D. 1971: Environmental significance of salt. *Bulletin of the American Association of Petroleum Geologists* 55, 810–25.

Marx, J. L. 1975: Air pollution: effects on plants. *Science* 187, 731–3.

Matley, I. M. 1966: The Marxist approach to the geographical environment. *Annals of the Association of American Geographers* 56, 97—111.

Matthews, W. H., Kellogg, W. W. and Robinson, G. D., editors, 1971: *Man's impact on the climate.* Cambridge, Mass.: MIT Press.

Maugh, T. H. 1979: The Dead Sea is alive and, well..., *Science* 205, 178.

May, R. M. 1979: Fluctuations in abundance of tropical insects. *Nature* 278, 505—7.

Mead, W. R. 1954: Ridge and furrow in Buckinghamshire. *Geographical Journal* 120, 34—42.

Mellanby, K. 1967: *Pesticides and pollution.* London: Fontana.

Mendelssohn, H. 1973: Ecological effects of chemical control of residents and jackals in Israel. In Farvar, H. T. and Milton, J. P., editors, *The careless technology.* London: Tom Stacey, 527—44.

Mercer, J. H. 1978: West Antarctic ice sheet and CO_2 greenhouse effect: a threat of disaster. *Nature* 271, 321—5.

Merryfield, D. L. and Moore, P. D. 1974: Prehistoric human activity and blanket peat initiation on Exmoor. *Nature* 250, 439—41.

Meybeck, M. 1979: Concentration des eaux fluviales en elements majeurs et apports en solution aux oceans. *Revue de Géographie Physique et Géologie Dynamique* 21, 215—46.

Micklin, P. P. 1972: Dimensions of the Caspian Sea problem. *Soviet Geography* 13, 589—603.

Mikesell, M. W. 1969: The deforestation of Mount Lebanon. *Geographical Review* 59, 1—28.

Miller, R. S. and Botkin, D. B. 1974: Endangered species: models and predictions. *American Scientist* 62, 172—81.

Milne, W. G. 1976: Induced seismicity. *Engineering Geology* 10, 83—388.

Ministry of Agriculture, Fisheries and Food. 1976: *Agriculture and Water Quality.* London: Her Majesty's Stationery Office.

Mooney, H. A. and Parsons, D. J. 1973: Structure and function of the California Chaparral — an example from San Dimas. *Ecological Studies* 7, 83—112.

Moore, N. W., Hooper, M. D. and Davis, B. N. K. 1967: Hedges. 1. Introduction and reconnaissance studies. *Journal of Applied Ecology* 4, 201—20.

Moore, P. D. 1973: Origin of blanket mires. *Nature* 256, 267—9.

Moore, R. M. 1959: Ecological observations on plant communities grazed by sheep in Australia. In Keast, A., Crocker, R. L. and Christian, C. S., editors, *Biogeography and ecology in Australia.* The Hague: Junk, 500—13.

Moore, T. R. 1979: Land use and erosion in the Machakos Hills. *Annals of the Association of American Geographers* 69, 419—31.

Morgan, R. P. C. 1977: Soil erosion in the United Kingdom: field studies in the Silsoe area, 1973—75. *National College of Agricultural Engineering, Occasional Paper,* 4.

1979: *Soil erosion.* London: Longman.

Morgan, W. B. and Moss, R. P. 1965: Savanna and forest in Western Nigeria. *Africa* 35, 286—93.

Mote, V. L. and Zumbrunne, C. 1977: Anthropogenic environmental alteration of the Sea of Azov. *Soviet Geography* 18, 744—59.

Moyle, P. B. 1976: Fish introductions in California: history and impact on native fishes. *Biological Conservation* 9, 101—18.

Mrowka, J. P. 1974: Man's impact on stream regimen and quality. In Manners, I. R. and Mikesell, M. W., editors, *Perspectives on environment*. Washington, DC: Association of American Geographers, 79—104.

Murdoch, W. W. 1975: Diversity, complexity, stability and pest control. *Journal of Applied Ecology* 12, 795—807.

Murozumi, M., Chow, T. J. and Patterson, C. 1969: Chemical concentrations of pollutant lead aerosols, terrestrial dusts and sea salt in Greenland and Antarctic snow strata. *Geochimica et Cosmochimica Acta* 33, 1247—94.

Murton, R. K. 1971: *Man and birds*. Glasgow: Collins.

Nakano, T. and Matsuda, I. 1976: A note on land subsidence in Japan. *Geographical Reports of Tokyo Metropolitan University* 11, 147—62.

National Academy of Sciences. 1972: *The Earth and human affairs*. San Francisco: Camfield Press.

Nature Conservancy Council. 1977: *Nature conservation and agriculture*. London: Her Majesty's Stationery Office.

Nesterov, A. I. 1974: The development of anthropogenic landscape science at the Geography Faculty of Voronezh University. *Soviet Geography* 15, 463—6.

Newman, J. R. 1979: Effects of industrial pollution on wildlife. *Biological Conservation* 15, 181—90.

Newton, J. G. 1976: Induced and natural sinkholes in Alabama: continuing problem along highway corridors. In Zwanig, F. R., editor, *Subsidence over mines and caverns*. Washington, DC: National Academy of Sciences, 9—16.

Nicholson, S. E. 1978: Climatic variations in the Sahel and other African regions during the past five centuries. *Journal of Arid Environments*, 1, 3—24.

Nikonov, A. A. 1977: Contemporary technogenic movements of the Earth's crust. *International Geology Review* 19, 1245—58.

Nossin, J. J. 1972: Landsliding in the Crati basin, Calabria, Italy. *Geologie en Mijnbouw* 51, 591—607.

Noy-Meir, I. 1974: Stability in arid ecosystems and effects of men on it. *Proceedings of the 1st International Congress of Ecology*. Wageningen, 220—5.

Nriagu, J. D. 1979: Global inventory of natural and anthropogenic emissions of trace metals in the atmosphere. *Nature* 279, 409—11.

Nye, P. H. and Greenland, D. J. 1964: Changes in the soil after clearing tropical forest. *Plant and Soil* 21, 101—12.

Oberle, M. 1969: Forest fires: suppression policy has its ecological drawbacks. *Science* 165, 568—71.

Oke, T. R. 1978: *Boundary layer climates*. London: Methuen.

Otterman, J. 1974: Baring high albedo soils by overgrazing: a hypothesised desertification mechanism. *Science* 186, 531—3.

Oxley, D. J., Fenten, M. B. and Carmody, G. R. 1974: The effects of roads on populations of small mammals. *Journal of Applied Ecology* 11, 51—9.

Pakiser, L. C., Eaton, J. P. Healy, J. H. and Raleigh, C. B. 1969: Earthquake prediction and control. *Science* 166, 1467—74.

Panel on Weather and Climate Modification. 1966: *Weather and climate modification problems and prospects.* Publication 1350. Washington DC: National Academy of Sciences.

Panofsky, H. 1976: Man's impact on climate. In Ferrar, T. A., editor, *The urban costs of climate modification.* New York: Wiley.

Park, C. C. 1977: Man-induced changes in stream channel capacity. In Gregory, K. J., editor, *River channel change.* Chichester: Wiley, 121—44.

Parsons, J. J. 1960: Fog drip from coastal stratus. *Weather* 15, 58.

Passmore, J. 1974: *Man's responsibility for nature.* London: Duckworth.

Pawson, E. 1978: *The early industrial revolution: Britain in the eighteenth century.* London: Batsford.

Peck, A. J. 1975: Effects of land use on salt distribution in the soil. *Ecological Studies* 15, 77—90.

1978: Salinization of non-irrigated soils and associated streams: a review. *Australian Journal of Soil Research* 16, 157—68.

Pennington, W. 1974: *The history of British vegetation* (2nd edition). London: English University Press.

Pereira, H. C. 1973: *Land use and water resources in temperate and tropical climates.* Cambridge: Cambridge University Press.

Perla, R. 1978: Artificial release of avalanches in North America. *Arctic and Alpine Research* 10, 235—40.

Petts, G. E. 1979: Complex response of river channel morphology subsequent to reservoir construction. *Progress in Physical Geography* 3, 329—62.

Petts, G. E. and Lewin, J. 1979: Physical effects of reservoirs on river systems. In Hollis, G. E., editor, *Man's impact on the hydrological cycle in the United Kingdom.* Norwich: Geobooks, 79—91.

Pimentel, D. 1976: Land degradation: effects on food and energy resources. *Science* 194, 149—55.

Pitt, D. 1979: Throwing light on a black secret. *New Scientist* 81, 1022—5.

Pluhowski, E. J. 1970: Urbanization and its effects on the temperature of the streams on Long Island, New York. *United States Geological Survey Professional Paper* 627—D.

Pollard, E. and Miller, A. 1968: Wind erosion in the East Anglian Fens. *Weather* 23, 414—17.

Poore, M. E. D. 1976: The values of tropical moist forest ecosystems. *Unasylva* 28, 127—43.

Pope, J. C. 1970: Plaggen soils in the Netherlands. *Geoderma* 4, 229—55.

Porter, E. 1978: *Water management in England and Wales.* Cambridge:

Sawyer, J. S. 1971: Possible effects of human activity on world climate. *Weather* 26, 251–62.

Schimper, A. F. W. 1903: *Plant-geography upon a physiological basis.* Oxford: Clarendon Press.

Schindler, D. W. 1974: Eutrophication and recovery in experimental lakes: implications for lake management. *Science* 184, 897–9.

Schmid, J. A. 1974: The environmental impact of urbanization. In Manners, I. R. and Mikesell, M. W., editors, *Perspectives on environment.* Washington, DC: Association of American Geographers.

⎯ 1975: Urban vegetation. *Research Paper: Department of Geography, University of Chicago.*

Schmieder, O. 1927: The Pampa ⎯ a natural or culturally induced grassland? *University of California Publications in Geography 2,* 255–70.

⎯ 1927b: Alteration of the Argentine Pampa in the colonial period. *University of California Publications in Geography 2,* 303–21.

Schumm, S. A. 1977: *The fluvial system.* New York: Wiley.

Schwarz, E. H. L. 1923: *The Kalahari or Thirsland redemption.* Cape Town and Oxford: Oxford University Press.

Scott, G. J. 1977: The role of fire in the creation and maintenance of savanna in the Montana of Peru. *Journal of Biogeography 4,* 143–67.

Scott, P. A. 1978: Tropical rain forest in recent ecological thought: The reassessment of a non-renewable resource. *Progress in Physical Geography 2,* 80–98.

Sears, P. B. 1957: Man the newcomer: the living landscape and a new tenant. In Russwurm, L. H. and Sommerville, E., editors, *Man's natural environment, a system approach.* North Scituate: Duxbury, 43–55.

Selby, M. J. 1979: Slopes and weathering. In Gregory, K. J. and Walling, D. E., editors, *Man and environmental processes.* Folkestone: Dawson, 105–22.

Shaler, N. S. 1912: *Man and the earth.* New York: Duffield.

Sheail, J. 1971: *Rabbits and their history.* Newton Abbot: David and Charles.

Sherlock, R. L. 1922: *Man as a geological agent.* London: Witherby.

Shirhata, H., Elias, R. W., Patterson, C. C. and Koide, M. 1980: Chronological variations in concentrations and isotopic composition of anthropogenic atmospheric lead in sediments of a remote subalpine pond. *Geochimica er Cosmochimica Acta* 44, 149–62.

Simmonds, N. W. 1976: *Evolution of crop plants.* London: Longman.

Simmons, I. 1979: *Biogeography: natural and cultural.* London: Arnold.

Simoons, F. J. 1974: Contemporary research themes in the cultural geography of domesticated animals. *Geographical Review 64,* 557–76.

Smith, C. T. 1978: *An historical geography of western Europe before 1800* (2nd edition). London: Longman.

Smith, J. E., editor, 1968: *'Torrey Canyon' Pollution and marine life.* Cambridge: Cambridge University Press.

Smith, K. 1975: *Principles of applied climatology.* London: McGraw Hill.

Smith, L. B. and Hadley, C. H. 1926: The Japanese beetle, *Dept. Circ. US Dep. Agric.* 363, 1—66.

Smith, N. 1976: *Man and water*. London: Davies.

Smith, W. H. 1974: Air pollution — effects on the structure and function of the temperate forest ecosystem. *Environmental Pollution* 6, 111—29.

Snelgrove, A. K. 1967: *Geohydrology of the Indus River, West Pakistan*. Hyderabad: Sind University Press.

So, C. L. 1971: Mass movements associated with the rainstorm of 1966 in Hong Kong. *Transactions of the Institute of British Geographers* 53, 55—65.

Somerville, M. 1858: *Physical geography* (4th edition). London: Murray.

Sopper, W. E. 1975: Effects of timber harvesting and related management practices on water quality in forested watersheds. *Journal of Environmental Quality* 4, 24—9.

Southwick, C. H. 1976: *Ecology and the quality of our environment* (2nd edition). New York: Van Nostrand.

Sparks, B. W. and West, R. G. 1972: *The Ice Age in Britain*. London: Methuen.

Spate, O. H. K. and Learmonth, A. T. A. 1967: *India and Pakistan*. London: Methuen.

Speight, M. C. D. 1973: Outdoor recreation and its ecological effects. A bibliography and review. *Discussion papers in Conservation, University College, London*, 4.

Spencer, J. E. and Hale, G. A. 1961: The origin, nature and distribution of agricultural terracing. *Pacific Viewpoint* 2, 1—40.

Spencer, J. E. and Thomas, W. L. 1978: *Introducing cultural geography* (2nd edition). New York: Wiley.

Sperling, C. H. B., Goudie, A. S., Stoddart, D. R. and Poole, G. C. 1979: Origin of the Dorset dolines. *Transactions of the Institute of British Geographers*, new series, 4. 121—4.

Speth, W. W. 1977: Carl Ortwin Sauer on destructive exploitation. *Biological Conservation* 11, 145—60.

Stephens, J. C. 1956: Subsidence of organic soils in the Florida Everglades. *Proceedings of the Soil Science Society of America* 20, 77—80.

Sternberg, H. O'R. 1968. Man and environmental change in South America. *Monographiae Biologicae* 18, 413—45.

Stewart, O. C. 1956: Fire as the first great force employed by man. In Thomas, W. L., editor, *Man's role in changing the face of the earth*. Chicago: University of Chicago Press, 115—33.

Stoddart, D. R. 1968: Catastrophic human interference with coral atoll ecosystems. *Geography* 53, 25—40.

   1971: Coral reefs and islands and catastrophic storms. In Steers, J. A., editor, *Applied coastal geomorphology*. London: Macmillan, 154—97.

Strahler, A. N. and Strahler, A. H. 1973: *Environmental geoscience: interaction between natural systems and man*. Santa Barbara: Hamilton.

Strandberg, C. H. 1971: Water pollution. In Smith, G. H., editor,

Conservation of natural resources (4th edition). New York: Wiley, 189–219.

Swank, W. T. and Douglass, J. E. 1974: Streamflow greatly reduced by converting deciduous hardwood stands to pine. *Science* 18, 857–9.

Swanston, D. N. and Swanson, F. J. 1976: Timber harvesting, mass erosion and steepland forest geomorphology in the Pacific northwest. In Coates, D. R., editor, *Geomorphology and engineering.* Stroudburg: Dowden, Hutchinson and Ross, 199–221.

Swift, J. 1974: *The other Eden. A new approach to man, nature and society.* London: Dent.

Swift, L. W. and Messer, J. B. 1971: Forest cuttings raise temperatures of small streams in the southern Appalachians. *Journal of Soil and Water Conservation* 26, 111–16.

Tajikistan Academy of Sciences. 1975: Induced seismicity of the Nurek reservoir. Dushanbe: Tajik Academy.

Taylor, C. 1975: *Fields in the English landscape.* London: Dent.

Thomas, W. L., editor, 1956: *Man's role in changing the face of the Earth.* Chicago: University of Chicago Press.

Thompson, J. R. 1970: Soil erosion in the Detroit metropolitan area. *Journal of Soil and Water Conservation* 25, 8–10.

Thompson, R. 1978: Atmospheric contamination – a review of the air pollution problem. *Geographical Papers, Department of Geography, University of Reading* 68.

Thornthwaite, C. W. 1956. Modification of rural microclimates. In Thomas, W. L., editor, *Man's role in changing the face of the Earth.* Chicago: University of Chicago Press. 567–83.

Tivy, J. 1971: *Biogeography. A study of plants in the ecosphere.* Edinburgh: Oliver and Boyd.

Todd, D. K. 1959: *Groundwater hydrology.* New York: Wiley.

1964: Groundwater, in Ven Te Chow, editor, *Handbook of Applied Hydrology*, Sect. 13. New York: McGraw Hill.

Tomaselli, R. 1977: Degradation of the Mediterranean maquis. *UNESCO, MAB Technical Notes* 2, 33–72.

Tomlinson, T. E. 1970: Trends in nitrate concentrations in English rivers in relation to fertilizer use. *Water Treatment and Examination* 19, 277–89.

Trimble, S. W. 1974: *Man-induced soil erosion on the Southern Piedmont.* Soil Conservation Society of America.

1976: Modern stream and valley sedimentation in the Driftless Area, Wisconsin, U.S.A. *23rd International Geographical Congress*, Section 1, 228–31.

Troels-Smith, J. 1956: Neolithic period in Switzerland and Denmark. *Science* 124, 876–9.

US Bureau of Entomology and Plant Quarantine 1941: *Insect Pest Survey Bulletin* 21, 801–2.

Usher, M. B. 1973: *Biological management and conservation.* London: Chapman and Hall.

Vale, T. R. 1974: Sagebrush conversion projects: an element of contemporary environmental change in the western United States. *Biological Conservation* 6, 274—84.

Vale, T. R. and Vale, G. R. 1976: Suburban bird populations in west-central California. *Journal of Biogeography* 3, 157—65.

Vankat, J. L. 1977: Fire and man in Sequoia National Park. *Annals of the Association of American Geographers* 67, 17—27.

Vendrov, S. L. 1965: A forecast of changes in natural conditions in the northern Ob' basin in case of construction of the lower Ob' Hydro Project. *Soviet Geography* 6, 3—18.

Vice, R. B., Guy, H. P. and Ferguson, G. E. 1969: Sediment movement in an area of suburban highway construction, Scott Run Basin, Fairfax County, Virginia, 1961—64. *United States Geological Survey Water Supply Paper* 1591—E.

Viessman, W., Knapp, J. W., Lewis, G. L. and Harbaugh, T. E. 1977: *Introduction to hydrology* (2nd edition). New York: IEP.

Viets, F. G. 1971: Water quality in relation to farm use of fertilizer. *Bio Science* 21, 460—7.

Vine, H. 1968: Developments in the study of soils and shifting agriculture in tropical Africa. In Moss, R. P., editor, *The soil resources of tropical Africa*. Cambridge: Cambridge University Press, 89—119.

Vita-Finzi, C. 1969: *The Mediterranean valleys.* Cambridge: Cambridge University Press.

Vitousek, P. M., Gosz, J. R., Gruer, C. C., Melillo, J. M., Reiners, W. A. and Todd, R. L. 1979: Nitrate losses from disturbed ecosystems. *Science* 204, 469—73.

Vogl, R. J. 1974: Effects of fires on grasslands. In Kozlowski, T. T. and Ahlgren, C. C., editors, *Fire and ecosystems*. New York: Academic Press, 139—94.

— 1977: Fire: a destructive menace or a rational process. In Cairns, J., Dickson, K. L. and Herricks, E. E., editors, *Recovery and restoration of damaged ecosystems*. Charlottesville: University Press of Virginia, 261—89.

Wagner, R. H. 1974: *Environment and man.* New York: Norton.

Waldichuk, M. 1979: Review of the problems. *Philosophical Transactions of the Royal Society* 286B, 399—429.

Wall, G. and Wright, C. 1977: The environmental impact of outdoor recreation. *Department of Geography Publication Series, University of Waterloo, Canada* 11.

Walling, D. E. and Gregory, K. J. 1970: The measurement of the effects of building construction on drainage basin dynamics. *Journal of Hydrology* 11, 129—44.

Wallwork, K. L. 1956: Subsidence in the mid-Cheshire industrial area. *Geographical Journal* 122, 40—53.

— 1960: Some problems of subsidence and land use in the mid-Cheshire industrial area. *Geographical Journal* 126, 191—9.

— 1974: *Derelict land.* Newton Abbot: David and Charles.

Wang, W. C., Yung, Y. L., Lacis, A. A., Mo, T. and Hanson, J. E. 1976:

Greenhouse effects due to man-made perturbations of trace gases. *Science* 194, 685–90.

Ward, R. C. 1978: *Floods – a geographical perspective.* London: Macmillan.

Ward, S. D. 1979: Limestone pavements – biologist's view. *Earth Science Conservation* 16, 16–18.

Warren, A. and Maizels, J. 1976: *Ecological change and desertification.* London: University College.

Warren, A. and Maizels, J. K. 1977: Ecological change and desertification, In United Nations, *Desertification: its causes and consequences.* Oxford: Pergamon, 171–260.

Watson, A. 1976: The origin and distribution of closed depressions in south-west Lancashire and north-west Cheshire. Unpublished B.A. dissertation, University of Oxford.

Weare, B. C., Temkin, R. L. and Snell, C. M. 1974: Aerosols and climate: some further consideration. *Science* 186, 827–8.

Weaver, H. 1974: Effects of fire on temperate forests: western United States. In Kozlowski, T. T. and Ahlgren, C. C., editors, *Fire and ecosystems.* New York: Academic Press, 279–319.

Weaver, J. E. 1954: *North American prairie*, Lincoln: Johnsen.

Wells, P. V. 1965: Scarp woodlands, transported grass soils, and concept of grassland climate in the Great Plains region. *Science* 148, 246–9.

Wendorf, F., Schild, R., El Hadidi, N., Close, A. E., Kobusiewicz, M., Wiekowska, H., Issawi, B. and Haas, H. 1979: The use of barley in the Egyptian late Paleolithic. *Science* 205, 1341–7.

Wertine, T. A. 1973: Pyrotechnology: man's first industrial uses of fire. *American Scientist* 61, 670–82.

Westing, A. and Pfeiffer, E. W. 1972: The cratering of Indochina. *Scientific American* 226 (5), 21–9.

Whitaker, J. R. 1940: World view of destruction and conservation of natural resources. *Annals of the Association of American Geographers* 30, 143–62.

Whittaker, E. 1961: Temperatures in heath fires. *Journal of Ecology* 49, 709–15.

Whyte, A. V. T., 1977: Guidelines for field studies in environmental perception. *MAB Technical Note 5.* UNESCO.

Wilken, G. C. 1972: Microclimate management by traditional farmers. *Geographical Review* 62, 544–60.

Williams, M. 1970: *The draining of the Somerset levels.* Cambridge: Cambridge University Press.

Williams, R. S. and Moore, J. G. 1973: Iceland chills lava flow. *Geotimes* 18, 14–17.

Wilshire, H. G. 1980: Human causes of accelerated wind erosion in California's deserts. In Coates, D. R. and Vitek, J. D., editors, *Geomorphic Thresholds.* Stroudsburg: Dowden, Hutchinson and Ross, 415–33.

Wilshire, H. G., Nakata, J. K. and Hallet, B. (in press): Field observations of the December, 1977 Windstorm, San Joaquin Valley, California. In Péwé, T. L., editor, *Desert dust: origin, characteristics and effects on man.* Geological Society of America.

Wilson, A. T. 1978: Pioneer agriculture explosion and CO$_2$ levels in the atmosphere. *Nature* 273, 40–1.

Wilson, K. V. 1967: A preliminary study of the effect of urbanization on floods in Jackson, Mississippi. *United States Geological Survey Professional Paper* 575-D, 259–61.

Winkler, E. M. 1970: The importance of air pollution in the corrosion of stone and metals, *Engineering Geology* 4, 327–34.

Winstanley, D. 1973: Rainfall patterns and general atmospheric circulation. *Nature* 245, 190–4.

Wolman, M. G. 1965: The metabolism of cities. *Scientific American* 213, 179–88.

Wolman, M. G. 1967: A cycle of sedimentation and erosion in urban river channels. *Geografiska Annaler* 49A, 385–95.

Wolman, M. G. and Schick, A. P. 1967: Effects of construction on fluvial sediment, urban and suburban areas of Maryland. *Water Resources Research* 3, 451–64.

Wong, C. S. 1978: Atmospheric imput of carbon dioxide from burning wood. *Science* 200, 197–9.

Wood, C. M., Lee, M., Linker, J. A. and Saunders, P. J. W. 1974: *The geography of pollution, a study of greater Manchester.* Manchester: Manchester University Press.

Woodwell, G. M. 1978: The carbon dioxide question. *Scientific American* 238 (1), 34–43.

Woodwell, G. M., Whittaker, R. H., Reiners, W. A., Likens, G. E., Delwiche, C. C. and Botkin, D. B. 1978: The biota and world carbon budget. *Science* 199, 141–6.

Wooster, W. S. 1969: The ocean and man. *Scientific American* 221, 218–23.

Worthington, E. B., editor, 1977: *Arid land irrigation in developing countries: environmental problems and effects.* Oxford: Pergamon.

Wrigley, E. A. 1965: Changes in the philosophy of geography. In Chorley, R. J. and Haggett, P., editors, *Frontiers in geographical teaching.* London: Methuen.

Wright, H. E. 1974: Landscape development, forest fires and wilderness management. *Science* 186, 487–95.

Wright, L. W. and Wanstall, P. J. 1977. The Vegetation of Mediterranean France: a review. *Occasional Paper no. 9. Department of Geography, Queen Mary College, University of London*, 44pp.

Yaalon, D. H. and Yaron, B. 1966: Framework for man-made soil changes – an outline of metapedogenesis. *Soil Science* 102, 272–7.

Yi-fu Tuan, 1971: Man and nature. *Commission on College Geography Resource Paper* 10.

Yorke, T. H. and Herb, W. J. 1978: Effects of urbanization on streamflow and sediment transport in the Rock Creek and Anacostia River basins, Montgomery County, Maryland, 1962–74. *United States Geological Survey Professional Paper* 1003.

Zaret, T. M. and Paine, R. T. 1973: Species introduction in a tropical lake. *Science* 182, 449—55.

Zimina R. P., Polevaya, Z. A. and Yelkin, K. F. 1972: The plowing up of the virgin lands and the Bobac Marot resources of Central Kazakhstan. *Soviet Geography* 13, 246—56.

Index

316